Madame Chu's
Chinese Cooking School

by

GRACE ZIA CHU

ILLUSTRATIONS BY GRAMBS MILLER

A Fireside Book
Published by Simon and Schuster

MANUFACTURED IN THE UNITED STATES OF AMERICA

1 2 3 4 5 6 7 8 9 10

LIBRARY OF CONGRESS CATALOGING IN PUBLICATION DATA

CHU, GRACE ZIA.
MADAME CHU'S CHINESE COOKING SCHOOL.
1. COOKERY, CHINESE.   I. TITLE.
TX724.5.c5c575   641.5'951   74-34310

ISBN 0-671-21974-x
ISBN 0-671-24209-1 PBK.

THIS BOOK IS
DEDICATED TO
MY FRIEND MARGARET SPADER

ACKNOWLEDGMENTS

- to Bettijane Eisenpreis, who helped find the right words
- to my daughter-in-law, Lucy Chu, who supplied the right Chinese characters
- to Julie Houston, my editor, who took out the wrong words
- to all my students, who inspired the book

Contents

Contents

Contents

Contents

Why Another Chinese Cookbook?

The beginning of the 1970s marked an explosion of interest in Chinese food and cooking. Traveling Americans, more than ever before, were bringing back to their home towns throughout the country a newly acquired taste for "exotic" food. Young Americans shunned prepared foods and began experimenting with natural fresh ingredients. The historic first visit of an American President to China spurred interest in all things Chinese. But even before that, an increasing number of Americans were eating at Chinese restaurants and experimenting with cooking their favorite dishes at home. Calorie-conscious Americans realized the benefits of combining relatively small quantities of meat with large amounts of healthful, low-calorie vegetables. And with prices rising, Americans became more willing to expend a little additional labor to save money by stretching small amounts of more expensive foods in a pleasant-tasting and nutritious manner.

Authors and publishers sensed the rising interest in Chinese food, and Chinese cookbooks began appearing by the hundreds. Why is another such book necessary?

This book is not simply "another Chinese cookbook." Every book has something unique to offer, and this one is a necessary supplement to and continuation of my first book, *The Pleasures of Chinese Cooking*, published in 1962, when there were only a handful of Chinese cookbooks available to the American public. That book presented the principles and methods used in Chinese cooking, along with basic recipes using those methods and inspired by those principles. After over ten years, it is still selling just as well as it did at the outset, and many of my students and friends have asked for a second volume.

This book, *Madame Chu's Chinese Cooking School*, takes advantage of my further experiences in teaching the art of Chinese cooking. After twenty-two years and more than three thousand students, I know the problems Americans face in learning how to prepare Chinese food. Americans are far more sophisticated now than they were in 1962, and many, many more Chinese food products are available in their supermarkets and in an ever-growing number of Chinese specialty stores throughout the country. More advanced and interesting dishes can now be made, but new, simple dishes are always welcome, too. This is why I feel a second volume is needed to round out the first.

The techniques and cooking processes in this book are genuine, firmly rooted in Chinese tradition. I have attempted to adapt these processes to modern American life. More culinary aids are available to cut down the man-hours needed in preparing the same delectable foods that were served in ancient China. The gadgets have to do the work that the abundant population of China performed in the past, and they can, with a little ingenuity. Do not be frightened because Chinese cooking is supposed to be time consuming. After a while, the chopping and slicing—most of which can be done beforehand—will be natural to you. Actual cooking times are short and last-minute preparation simple.

When I first started teaching, my students asked many questions. The questions were very useful; the answers informed not only the one who asked but the whole class. The students wanted to know, not only about basic techniques, but about the cultural and historical reasons behind them. Now when I teach, there are fewer questions because I have learned to anticipate many of them. Indeed, many of the questions asked by friends and students have been incorporated into one section of this book. They may surprise even those who feel they know a good deal about Chinese cooking. Some may know more of the answers and some less, but I feel everyone will find out something by reading the section.

The Pleasures of Chinese Cooking is organized in menus, ranging from the very simple to the more complex. When that book was published, few Americans had experience in planning a Chinese meal, balancing the dishes, and knowing how to blend tastes and textures. Now, with Americans becoming more sophisticated, I feel I can return to a more traditional method of cookbook arrangement, listing foods by categories: soups, salads, fish, chicken, eggs, meats, and so forth. Sample suggested menus are given separately, along with the principles of menu arranging, but part of the pleasure of Chinese cooking is constructing menus of your own. The Chinese have no "main course." A Chinese meal consists of many one-dish "courses," each equally important for a different reason. How and why they are balanced will be explained in this book.

My aim is not solely to teach Americans how to cook a Chinese dinner, from soup to nuts (or soup to soup in the real Chinese fashion). I hope, after cooking these recipes for a while, that American cooks will begin to use them out of context as well as in it. Try one heavy meat, cooked Chinese style, along with your usual vegetable, salad, bread, and dessert. Or serve an American meat, but try preparing the vegetable the Chinese way, stir fried in a little polyunsaturated oil, which preserves its color and nutritional value and tastes so good, too.

The recipes given here are not from any one region. No American would eat the food of the South or New England exclusively; so why should he arbitrarily decide to eat only Cantonese or Szechuan food. The great majority of recipes in this book could be found, with variations according to local products and tastes, in all parts of the country. For instance, in Soochow, Wusih,

Shanghai, and Hangchow and environs, a little sugar is often included in the seasoning of a dish. In other areas, the same dish might be prepared but the sugar omitted and other seasonings substituted. In less affluent areas like Shansi, Hupeh, and Kweichow, the food is made very salty so that little food but much rice will be consumed. In all the large cities of China, restaurants serve food common to all parts of China as well as regional specialties. Even restaurants named after a particular "school" or city have dishes from other cities on their menus.

A menu of dishes from one region alone would be too limited, too monotonous, and in areas where the food is hot or salty, bad for the health of the diners. As a matter of interest, however, I have listed the regional dishes contained in this book and indicated the page on which each can be found.

Whenever it is possible, I have included the story behind each dish or the reason for its inclusion in my book. I feel that the more the American cook knows about the history or preparation of the meal she is cooking the more interested she will be in making it and the happier she will feel to try it.

At the end of most of the recipes is a section labeled "Tips." This is designed to make preparation easier. You will learn which recipes can be made in advance or even frozen, how to make cooking easier, and what to substitute if something is unavailable or if you wish to vary the dish. Chinese cooking is infinitely variable. There are over two hundred and fifty ways of cooking pork, nearly two hundred different recipes for chicken, and at least one hundred for beef, just to mention a very small area of the Chinese cuisine. The student could study Chinese cooking for a whole lifetime and still have many things to learn—which is part of the pleasure of this fascinating art. I have tried in my two books to give an idea of the basic principles of Chinese cooking, the methods of cutting and cooking, and some of the many ingredients that can be used. Every recipe given here can be turned into several different recipes, once you have mastered the techniques involved. So, though this volume may look slim, its possibilities are endless.

My answer to the question, "Why another cookbook?" is, after all, a simple one. I want *Madame Chu's Chinese Cooking School* to teach more students than my classes could possibly reach *more* pleasures of Chinese cooking.

HOW TO PLAN
A CHINESE DINNER

In Western countries, menu planning is often fairly automatic. Once the main meat has been chosen, the balance of the dinner falls into place. Turkey means dressing, cranberry sauce, sweet potatoes, and gravy. Steak brings to most Americans immediate visions of baked or French-fried potatoes and tossed salad. I have even heard of a Viennese gentleman who threatened to divorce his wife because she dared to serve creamed spinach with Wiener Schnitzel instead of the mandatory oven-browned potatoes and head of lettuce.

The fact that a Chinese meal has no "main course" frightens many American housewives. They may have studied Chinese cooking and bought several Chinese cookbooks, but when the challenge is to put together a complete meal, they are at a loss. How many dishes should each meal include? What kinds of dishes should they be? What is a balanced menu? Is it true that a whole fish and a whole duck can be served at the same meal?

I feel that some explanation and direction will help readers of this book, as it has helped my students in the past. There are a few basic rules to follow in planning a Chinese dinner. These will help host and hostess to stay calm, and allow everyone to enjoy a pleasant new experience.

First, start small. The novice in Chinese cooking is too often tempted to begin with too many dishes or guests the first time she entertains. The diners may enjoy themselves, but the harried hostess often becomes so exhausted that she never again attempts a Chinese meal.

Chinese food may be served at "sit-down" or buffet dinners. By "sit-down," I do not mean a formal banquet, but simply that several Chinese dishes are put in the center of the table and the host, hostess, and guests help themselves. The Chinese buffet consists of foods that can be made in advance and kept warm or served cold. They are put on a side table, and all walk around and help themselves. The seated dinner may require slightly fewer dishes but more last-minute cooking. The buffet, cooked entirely in advance, may be more work but less nerve-wracking.

First, let us look at the sit-down dinner. For a beginner, six people, including the host and hostess, make an ideal-sized group. For this party, plan no more than four dishes in addition to soup, rice, dessert, and tea.

What should the dishes include? The first should be a meat dish that can be prepared in advance, that does not require last-minute stir-frying. The meat may be beef, pork, or chicken, in such combinations as Curry Beef (page 116), Chicken with Chestnuts (page 150), or Red-Cooked Pork Cubes with Braised Bamboo Shoots (page 138).

A fish or seafood dish comes next. Steamed fish, such as Steamed Floured Carp (page 184), or Steamed Sea Bass (*Pleasures of Chinese Cooking*, page 133), requires very little preparation, either in advance or at the last minute. It may be seasoned according to directions and then put into the steamer while the guests have their cocktails. Dishes like Shrimp and Kidney (page 191), Shrimp in Wine-Rice Sauce (page 194), and Lobster Cantonese (page 190), require advance preparation of ingredients, but can be cooked easily and quickly right before the meal is served.

Some combination of meat and vegetables would be good for the next course. Home-Style Bean Curd (page 236), which combines pork, bean curd, and vegetables, and Flank Steak with Preserved

Mustard Greens (page 118), a form of beef and oyster sauce, are excellent examples, though there are many possible combinations.

Last comes a simple vegetable dish. Both Chinese Cabbage (Bok Choy) (page 208) or String Beans with Soy Sauce (page 213) can be washed, cut, and laid out ready for cooking beforehand, then stir fried just before serving time. If, however, you wish to eliminate the extra pot to wash, a vegetable salad like Celery and Soy Sauce—Pressed Bean Curd Salad (page 100), or Water Chestnut and Broccoli Salad (page 112) can be substituted.

Cook-in-advance courses like curries and red-cooked dishes should be made the day before and left at room temperature or in the refrigerator overnight. All vegetables and meats for stir-fry should be cut up on the morning of the party and put in the refrigerator in plastic wrap. About an hour before, arrange premeasured seasonings and all necessary cooking utensils near the wok or skillet, where you will need them. About ten minutes before mealtime, excuse yourself and stir fry one or two dishes.

A word to the wise: Everything in this book will work successfully if directions are followed. Nevertheless, do not try a recipe for the first time at a dinner party. Cook each recipe for the family before trying it on company. Quantities of seasonings have been prescribed to suit general tastes, but you may always decide you like more or less sugar, salt, and so forth. Read through the whole book and try recipes that appeal to you one at a time with your family, getting their suggestions as to the adjustments needed.

If, after one experience with four guests, you wish to invite six, add one or two dishes, but never include more than two stir-fry dishes at one meal. Another precooked dish, such as Red-Cooked Whole Shoulder of Pork (page 139) or Spiced Roast Duck (page 172), or a "cold mix," like Szechuan Peppercorn Chicken (page 161) or Chicken and Agar-Agar Salad (page 105), might be the additional courses.

You do not need to cook ten main dishes for a party of ten. At most, six or seven will be ample.

Buffet entertaining, Chinese style, can be very interesting for both host and guests. It requires advance planning, but any party should be planned, and this kind will be much appreciated. Many of the rules are the same as those just given for seated dinners. Balance meat, seafood, mixed, and vegetable dishes, including about four main dishes for six people, five or six for eight, seven for ten, and so on. The only difference is that one stir-fry dish is the most you should include in a buffet. Only dishes that can be done well ahead of time and reheated, served cold, or cooked half an hour in advance and kept warm in a casserole should be included.

My student Bettijane Eisenpreis and I have worked out some menus that adapt Chinese recipes to American buffet-style entertaining. Here are three of them:

Bok Choy and Bean Curd Soup (page 86)*
Flank Steak Shreds with Rice Sticks (page 117)
Lion's Head (page 133)
Steamed Floured Carp (page 184)
Lotus Seeds in Syrup (page 230)*
Oolong tea*

Chicken Watercress Soup (page 87)*
Bettijane Eisenpreis's Pork with Mandarin Oranges (page 259)
Bacon Fried Rice (page 245)
Szechuan Peppercorn Chicken (page 161)
Broccoli Stem Salad (page 102)
Wine-Rice Mandarin Orange "Tea" (page 232)*
Black tea*

Peking Sour and Peppery Soup (page 93)*
Curry Beef (page 116)
Pork Lo Mein (page 240)
Chicken and Agar-Agar Salad (page 105)
Asparagus, Chinese Style (page 201)
Longan and Loquat Delight (page 229)*
Chrysanthemum tea*

* Items marked * are optional.

Below are sample sit-down menus from dishes in this book:

Dinner for 2:
    Steak Slices with Onion (page 120)
    Straw Mushrooms, Bamboo Shoots, and Fresh Water Chestnuts
        (page 211)
Dinner for 4:
    Szechuan Shredded Beef (page 121)
    Chinese Roast Pork with Snow Peas (page 129)
    White-Cut Chicken (page 164)
    Broccoli Florets with Water Chestnuts (page 206)
Dinner for 6:
    Curry Beef (page 116)
    Ground Fresh Pork with Cellophane Noodles (page 132)
    Szechuan Peppercorn Chicken (page 161)
    Chicken Breasts with Mung Bean Sprouts and Pickled Cucumber
        Shreds (page 148)
    Red-Cooked Fish with Fresh Bean Curd (page 181)
    Brussels Sprouts with Ham Squares (page 207)
Dinner for 8:
    Shrimp Susanna (page 193)
    Tricolored Meat Platter (page 122)
    Dried Bean Curd with Pork Slices (page 130)
    Orange-Spiced Duck (page 165)
    Chicken with Chestnuts (page 150)
    Poached Fish, Canton Style (page 183)
    Fresh Bean Curd Salad (page 106)
    Chinese Cabbage (Bok Choy) (page 208)

Boiled rice and tea should be served with each meal. In addition, you can choose one soup and one dessert from the book to complete each of these meals.

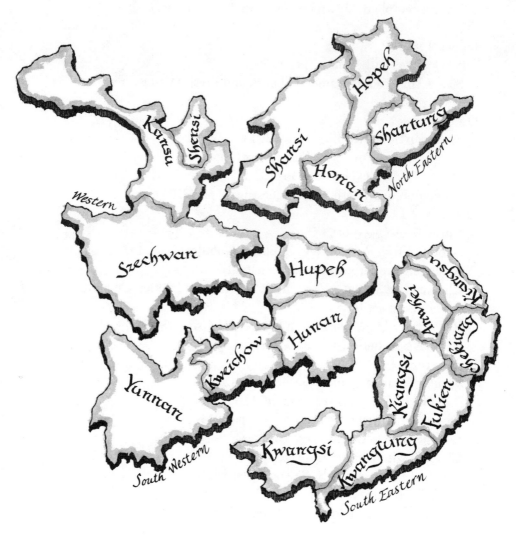

The four culinary sections of China

ALL OF CHINA IS A SCHOOL

Americans interested in Chinese food hear and speak a great deal about "the five major schools of Chinese cooking." Actually, there is no such hard and fast distinction, and no Chinese would refer to "schools of cooking."

In *Musings of a Chinese Gourmet*, published in England in 1954, F. T. Cheng, former ambassador to the Court of St. James, did suggest that one might be able to identify five major "schools" of Chinese cooking. This gave rise to many learned discussions among gourmets on the merits of the various schools.

But China is a vast country, so there are many more, different regional Chinese cuisines. Until recent times, transportation and communication between areas ranged from poor to nonexistent. In the days when the classical Chinese cuisine was developed, refrigeration was unknown. Each area was forced to depend on its own resources. Methods of cooking—stir frying, steaming, red cooking, and so forth—did not vary from one area to the next, but ingredients and seasonings were determined entirely by what the area raised, how rich or poor it was, and how accessible it was to the outside world.

Located on the seacoast, Canton was ideally suited for becoming a center of culinary excellence. Its climate favors agriculture. Fish and seafood are plentiful. The Cantonese are ingenious and resourceful, inventive chefs and appreciative eaters. For years, the only Chinese cooking Americans knew was Cantonese, because Cantonese were the first to emigrate. What Americans did not know was that, even among knowledgeable Chinese from other areas, Cantonese food is highly esteemed. To hire a Cantonese chef in China is similar to employing a French chef in America or Europe.

Shantung, in northern China, is the place of origin of many dishes now known by the name of "Peking." Shantung is near Peking, and since the Imperial Court resided at Peking, many fine Shantung foods were adopted by the aristocracy and became their own. "Peking Duck," for instance, is really "Shantung Duck." Shantung cooking is distinguished by the use of large cuts of meat and the fact that there is very little stir-frying. Leek, scallions, onions, and garlic are favored seasonings. Wine stock is used frequently. And due to the presence of the court in nearby Peking, many banquet dishes are from Shantung.

Szechuan, in southwestern China, was neither near the sea, like Canton, or near the aristocracy, like Peking. Until recently, food from this relatively isolated area was not very well known. The so-called Szechuan school comprises foods of the inland provinces of Szechuan, Yunnan, and Kweichow, of which Szechuan is the best known. The area is difficult to farm, the weather humid and muggy but it does have redeeming features. Spices of all kinds grow well there, as do mushrooms, because the area has a great deal of rainfall. The Szechuan peppercorn is a delicate, aromatic spice highly prized throughout China, but the chili pepper, grown in the three provinces, is the distinctive spice of the region. Children who had no food other than rice would take a small bottle of chopped fresh chili pepper, mixed with salt, to school in order to make the bland rice palatable. Workers and farmers also relied on pepper to season their rice or the meager meat or vegetable that might be served with that rice. However, though the term "Szechuan" has come to mean "hot," elegant food, even in Szechuan, is never overly spicy. The inhabitants of all three provinces never seasoned banquet dishes with chili pepper, feeling that it masked delicate flavors. Good food need not be hot.

There are many other provinces and areas in China, all of them with regional dishes and many with well-developed cuisines. Honan, for instance, is famous for sweet-and-sour sauce, adopted by the Cantonese. Fukien produces the best soy sauce in China, and being on the sea, it is famous for fish and seafood as well as for excellent clear soups. Then there are "minor" schools like Hunan and Kiangsu, each of which originated one or two dishes famous throughout China, such as Lion's Head from the city of Yangchow, Kiangsu. It is impossible to say that there are three or five or even twenty schools of cooking, since a dish that begins in one area may quickly become popular in several.

Besides the so-called "schools," there are two other types of Chinese cooking to consider. One is Mandarin. The term "Mandarin cooking" is unknown in China. The expression originated in the United States, but it describes a style of cooking that exists all over China. Mandarin dishes are universal Chinese dishes, typical of the best in Chinese food. They are tasty, wholesome, easy to prepare, and while they are usually served in fine Chinese restaurants, they are not necessarily banquet dishes, and it is quite possible to make them at home.

Many recipes in this book come under the heading of "home cooking." Home cooking is distinguished by the fact that the dishes prepared this way are low in calories and consist of simple, basic ingredients. Home-cooked dishes like Shrimp with Cucumber or Soy Sauce Spiced Beef (both in *The Pleasures of Chinese Cooking*, pages 95 and 77) are less oily than other kinds of Chinese food. Ingredients are relatively few and easy to obtain. Color and eye appeal are a hallmark of home-cooked dishes, of which Chicken Breast with Sweet Pepper (*The Pleasures of Chinese Cooking*, page 90) is typical.

This book contains examples of Mandarin dishes and home-cooking dishes, as well as foods representative of many different "schools." The reader should remember that he or she has an advantage over the Chinese who developed this cuisine. Chinese of one region never had a chance to taste food from other areas. Many poor people—the great majority of Chinese—spent their lives eating a very limited diet. American lovers of Chinese food can have a little of everything.

Indeed, balance is essential in enjoying Chinese food to the fullest. One Szechuan dish in a meal is fine, two is one too many. Balance the seafood dishes of Fukien with the meats of Shantung and the stir-fry of Canton. Mix spicy, bland and sweet-sour tastes.

Blend intricate, banquet-type dishes with the simple, but just as authentic, home-cooking variety. Do not feel you must champion one "school" over another. Variety is not only the spice of life, it is the essence of Chinese cooking.

Dishes Typical of Eastern China

Clam and Icicle Radish Soup
(page 88)
Laver and "Egg Flower" Soup
(page 91)
Steamed Eggplant Salad
(page 110)
Fresh and Salt Pork Casserole with Summer Bamboo and Thinly Pressed Bean Curd
(page 125)
Lion's Head
(page 133)
Red-Cooked Pork Cubes with Braised Bamboo Shoots
(page 138)
Red-Cooked Whole Shoulder of Pork
(page 139)
Wu-Sih Pork
(page 144)
Chicken with Chestnuts
(page 150)
Stuffed Boneless Chicken
(page 155)
Spiced Roast Duck
(page 172)
Red-Cooked Fish (Whiting)
(page 178)
Red-Cooked Fish with Fresh Bean Curd
(page 181)
Steamed Floured Carp
(page 184)
Watercress, Shanghai Style
(page 217)

Dishes Typical of Southern China

Chicken Watercress Soup
(page 87)

Dried Lotus Root and Sparerib Soup
(page 89)

Peanut and Hog's Maw Soup
(page 92)

Flank Steak Shreds with Rice Sticks
(page 117)

Flank Steak with Preserved Mustard Greens
(page 118)

Chinese Roast Pork with Snow Peas
(page 129)

Steamed Ham with Chicken and Chinese Mustard Greens
(page 153)

Orange-Spiced Duck
(page 165)

Pressed Duck with Almonds
(page 167)

Roasted Stuffed Boneless Duck
(page 169)

Minced Squab
(page 174)

Poached Fish, Canton Style
(page 183)

Clams in Black Bean Sauce
(page 187)

Lobster Cantonese
(page 190)

Roast Pork Lo Mein
(page 240)

Chinese Pork Sausage and Mushroom Rice
(page 247)

Dishes Typical of Western China

Pork, Cellophane Noodle, and Szechuan Preserved Kohlrabi Soup
(page 95)

Pickled Assorted Vegetables
(page 220)

Pork, Bamboo Shoots, and Szechuan Preserved Kohlrabi Shreds
(page 134)

Szechuan Peppercorn Chicken
(page 161)

Braised Eggplant, Szechuan Style
(page 203)

Silver Fungus in Syrup
(page 231)

Szechuan Spicy Bean Curd
(page 238)

Dishes Typical of Northern China

Peking Sour and Peppery Soup
(page 93)

Lamb Shreds with Scallions
(page 123)

Cassia Pork
(page 126)

Pork Shreds with Pressed Bean Curd and Chinese Chives
(page 136)

Velvet Chicken
(page 162)

Shrimp in Wine-Rice Sauce
(page 194)

Taro and Scallions
(page 215)

Glazed Yucca
(page 227)

Wine-Rice Mandarin Orange "Tea"
(page 232)

Peking Noodles with Meat Sauce
(page 242)

Chinese Steamed Buns
(page 248)

Buns with Roast Pork Filling
(page 250)

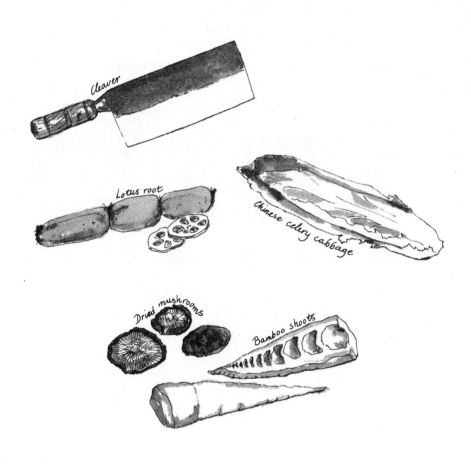

Cleaver

Lotus root

Chinese celery cabbage

Dried mushrooms

Bamboo shoots

Brushing Up on Techniques

PREPARATION OF FOOD: CUTTING

This book is designed for beginning and experienced Chinese cooks alike. Some may have read my first book or another book on Chinese cooking. Some may have taken one or more Chinese cooking courses; others may have no previous experience. Knowing this, I will review briefly the basic techniques of food preparation and cooking. Although many of the techniques described here are also mentioned in Questions and Answers (page 41) or the Glossary (page 269), I feel that it is helpful to have the principal techniques listed in one section.

Preparation is more than half the battle. China is a land with little fuel and many people. Therefore, the Chinese have evolved a system of food preparation based on cutting food into small pieces, which cook quickly with little fuel wasted. From this basic principle came the art of Chinese cutting. Foods are not chopped up at random, they are cut into certain basic shapes. The nature of the main ingredient, efficiency in cooking, flavor, and aesthetic considerations, all determine these shapes. For instance, vegetables added to fried rice are cut into small dice or minced to match the rice grains, while those used in *lo mein* are shredded into noodle-like pieces. Pieces must be the same size for even cooking; it would be bad if the scallions burned while the pork was undercooked. Eye appeal figures in as well: triangles of red bell pepper add beauty as well as flavor.

Because so much cutting is done, the Chinese use a most serviceable knife—the cleaver. Unlike the more familiar meat cleaver, the Chinese cleaver is a slicing knife. It has a short, round, wooden handle and a rectangular blade. To cut with the cleaver, place food on a wooden chopping board. Hold the cleaver in your right hand (unless you are left-handed) and the food to be cut in your left. Grasp the cleaver handle gently but firmly, allowing thumb and forefinger to fall on either side of the blade; do not stick your forefinger straight out along the edge of the blade. Meanwhile, curve the knuckles of your left hand down and in, letting the top knuckles extend a little beyond the second knuckles. Place the cleaver parallel to the line formed by the knuckles and use the knuckles as a guide. As long as your fingertips are curved inward, you will not have any accidents.

Press forward and downward with the cleaver while cutting. Never use a sawing motion. When you find that you must saw, have the cleaver sharpened.

Although there are many variations, here are the basic ways of cutting:

Slicing needs no explanation, other than to say that there are two main types, straight and slant. *Straight slicing* is done with the vegetable or meat perpendicular to the broad side of the cleaver. Usually the slices are quite thin, although thickness differs from recipe to recipe. Meat should be sliced partially frozen when the thinnest slices possible are desired. *Slant slicing* is performed with the food at a 45-degree angle to the cleaver blade.

Shredding is also self-explanatory. Simply cut the food into thin slices and then cut these into very thin strips (shreds). To speed up the process, several slices may be piled on top of each other before shredding.

Mincing is the next step. To mince, first shred, then cut the shreds at right angles into very fine pieces.

Dicing is somewhat like mincing, but the pieces are larger. Cut the food lengthwise into strips about ½ inch wide, then cut these into small cubes or dice.

Oblique cutting is harder to describe than to do. Sometimes vegetables are "stringy" or fibrous, or we want them to absorb as much flavor as possible. Oblique cutting breaks up the fibers and creates a maximum number of surfaces to absorb flavor. In this book, the potatoes in Curry Beef (page 116) are cut obliquely. The result is a tasty and thoroughly curry-flavored dish.

To make an oblique cut, first make a slant slice. Then roll the vegetable a quarter turn until the cut surface faces directly upward. Now slice diagonally through the cut surface. Then roll it another quarter turn and repeat the process until the entire vegetable is sliced into oblique pieces.

When you first start using your cleaver, allow plenty of cutting time. Do it several hours before the meal and store the cut food in the refrigerator in plastic bags. Gradually your speed will improve —but never rush while preparing Chinese food. Remember, most recipes take very little time to cook; so a little extra preparation just "evens things out."

METHODS OF COOKING

Many beginning students confess to me that they are afraid they can never serve a complete Chinese meal to their families. "I hear it all has to be cooked at the last minute," they say. "How can I make two or three dishes at the same time?"

This mistaken belief arises from the fact that many people think stir frying, the most common method of Chinese cooking, is the *only* method. Stir frying is only one of several ways in which the Chinese prepare food. It may be the most uniquely Chinese, but not even the Chinese stir fry every dish served at a single meal.

Stir frying is tricky, but not too difficult. It includes four essentials. Small pieces of food are cooked in (1) a small amount of oil over (2) a high flame for (3) a short period of time and (4) tossed and turned continuously. If you remember to have all ingredients ready and close at hand, and if the wok or frying pan is well heated, stir frying should be easy. Don't stop tossing and turning the food to go and find the salt; the food will stick to the pan and burn.

Shallow frying, using more oil than stir frying, is more like American frying or French sautéing. Food is cooked over medium heat for a longer period of time, and turned only once or twice during the cooking period. This method is usually reserved for food that has already been partially cooked.

Deep frying is a process shared by many ethnic cultures. At least a cup of oil must be used, preheated to 375 degrees in a deep-fryer or other utensil in which the oil will stand at least 1 inch deep. The food is dropped gently into the hot oil and fried until it is golden brown and thoroughly cooked.

Clear simmering means cooking in plain water for several hours. Meats and vegetables are prepared this way, yielding, when strained, a very clear and flavorful soup. Salt is added at the end of the cooking period.

Red cooking (red stewing), a technique used several times in this book, is a favorite way of preparing whole poultry, fish, and meats that require a long cooking period. Food is cooked slowly in large quantities of dark soy sauce, which gives it a dark reddish-brown color. Sherry, ginger, and scallions are usually added. Foods cooked this way can be reheated, and taste even better the second or third time.

Steaming to the Chinese means "wet steaming." The food is placed in a container with holes in the bottom. This is set on top of a pan of rapidly boiling water and the whole thing is covered. The steam then circulates around the food and cooks it. Do not boil the food and do not use a double boiler, which dry steams, unless this is specifically indicated.

Fermented black beans

Soy sauce

Sesame oil

Oyster sauce

Hoisin Sauce

HOISIN SAUCE

Dried Shrimp

Bok choy

Bean curd

A Chinatown
Shopping Tour

Shopping for Chinese ingredients need not be a difficult or confusing chore. How much or how little Chinese shopping you do will be determined by how much time you have and how many Chinese grocery stores there are in your community. If there is no Chinatown near you, you can order dried and canned staples by mail and use meats and vegetables available in American markets. You can grow your own bean sprouts indoors, and snow peas will thrive in American outdoor gardens. Health food stores carry Oriental sesame seed oil, and many supermarkets stock soy sauce, canned bamboo shoots, and canned water chestnuts.

However, if there is a Chinese market or a Chinatown in your city, you can really enjoy shopping there. In this section I will describe how I introduce beginners to Chinese food and food stores, hoping that it will help you feel confident when you venture forth. Those who have no Oriental market nearby can refer to the list of staples given here, and do their ordering by mail.

I feel it is helpful for students of Chinese cooking to go through the markets with an experienced Chinese shopper, usually their teacher. Therefore, I have always included a Chinatown grocery tour in my basic cooking classes.

Upon arrival in Chinatown, I point out the fresh seasonal vegetables in the windows of the greengrocers' shops. I want my students to be able to identify these vegetables, even though we may not cook them in class, as my class recipes are selected for year-round use. However, I do use a few seasonal vegetables in this book: icicle radish, sold mostly in winter, and *kai-lan* (Chinese broccoli) are two examples. I point out others—fresh red or green amaranth, chrysanthemum *choy*, and pole beans in spring; snow peas, loofah, fresh kohlrabi in summer. It has always been important to the Chinese, who were unable to preserve vegetables by canning or freezing, to use fresh, natural ingredients. Now Americans, observing the trend toward "natural" foods, are cooking more like the Chinese always did.

Also in the windows are important staple vegetables, available most of the year. These include fresh ginger, water chestnuts, bean sprouts, *bok choy*, and celery cabbage. Except for the ginger, these foods must be bought as needed, as they stay fresh for a limited time.

Next, we go into a store and choose items we will use in class. Our shopping list can serve as a guide for anyone who wishes to keep some staples on hand. The list includes:

Dark or heavy soy sauce	Dried tiger-lily buds
Light soy sauce	Fermented black beans
Oriental sesame seed oil	Fresh ginger
Hoisin sauce	Cellophane noodles
Oyster sauce	Canned bamboo shoots
Plum sauce	Canned water chestnuts
Hot pepper oil	Star anise
Dried Chinese mushrooms	Szechuan peppercorns
Dried tree (cloud) ears	

Although "the story of tea" is a lecture that I give in class later on, I do point out the basic varieties of tea while we are in the store. These include fully fermented, or black; semifermented, or oolong; unfermented, or green; and scented, of which the best-known example is jasmine.

As an item of interest, we look at some exotic foods, not normally used in home cooking. Bird's nest, shark's fin, sea cucumber, dried abalone, dried shrimp and mussels are all used in banquet recipes. Dried shrimp and shark's fin are included in this book for more adventurous or experienced cooks, but I do not instruct my beginning students in their use.

Now we come to cooking utensils. I do not insist that my students buy any, but I do feel that the following few items facilitate Chinese cooking: chopsticks for eating and cooking, a 12- or 14-inch (diameter) wok, a ring to support the wok on a gas range, and a No. 3 cleaver for cutting and slicing (not for chopping through bone).

I also show the students fresh noodles, egg-roll wrappers, wonton wrappers, and doilies for Mo-Shu-Ro and Peking Duck. These perishable items are stored in refrigerator cases and should be purchased later, as needed.

After we have shopped for necessities, we browse. My students look at and smell exotic Chinese spices like tangerine peel, *Wei-san*, *chi-tzu*, and others. Everyone is intrigued by the "thousand-year eggs." Roasted meats, prepared commercially in Chinatown as in China, hang from overhead racks. Roast pork, roast duck, and roast chicken are always on display. Roast pig, roast squabs, hog's maw, and even hog's ear and snout may be there as well, depending on the size of the store.

At the end of the tour, we usually go to a restaurant in the area, where we savor what professional chefs can do with some of the ingredients we have just seen and purchased.

HOW TO STORE SOME COMMON CHINESE FOOD PRODUCTS

Foods that can be put on the shelf:

Fermented black beans
Fermented bean curd
Dried bean curd layers
Dried beans
Dried bird's nest
Spices
Thousand-year eggs
Salted duck eggs
Flour (regular all-purpose flour)
Jujube
Lotus seed
Lotus root
Shrimp chips
Bead molasses
Oriental sesame seed oil and paste
Soy sauce
Oyster sauce
Hoisin sauce
Hot pepper oil
Madame Chu's Plum (duck) Sauce

Shrimp sauce (paste)
Dried mushrooms
Tree (cloud) ears
Dried silver ears (silver fungus)
Cellophane noodles
Rice sticks
Rice, all kinds
Rock candy
Dried oysters
Dried scallops
Dried sea cucumber
Dried seaweed
Dried shark's fin
Dried shrimp
Dried squid
Dried tiger-lily buds
Dried turnip
Preserved turnip
All seeds

Refrigerate the following canned foods, after opening:

Abalone
Bamboo shoots (in fresh water, changing every third day)
Braised bamboo shoots
Red bean paste
Dragon's eye
Lichees
Szechuan preserved kohlrabi
Water chestnuts (in fresh water, changing every third day)

Refrigerate the following non-canned foods:
Thinly pressed bean curd
Chinese sausages
Preserved duck
Egg-roll skin or wrapper
Wine yeast
Bean sprouts (Wrap in a dry paper towel, and store in the refrigerator in a plastic bag or container. After 3 days, change the towel, which will now be wet. Will keep 1 week.)
Fresh gingerroot (Wash and scrape with a vegetable peeler. Store in a glass jar and cover with dry sherry. Will keep in refrigerator for months.)
Sliced dried jellyfish (Thoroughly wash off all salt. Rinse several times in cold water, then put in a wide-mouthed container and cover with water. Cover and refrigerate. Do not change water, as with water chestnuts and bamboo shoots. Will keep several months.)

The following can be frozen. First, wrap each item carefully in aluminum foil. Then wrap in freezer paper and seal. Label each item with its name and the date it was frozen.
Sausages
Smithfield ham, cooked or uncooked
Fish maw
Preserved duck
Roast pork
Roast pig
Wonton wrappers
Egg-roll wrappers
Fresh egg noodles

Steamer

Casserole

Spatula

Ladle

Wok

Questions and Answers

IN GENERAL . . .

Q: *What school of cooking do the Chinese themselves prefer?*

A: Strange as it may seem, the Cantonese school is the most popular, for several reasons.

Food is very important to the people of Canton Province. Generally speaking, the Cantonese prefer to spend money on food as opposed to clothes or housing, and good, well-prepared food is the number-one priority. The Cantonese are the gourmets of China, so many good cooks live in that area.

Secondly, the soil and climatic conditions in the area around Canton are extremely congenial for the cultivation of fruits and vegetables. Plentiful feed for livestock makes meat abundant and of high quality. The sea is nearby, rich in fish and shellfish. So all the raw materials for a varied and sophisticated cuisine are at hand.

The third reason lies in the character of the Cantonese themselves. They are, as a whole, adventurous; for example, they were the first group of Chinese to migrate to the United States.

At times this daring extends to their eating habits, to include types of food that appear strange and unpalatable not only to the Western tongue but also to the majority of other Chinese. In the Canton area foods are eaten that most Chinese shun: sparrows, certain species of white mice, snakes, snails, and so on. Since the Cantonese are adventurous, they are innovative and creative cooks, and have over the years developed many exciting dishes.

Q: *Is there a modern Chinese cuisine as opposed to a traditional one, or have cooking methods and dishes remained unchanged?*

A: Basically, there has been very little change in Chinese cooking techniques through the centuries. Now, with more Chinese able to take advantage of modern facilities, shortcuts are often taken to arrive at traditional dishes. Frozen vegetables and other prepared foods are used, but the end result is not much different from the dishes of years gone by.

Q: *What school of Chinese cooking appeals most to Americans?*

A: At present, the Szechuan and Hunan cuisines are enjoying immense popularity in eastern America because of the hot, spicy dishes.

It is important for Americans to understand something about Szechuanese cooking, and not to overemphasize the importance of hot food in the Chinese cuisine.

The climate of Szechuan Province is wet, muggy, and unpleasant for man and beast. Animals do not thrive well there, so meat is often tough and stringy. The only vegetable growth that flourishes is that of such spices as chili peppers and Szechuan peppercorns, and fungi like mushrooms, tree (cloud) ears, and silver fungi. The people in the area are comparatively poor, and many cannot afford meat. Therefore, they use chopped chili peppers and other spices to make palatable the two or three bowls of rice that often make up their entire meal. Sometimes this hot spice is combined with a tiny bit of meat; sometimes it is mixed with bean curd or vegetables. By making the meat or vegetable very spicy, the Szechuan laborer needs only a very tiny portion, and then eats large quantities of rice to cool his palate.

Whenever people in Szechuan entertain or have banquets, hardly any hot dishes are served. When food is plentiful, hot spices are not needed, since they kill the taste. Constant consumption of excessively spiced food is a health hazard, and this cannot be pointed out too strongly to Americans caught up in the current fad for Szechuanese cooking. Overuse of pepper may lead to indigestion at the least, and peptic ulcers at the worst. One hot, spicy dish in a menu should be complemented by a bland dish, a sweet-sour dish, and other tastes and flavors for balance.

Q: *My children are somewhat cautious about eating Chinese food, especially as it is "all mixed up." How can I cook Chinese style for my husband and myself and avoid making a separate meal for the kids?*

A: Apparently, children are very much the same the world over. Even some Chinese children, exposed from birth to food mixed together, prefer to eat things separately if given a choice. Chinese children, while watching their elders mixing food with rice, often save the rice until last and eat it bland, without sugar, salt, or cream. This is unthinkable to a Chinese adult.

Actually, it is quite easy to serve your children Chinese food the way they like it. Almost all recipes require cooking the meat first and then adding the vegetables. Just remove some of the meat and put it in a separate dish; do the same with the cooked vegetables. You will find that the children will eat the meat, and maybe even the vegetables, too.

Q: *How does Chinese food differ from that of other Asian peoples, such as the Japanese, Thai, or Vietnamese?*

A: The civilization of China is one of the oldest in the world. The basic culinary techniques evolved by the Chinese were adopted by other Southeast Asian peoples many centuries ago and incorporated into their own cultures. Over the years, each country has developed its own body of culinary lore, determined by geographical environment, foodstuffs available, and the cultural background of its people. The methods employed—the arts of cutting, cooking, and serving—are somewhat similar throughout the Orient, but the actual foods eaten depend on what is available locally. In Japan, for example, the average diet is heavy on fish and seafood. Thais and Vietnamese eat many curries and spicy foods because they live in hot climates.

Nowhere is there a cuisine as varied as that of China. China is so vast and so old that many regional and historical influences are combined in its cuisine. In certain parts of China there are dishes that resemble those of other countries because they share certain geographic characteristics, but in each of these countries there is a more limited choice of dishes than in China as a whole.

Q: *Have the Chinese adopted any foods besides curries from other cultures?*

A: We love Hungarian goulash! As a matter of fact, stews of all kinds are popular in China. Like Chinese dishes, stews blend meat and other ingredients, but since they are different from Chinese stir-fry dishes, they are a rare and exotic treat for us.

Q: *Has Chinese cooking had any influence on European cooking through the centuries, as Chinese furnishings had on Chippendale furniture?*

A: Marco Polo imported many Chinese foods into Europe, and others may have done the same. It has been said that he brought the Chinese *mein* (noodles) the forerunners of spaghetti, into Italy. We also heard that he brought fava beans and sesame seeds, although the sesame seed oil made by the Italians differs in color and texture from Oriental sesame seed oil because it is made from untoasted seeds.

Q: *Is there an established protocol as to where members of a Chinese family and their guests sit at the dinner table?*

A: Yes, the traditional Chinese family has definite rules of etiquette governing places at table.

Traditionally, a Chinese family included three generations: the grandparents, who owned the home, their sons and the sons' wives, and their grandchildren.

The average Chinese family uses a square table for informal dining at home. The head of the table is the side farthest from the door. Here the grandparents sit, facing the door. On their right sit their sons; and the daughters-in-law sit on the left.

Grandchildren sit at the foot of the table. Should there be only one married son and should close friends come for dinner, the friends sit on the grandfather's right and son and wife sit together on the left.

Formal dining, either at dinner parties at home or in restaurants, takes place at a round table. Members of the oldest generation, when present, sit at the head of the table. The guest of honor sits on the right of the oldest person, and the host and hostess sit together at the foot of the table.

The reason for using square tables for family dining and round tables for company is that only eight can sit at the square table, while ten can fit at a round one. The Chinese believe that food should be placed in the center of the table where all can reach it; it is held to be inconsiderate to trouble your neighbor to pass the food.

Q: *Do the Chinese have birthday parties? If so, what foods are served?*

A: Yes, the Chinese have birthday parties. We do not celebrate every year, but have parties for each decade year: ten, twenty, and so on. In addition, parties are given on the one-month and one-year birthdays of baby boys.

Noodles are a must for birthdays. They are served long, never cut, symbolizing a wish of long life for the celebrant. Peaches, the longevity fruit, are molded out of dough, colored red and green, and filled with a sweet filling. These take the place of birthday cake.

Q: *Do the Chinese consider any foods especially lucky?*

A: Many foods have special meanings to the Chinese people. For instance, the noodles that are eaten uncut on birthdays are symbols of long life. The Chinese venerate old age, feeling that added years mean added wisdom; so longevity and good luck are synonymous.

Each fruit has a symbolic meaning. The peach is a symbol of longevity. Oranges stand for happiness; pomegranates, fertility; pears, prosperity. The apple is called "peace fruit," and bowls of apples are often used to decorate the table at banquets, symbolizing peace. After the meal is over, the apples are sliced and eaten. The Chinese are a practical people, and often use fruit as a table decoration. After all, you can't eat flowers!

Q: *Are fortune cookies authentically Chinese?*

A: The answer to this question is yes and no.

There are flat wafers made of dough similar to that of the fortune cookies in China, as well as precedents for writing messages inside cakes or cookies. Birth announcements have been known to be sent wrapped in sweet dough. In one ancient Chinese parlor game, players were instructed to compose wise or witty sayings and write them on a scrap of paper inside a twisted cake.

However, the fortune cookie as we Americans know it was invented in the United States. George Jung, who immigrated to Los Angeles in 1911 and founded the Hong Kong Noodle Company in 1916, is credited with the invention. One story tells that Jung felt sorry for the tired and lonely people he saw in Los Angeles after World War I and invented the cakes to send them cheering messages. Another version states that he invented them to amuse diners in Chinese restaurants while they waited for their orders.

The fortunes themselves have undergone many changes since 1918 or 1919, when the cookies were invented. At first, verses were selected from the Bible by a Presbyterian minister. Later, the wife of the man who printed the messages was hired to compose four hundred sayings, subsequently supplying fifty new ones every year to replace worn-out truisms. Now fortune cookie bakeries get slogans from volunteers, from contests, and from professional writers. Fortunes range from funny to risque to downright vulgar. The cookies have been used in advertising campaigns, especially for the film, *The Fortune Cookie*.

If you wish to make your own cookies and write fortunes for your friends, a recipe may be found on page 86 of *The Pleasures of Chinese Cooking*.

Q: *I know chop suey was invented by Chinese in America. Is chow mein a similar invention, or is it authentically Chinese?*

A: The crispy fried noodles in chow mein are an American invention. We do have noodles in China, but we never fry them in this way.

The method of cooking used for chow mein is a poor imitation of Chinese stir-fry.

Q: *Do "subgum" and "chop suey" mean somewhat the same thing?*

A: Yes; "subgum" means, literally, "assorted." "Chop suey" means "mixed assorted"—the word itself is redundant.

Subgum, used in conjunction with fried rice, *lo mein*, or similar dishes, means that several different meats and vegetables have been added to the basic dish.

Q: *Is there any truth to the American cliché that one becomes "hungry an hour after eating Chinese food"?*

A: I think this saying may be true for a great many Americans.

Large pieces of meat, such as the steak or roast beef often eaten by Americans, require several hours to be digested. Chinese food, on the other hand, includes much less meat, and that meat is already cut into small pieces and mixed with light, easy-to-digest vegetables so that it can be digested quickly.

Chinese people do not get as hungry as quickly as Westerners because they always eat several bowls of rice with each meal. Carbohydrates from this rice provide them with sufficient energy to go on until the next meal.

When food is easy to digest, it is much better for the digestive system, but one does become hungry more quickly.

Q: *Is Chinese food fattening?*

A: All food is fattening if consumed in unrestricted quantities. However, Chinese food is not fattening when eaten in moderation.

Most Chinese meat dishes contain a relatively small amount of meat, mixed with vegetables that have far fewer calories than the meat itself. Cream and butterfat are not used in Chinese cooking; the amount of vegetable oil in most dishes is minimal. Dieters should avoid the few deep-fried dishes the Chinese serve. Rice is a good source of carbohydrates, needed for energy, and contains fewer calories than a similar amount of potatoes or pasta. All in all, Chinese food is less fattening than most other famous cuisines.

Q: *Is it true that Chinese people do not have high blood pressure? If so, could this be related to their diet?*

A: Chinese people do get high blood pressure, but the condition is not nearly so prevalent as it is among Americans. I do believe the low incidence of high blood pressure is related to the Chinese diet.

   The Chinese eat much less meat and animal fats and much more vegetables and rice than do Americans. As for salt intake, the Chinese frequently use soy sauce, which is lower in sodium than salt.

Q: *I am on a low-fat, low-sodium diet. Can I eat Chinese food at home? At restaurants?*

A: You can certainly eat Chinese food at home. When preparing any dish, use the minimum amount of oil necessary to prevent food from sticking to the pan. You probably should avoid deep-fried foods, but there are relatively few of them in Chinese cooking.

   As for sodium, do not use salt but substitute a small amount of soy sauce, which has a lower sodium content and adds color as well as taste.

   Eating in Chinese restaurants poses a problem for those on restricted diets, just as eating in any restaurant does. The diner cannot control the way food is prepared in the restaurant kitchen. The best advice I can give is, just take a taste of each dish and eat a good-sized portion of rice. Also, don't plan on going to Chinese restaurants too frequently.

Q: *Since so much Chinese food is cut into pieces that do not require much chewing, and since their diet is low on the calcium derived from milk, how do the Chinese preserve their teeth?*

A: I am not an expert in this field, but some claim strong teeth may be a racial characteristic.

   Also, while it is true that the Chinese do not exercise their teeth by chewing on large pieces of meat as Americans do, they are not in as much danger of having shreds of meat lodge between their teeth and cause decay. They eat very few sweets, which are harmful to healthy teeth.

The Chinese do chew, however. They are fond of eating nuts and hard fruits, and they often chew on pieces of sugar cane, extracting the sweet juice and discarding the hard part after chewing.

Q: *What is "Chinese restaurant syndrome"?*

A: "Chinese restaurant syndrome" is a term that has only recently come into use. Its principal symptom is a headache or feeling of pressure in the head, though there may be other symptoms as well. The "syndrome" is temporary, and while uncomfortable, does no permanent harm to the sufferer.

Chinese restaurant syndrome is caused by a sensitivity (not an allergy) some people have to monosodium glutamate, an additive used in Chinese restaurants to bring out flavor in food. Because of the large quantity of any dish a restaurant prepares at one time, it is difficult to control the amount of MSG used. A tiny amount will do the job, but many restaurants tend to use more than required.

When cooking at home, use ⅛ teaspoon of MSG or less, or omit it entirely if you do not feel it makes a difference in flavor. Some people, especially Orientals, feel that it brings out the flavor of food immensely. Others cannot taste any difference, and they need not use it at all.

CHINESE EATING HABITS

Q: *What do Chinese people eat for breakfast? What do they eat for lunch?*

A: For almost all Chinese, lunch and dinner are exactly the same. If a family normally eats four dishes for lunch, they eat four dishes for dinner. If you eat rice at lunch, you eat rice again for dinner. If bread is the staple served at lunch, it is also served at dinner.

Once in a while, when the family is too busy or when friends drop in, they will have a snack lunch, called *dem sin* by the Cantonese. For the average Chinese, this will not be as elaborate as the many meat- and fish-filled pastries and dumplings served in the United States at tea houses and restaurants and called *dem sin*. It may consist simply of soup noodles or soup wonton, which differ from noodle soup and wonton soup in that there is very little liquid and mostly noodles or wonton.

Breakfast is a very light and nutritionally poor meal. A very liquid gruel made from rice is served warm with salted pickles or other salted vegetables instead of milk or sugar. Recently, steamed buns dipped in sugar have begun to be served with this gruel. Some people also eat peanuts, which give added energy. I don't recommend that anyone try a Chinese breakfast, unless it is something like a light lunch—soup noodles or *dem sin*, for instance.

Q: *What kinds of food do the Chinese carry with them for school lunches, lunches for workers, or snacks on trains?*

A: The Chinese believe strongly in a hot lunch. As I have said before, the Chinese family eats the same kind of meal at midday as it does in the evening.

When it is impossible for a student or worker to get home for lunch, he usually eats a hot lunch in his school or place of business. There are special containers for delivering a hot lunch to the student who does not board at school or the worker who wishes food from home. Unlike American lunchboxes, these are tin dishes that nest on top of each other, with a cover over all and a slot near the handle to hold chopsticks. The bottom dish holds rice, the next meat, the next vegetables, and the top one soup.

Meat-filled buns (*bao*), tea eggs, or cold cooked meats are popular portable foods, but these are regarded as snacks, not as a meal. Tea is sold on trains or anywhere the diner may find himself at lunchtime.

Q: *Do Chinese children drink milk?*

A: Cow's milk is not available in China in any appreciable quantities. Chinese babies are usually breastfed, or in some cases, similar to formula-fed American babies who are allergic to cow's milk, given soy-bean milk. Older children do not drink milk because dairy products are not available.

Q: *What kinds of foods do the Chinese nibble between meals?*

A: No matter how unexpectedly guests arrive, a Chinese host or hostess must offer them tea and something to eat—never tea alone. When there is nothing prepared, Chinese offer snack foods, including watermelon seeds, dried preserved fruits such as lichees or apricots, sesame seed candies or cakes, or nuts. Usually four different varieties of snacks are served, and the company can then "drink tea, crack nuts, and have fun."

Q: *What do the Chinese eat in the summer? Is this different from their winter diet?*

A: Yes, summer and winter menus differ widely.

Chinese menus depend heavily on availability. In summer the Chinese eat more fresh vegetables and other foods abundant at that season.

Light, easily digested foods that require little cooking are preferred for summer consumption, while winter food tends to be deep fried, rich, and warming. Roasted Stuffed Boneless Duck (page 169) and Red-Cooked Whole Shoulder of Pork (page 139) are typical winter foods. Szechuan Peppercorn Chicken (page 161), Fresh Bean Curd Salad (page 106), and Mung Bean Sprout Salad with Egg Strips (page 107) are more likely to be served in summer.

Q: *Do the Chinese consider one of the dishes served at each meal a "main dish" in the same way Americans do (i.e., a "turkey" dinner)?*

A: No, no single dish is the main dish in an ordinary Chinese meal. A variety of dishes—meat, fish or seafood, vegetable, or egg— may be served at one meal, each in smaller quantities than an American main dish. No one of these is considered superior to the others in importance.

In banquets, too, dishes are of equal importance, although they are served one at a time and not all put on the table at once.

The "main dish" is not a Chinese concept.

Q: *When is soup served in a Chinese meal?*

A: Soup is eaten throughout the meal.

Actually, soup, not tea, is the principal beverage accompanying a Chinese meal. Tea is served before and immediately following each meal, but soup is served throughout.

The Chinese never drink cold water while eating. Since all their cooking is done with oil, and they feel oil and water do not mix well healthwise, each diner is given a bowl of soup to accompany his food. If the meal is long, hot soup is brought to the table in the middle of the meal to replenish the supply.

The Chinese in China eat much more rice and less of other dishes than they do here. The hot, slightly salty soup helps to wash down the bland rice.

Q: *Do the Chinese eat raw vegetable salads like we do?*

A: No. Raw fruits and vegetables are thought of as unsafe in China, and often are. Lettuce and tomatoes are not native to China, but tomatoes, introduced recently, are not eaten until boiling water is poured over them and the skin is removed.

What is translated into English as Chinese "salads" is really a term meaning "cold mix." These cold mixed dishes may contain cooked meats and lightly parboiled vegetables, such as the Mung Bean Sprout Salad with Egg Strips on page 107, but they are seldom composed of uncooked vegetables. They are served cold or at room temperature, usually with a soy sauce-based dressing.

Q: *Do the Chinese eat fruit raw or cooked? How is the fruit cut and served? Do they have any special utensils for eating it?*

A: The Chinese do eat fruit raw, even though it is not necessarily safe from a hygienic point of view. The average Chinese develops a certain degree of immunity through exposure to the bacteria present in the fruit, and is therefore not as badly affected as Westerners who have been protected from these bacteria.

The Chinese who are more educated on the dangers of eating

raw fruit do take certain precautions. Fruit like bananas and apples is peeled. Berries and other nonpeelable fruits are washed in cold water, but because water from natural sources is also suspect, they are then washed in a diluted solution of potassium permanganate, an antiseptic solution.

As to the preparation of fruit, the Chinese first cut oranges into four or eight sections with the peel, but always peel apples before sectioning and eating, contrary to American habits.

Like Americans, the Chinese use no utensils for eating fruit other than a knife to cut it. The fruit is picked up and eaten with the hands.

Q: *Do the Chinese eat bread?*

A: In the north, where one-third of the population lives, there are high plains unsuitable for rice cultivation. The people of that area depend on wheat for their staple food. This wheat is made into bread and noodles as well as dumplings, pancakes, and so forth.

The dough for Chinese bread is almost identical to the yeast dough used in making Western white breads. The difference comes in the method of cooking. Since the great majority of Chinese do not have ovens, bread is not baked but wet steamed. Wet steaming is a relatively slow process, so the bread is made into small buns, which can be cooked faster and more thoroughly than loaves. These fluffy white buns may look more like dumplings than bread to Americans, but they are delicious, especially when served with dishes having a pungent sauce.

Q: *Do the Chinese eat Western-style desserts? If not, when do they eat sweets and what form do these sweets take?*

A: No, the Chinese never eat heavy pastries like cake and pies for dessert. Almost every day a Chinese family will finish its meal with fresh fruits in season—pomegranates or peaches, for example.

The so-called desserts in this book, such as Longan and Loquat Delight (page 229) or Wine-Rice Mandarin Orange "Tea" (page 232), are not considered desserts in China. They are the warm or cold sweet courses served between courses in Chinese banquets to clear the palate and whet the appetite for the courses to follow.

The Chinese have delicious candies made of sesame seeds, apricots, and so on, and these are nibbled between meals just as Western candies are.

Q: *Do the Chinese have cakes of any kind? When are these served?*

A: Yes, we do have cakes, but they are not served as dessert.

Chinese cakes are used for between-meal entertaining. They are small and light, and are usually steamed rather than baked. They are not rich like American or European pastries, because cream and butter are not available.

The Chinese serve their cakes warm, usually immediately after they are cooked. For this reason, cake is never served to unexpected company but rather to guests who have been invited for tea.

Q: *Are ice cream and sherbet, often served in Chinese restaurants, authentically Chinese?*

A: No, ice cream and sherbet are not Chinese. The Chinese are limited on desserts and usually eat fresh fruit at the end of a meal. If no sweet is served, tea is used to end the meal.

It is interesting that not only are ice cream and sherbet served at all Chinese restaurants in America, but that all Chinese who have had the opportunity to taste them love ice cream and sherbet. This is one form of non-Chinese food that has had almost unanimous acceptance among Chinese people. They like it better than apple pie.

Q: *What is the Chinese food, comparable to milk toast or chicken soup, for invalids?*

A: *Congee,* or rice gruel, the traditional Chinese breakfast, is also served to people who cannot tolerate regular food.

Congee is made by combining 1 cup of rice with 8 cups of water and cooking 40 minutes or longer. It can be served plain or combined with fish fillet, chicken, meat, or vegetables, in small quantities. Vegetables, meats, or fish are always added at the end of the cooking period. Soy sauce or a little salt can be used to season the *congee.*

Q: *Are there any foods the Chinese find distasteful? Generally? In specific regions?*

A: The foods any group of people enjoy are those which their area produces and to which they have become accustomed from youth. Most Chinese are unfamiliar with lamb and beef because the country is largely unsuitable for raising sheep and cattle. Lamb is especially distasteful to them, as it has a decided flavor and is hard to adapt to unless one has eaten it from birth. Only in Mongolia do the people eat lamb; in other parts of China it is rarely served.

Taste varies from region to region. In the northeastern section of China, garlic, scallions, shallots, onions, leeks, and so on are used liberally to season food. In other areas they are frowned on, and while used in cooking, where their flavor becomes merged with other flavors and hard to recognize, Chinese from these sections have been known to pick out bits of raw scallion from their soup rather than eat it.

In the middle section of China, sugar is added with salt as a seasoning, while inhabitants of other areas do not like anything sweet. Also, while most spices produced in Szechuan Province are used all over China, the chili pepper eaten in Szechuan is frowned on elsewhere. Those Chinese who have not grown used to chili pepper from birth do not like the taste, and they fear, with some justification, that eating too much of such a hot spice will cause gastric disorders.

PLANNING AND PREPARATION

Q: *How should I plan a Chinese dinner for six people?*

A: A meal for six people should include five or six dishes. One possible combination would be a soup, a salad or cold-mix dish, a dish that can be cooked the day before or even cooked in ad-

vance and frozen, a dish that can be cooked one-half hour before, and one stir-fry dish.

These dishes should present a contrast in taste and texture,
but the actual composition should be dictated by the foods
available regionally and seasonally. Decide roughly the kinds
of dishes you need and then go shopping with an open mind. If
broccoli is fresh and in season, you may decide to have Broccoli Florets with Water Chestnuts (page 206) as one dish. If
pork is not too expensive or fatty, Red-Cooked Whole Shoulder of Pork (page 139) could be the dish you prepare the day
before. Do not—as one of my students did—decide in advance
that you must use fresh asparagus in New York in January. She
did, and the fresh asparagus salad cost more than all the meat
consumed in the entire meal.

Q: *Does a Chinese banquet really have twenty-five courses or
more? How can the Chinese eat so much? Why don't they get
fat?*

A: Many years ago, in the Emperor's court, a royal banquet might
have as many as two hundred courses. That kind of meal was
only served to royalty. However, only thirty years ago, I
would have served a thirty-course banquet to company, and a
Chinese banquet may still consist of up to twenty courses.

When the Chinese say "course" they mean one dish, such as
Shark's Fin Soup (page 96) or Stuffed Boneless Chicken (page
155), not a main dish—that is, "a meat course"—and several side
dishes. Also, each diner is expected to take one small spoonful
of each dish. Americans eat much larger quantities of each
Chinese dish than Chinese would. A dish that serves four Americans would serve six or eight Chinese, but the Chinese might
order more dishes.

No Chinese eats banquets very often, any more than any
American has Thanksgiving dinner 365 days a year.

Q: *Are banquet dishes different in kind or only in number from
everyday dishes?*

A: Banquet dishes are very different in every respect. Unlike
everyday dishes, they are served one at a time. Banquets are
never given at home, unless they are catered by an outside

caterer who provides all the food, servants, and appointments. No home chef would ever attempt a banquet.

In the past, banquets included twenty to thirty different dishes. Now the number of dishes has been cut to about ten or twelve, but since the number of diners is generally less than in the past, the rule of about one dish per person still holds.

No rice is ever served at an authentic Chinese banquet. In the United States only, some Cantonese restaurants have added fried rice to the banquet menu.

Hardly any vegetables are served, and beef, too, is seldom seen at a banquet. Pork, because it is the staple meat of the Chinese diet, is excluded. However, seafood such as fish, lobster, shrimp, snails, and oysters, prepared in exotic, delicate ways, are frequently served at banquets, and whole rather than cut-up poultry—ducks, chicken, squab, and other fowl—attractively garnished, are common banquet dishes. Shark's fin, bird's nest, and sea cucumber are exclusively banquet foods. All foods are cut decoratively and carefully arranged.

Q: *Can I improvise Chinese dishes once I have learned some basic techniques?*

A: I would not advise American students to try and invent Chinese-style dishes.

However, once you have followed the recipe closely you can make substitutions in Chinese recipes. For instance, veal can be substituted for pork, or meat can be omitted altogether from a dish that includes one meat and several vegetables. And you may alter seasonings to your own taste if you find the amount specified too mild or too sharp.

In altering any recipe, remember not to combine differently sized or shaped pieces of food, such as a chunk with a shred or a dice with a slice. Not only do these pieces require different cooking times, but a dish combining different shapes and sizes would be unattractive and difficult to eat.

Q: *Can I include one Chinese dish in an otherwise American meal? If so, what sort of dish should this be?*

A: Absolutely yes. My aim is to make you so used to cooking Chinese food that Chinese dishes will become a regular part of your family's diet. If you do not wish to make an entire Chinese meal or are short of time, you can always incorporate one dish into a meal composed of more familiar foods.

Soy Sauce Spiced Beef (*The Pleasures of Chinese Cooking*, page 77) is one authentic Chinese dish that can be cooked ahead of time. If you do not feel like cooking rice and preparing other Chinese food to go with it, serve it with noodles and a tossed salad. You may wish to stir-fry a Chinese vegetable dish such as Straw Mushrooms, Bamboo Shoots, and Fresh Water Chestnuts (page 211) or Chinese Cabbage (Bok Choy) (page 208) to go with your roast. Fried Rice (page 245) is excellent with turkey or chicken, and Mung Bean Sprout Salad with Egg Strips (page 107) can be substituted for your regular salad. There are endless ways Chinese dishes can be incorporated into American menus.

Q: *I work, but would like to cook Chinese food. How can I prepare it in advance?*

A: Most of the preparation for a Chinese meal can be done in advance. Plan only one stir-fry dish per meal, and cut all the meat and vegetables for that ahead of time so that only the few minutes of actual cooking must be done at mealtime. The rest of the meal can be cold-mix or salad dishes, such as the Szechuan Peppercorn Chicken (page 161) or Mung Bean Sprout Salad with Egg Strips (page 107); heavy meats, like Red-Cooked Whole Shoulder of Pork (page 139); or dishes that can be reheated, like Bacon Fried Rice (page 245) and Chicken with Chestnuts (page 150). All these can be prepared in advance. In the case of salads, only the mixing of sauce and salad is done at the last moment.

Q: *Why do Orientals make such a point of decorating platters of food?*

A: The Chinese think of eating as a total experience. Food must appeal not only to the nose and the taste, but to the eye and even the ear. Sizzling rice, for instance, is interesting partly because of its crackling sound.

Much Chinese food is inherently pretty. Chicken cubes mixed with green or red peppers and black mushrooms present a pleasing contrast of colors, and need no decoration. On the other hand, the stuffed chicken recipe given in this book (page 155) is a uniform, dull color, so, though delicious, the dish does not look particularly enticing, and therefore invites decoration.

Garnishes need not be elaborate to be effective. Use vegetables and fruits available in the market: cherry tomatoes, regular tomatoes, icicle radishes, kumquats, loquats (on the West Coast), carrots, potatoes, pomegranates, and greens such as watercress, parsley, and Chinese parsley (cilantro). Small vegetables and fruits, such as cherry tomatoes and kumquats, can be used as is, on a bed of greens around the edges and in the center of the dish. Tomatoes can be sliced, cut into wedges, or carved into flowers.

A pomegranate makes an inexpensive, exotic decoration. Starting at the top, remove about a fifth of the peel, to reveal the four or five natural segments. Open it into a blood-red pomegranate flower and remove the white membranes. Place the open pomegranate on a bed of greens, such as parsley or cilantro, to complete the effect.

Potatoes are excellent for carving. Peel an Idaho potato, cut a slice off the side, and then carve into a figure, such as a reindeer, rabbit, or bird. Once the carving has been made, slice the potato into numerous flat figures and sprinkle with lemon juice to prevent them from turning color. Potato carvings can also be made by forcing the potato through special cutters and then cutting into slices. The finished carvings can be combined with greens or contrasted with slices of tomatoes, peppers, or kumquats, or strips of carrot, for added color.

Q: *Why is food in Chinese recipes cut into such small pieces and so many different shapes, that is, dice, shreds, oblique cut, etc.? Is this simply for appearance or are there other reasons?*

A: Food is cut into small pieces in China mainly to conserve fuel. Unlike the United States, where gas and electric stoves are common, the mass of 750 million Chinese have to use native stoves, which burn straw, leaves, bamboo, briquets, coal, or wood, depending on what the area produces. It is the responsibility of the cook either to buy or make the fuel; so the less fuel used, the less time and money is spent. On the other hand, it is easy to obtain help in chopping or slicing food into small, quickly cooked pieces, as manpower is abundant.

Since it would also be monotonous to cut everything into the same shape and size, the art of cutting grew from the necessity of saving fuel. Specific sizes and shapes are determined by taste, appearance, material available, and variety.

When tiny particles of food are mixed together, the flavors merge into a unique blend, making the dish a "marriage of flavors." Broccoli Stem Salad (page 102) is a perfect example of how careful cutting improves taste.

Often the shape of the pieces used in a given dish is determined by the shape of the ingredient central to that dish. For example, in Bacon Fried Rice (page 245), everything is cut into small pieces somewhat like grains of rice. If noodles are the main ingredient (Roast Pork Lo Mein, page 240), the other ingredients are shredded to match.

Both for appearance and for variety, dishes featuring different-shaped pieces are used in each meal, and the same ingredients are cut different ways and used in different combinations. Some good chefs boast that they can cook for a year without repeating a dish simply by varying the combination of ingredients and the method of cutting.

Q: *Exactly what do you mean when you use the term "mincing"?*

A: Mincing is chopping very fine. To mince food, first make very thin slices. Next, cut the slices into thin shreds, and finally, chop these shreds as small as possible. The result is minced food.

Q: *What do you mean by "stir fry"?*

A: To stir fry means to cook with a little bit of oil, over a high flame, tossing and turning the food continuously, for a short period of time.

Seventy-five percent of Chinese food is stir fried because the short cooking time required saves fuel and also because food cooked this way tastes so good. Manpower has always been plentiful in China, so there was always someone (cook, housewife, or relative) in the kitchen to do the last-minute cooking.

Some dishes need a longer period of cooking time. They can be stir fried first, then the heat turned down, the wok covered, and the cooking process completed.

The stir-fry technique is easy to learn but hard to master.

Q: *I know stir-fried foods must always be prepared at the last minute. Does this mean they can never be reheated when some is left over?*

A: For the best taste and appearance, foods should be stir fried just before eating. However, there is nothing wrong with eating leftovers of stir-fried foods. Your family will enjoy them, though they might not look right to serve for company.

To reheat, place leftovers in a small skillet and heat quickly on top of the range until hot, stirring constantly. Serve at once.

Q: *Can food like pork and shrimp be cooked thoroughly when stir fried only a few minutes? Is it safe to eat?*

A: The technique of stir frying is designed to cook food thoroughly in a relatively short time period. First, the food is cut into very small pieces. Pork, for instance, is ground, diced, sliced, or shredded before stir frying. The heat is very high, and the meat is tossed and turned so that all pieces receive equal heat. Pork is never considered cooked until all traces of pink have disappeared, so when the Chinese cook pork by a method other than stir frying, and when they use large pieces, as in Red-Cooked Whole Shoulder of Pork (page 139), the pork is cooked for long periods (5 hours in this last recipe, for example).

Shrimp, chicken, and beef differ from pork in that undercooking, while unappetizing to many Westerners, is not dangerous to health. It may seem to you that Orientals undercook these meats, and you may wish to lengthen the cooking time very slightly if they really taste raw to you. However, try them the way the recipe specifies first; you may be surprised how good they taste cooked quickly. If shrimp seem slightly undercooked before vegetables or additional ingredients are put in, remember they will receive several more minutes of cooking along with the vegetables. Overcooking toughens shrimp and chicken and destroys the unique taste of stir-fried food.

Q: *Many Chinese recipes specify "steaming" as a cooking method. What is the Chinese method of steaming, and does it differ from the American way?*

A: Americans often steam food in the top of a double boiler, so that the steam does not actually touch the food, but the food is cooked by the heat of the steam. Chinese use live, or "wet," steam. A Chinese steamer consists of a large pot with a perforated top section fitting over the bottom half and equipped with a tight-fitting lid, which covers the entire pot. Food is placed in the top half, boiling water in the bottom. If the food to be cooked is fish, meat, eggs, or the like, it is placed in the top of the steamer on a heatproof plate or bowl, to save the juices. If pastry or rolls, the most commonly steamed foods, are to be cooked, they are placed directly over the steam. If the holes in the top of the steamer are too large, cheesecloth or paper toweling can be placed on the rack to prevent bits of rice or other food from falling through the holes.

Q: *How can I make a steamer?*

A: A steamer can be improvised from a large pot or soup kettle. Fill the pot to a depth of about 2½ inches of water and place in it a tin can, about 3 inches high and 4 inches in diameter, with the top and bottom removed. Place an ovenproof dish or wire rack (for rolls) over this ring and cover the whole pot tightly so that steam circulates around the food and does not escape. Steam as long as the recipe specifies.

The tight-fitting cover is an important part of any steamer. It must cover not only the food but the entire pot, so that no steam escapes.

UTENSILS

Q: *What are the basic utensils needed for preparing Chinese food in an American kitchen if no Chinese utensils are available?*

A: If no Chinese utensils are available, regular knives and French knives can be substituted for cleavers, and a frying pan 10 to 12 inches in diameter can be used in place of a wok. Whisks, forks, and spoons may take the place of chopsticks for beating and stirring, and finally, a regular pancake turner will serve instead of a Chinese spatula.

Q: *Woks are becoming increasingly available in American stores. Must I buy one in order to cook Chinese dishes? Must I buy the utensils sold with the woks?*

A: Although Chinese food can be cooked without a wok, it certainly is a useful item to have if you plan to do a lot of Chinese cooking. Woks are specifically designed for cooking Chinese food, they are fun to use, and you will use less oil by cooking with a wok. To hold the wok steady on an American gas range, the "ring" sold with it is absolutely necessary. Other accessories are optional: a large saucepan lid will do for a cover, and regular kitchen spoons, spatulas, and so on, are all the utensils you will need. If, after you have cooked with the wok for a while, you find that you would like to buy one Chinese-style utensil, such as a flat, long-handled strainer for deep-frying, you can always purchase it separately.

Q: *A friend of mine bought a wok and it turned the food gray. What did she do wrong? Is the food edible?*

A: Your friend may not have "seasoned" her wok correctly before using, or she may have used a detergent to clean it. She should not eat the gray food.

A detailed description of seasoning a wok is given in *The Pleasures of Chinese Cooking* (page 32). Briefly, however, the wok should be washed with soap and water, then greased with vegetable oil, heated over a high flame, and rinsed with warm water. This process of greasing with oil should be repeated several times until the wok is well seasoned. Once the wok is seasoned, never use soap, detergent, or cleansing powders, but wash the wok with a stiff brush and hot water, and then dry it immediately.

Q: *Do stainless-steel or enameled woks, now being sold in America, require seasoning? Do you recommend buying this kind?*

A: Stainless steel and enamel woks do not need to be seasoned, but nevertheless, I do not recommend that you buy either kind.

A traditional iron wok, once seasoned, is far more satisfactory for stir frying, and also far less expensive. Enamel and stainless-steel woks are woks only in shape. They neither get as hot nor cook as evenly as the traditional kind.

However, if you are the recipient of a stainless steel wok, do use it. Simply allow a little extra time for preheating it.

Q: *Can I cook Chinese food on my electric range?*

A: A gas range is better suited for Chinese cooking, because it can reach high heat as soon as it is turned on and can then be turned off or to medium heat. Electric stoves take a few minutes to heat up and cool down, and cannot achieve the quick temperature changes required in Chinese cooking.

However, since so many of my students have only electric ranges, I have devised a system for cooking Chinese food on an electric stove.

Before cooking, read the recipe carefully. Then turn one of the units on your range on and allow it to reach maximum heat. Do not start to stir fry until the unit is all red and as hot as it can get.

At the same time, if the recipe requires additional cooking at medium or low heat, heat another unit to that temperature. When the initial stir frying is completed, move the entire pan to the next unit. Do not try to cool one burner down in time to do all the cooking.

An excellent example is rice, which must be boiled at high

heat, simmered for 20 minutes, and then allowed to "relax" at no heat for another 20 minutes. First, place the rice on the pre-heated hot unit. As soon as the rice has reached a full boil so that even the middle of the pot is bubbling hard, push the whole pan onto the back burner, which has been heated to "simmer." When the rice has finished simmering, remove it from the range entirely and allow it to relax. If left on the range, the rice will be burned by leftover heat.

It is important to remember to preheat all units to the de-sired temperatures before starting to cook.

Q: *Should I use the traditional Chinese wok and ring on my electric range?*

A: No. To cook on an electric stove, the bottom of any pot used must come into direct contact with the calrod in the center of the cooking unit. The ring used to steady a wok on a gas stove keeps the bottom of the wok slightly away from the heat so that air and heat can circulate around the bottom of the wok.

If you want to use a wok on an electric stove, buy one of the new variety that are slightly flattened on the bottom so they can rest directly on the stove without a ring. Then the calrod will be activated and the wok will heat properly.

Q: *I notice that there are electric woks on the market. Do you recommend buying an electric wok?*

A: Electric woks are no substitute for a traditional wok used on a gas range. However, they are excellent if you have only an electric range, or for use anywhere that the kitchen facilities are limited, such as a summer home. I have used one to demonstrate Chinese cooking in a room without a stove, and find it much more satisfactory than a traditional wok used on a camp stove.

Q: *What is a Mongolian fire pot? Should I buy one? How can I improvise one?*

A: There has been much confusion about the term "fire pot." Many people believe that all fire pots are Mongolian. Actually, there are three kinds: regular, chrysanthemum, and Mongolian.

A fire pot is a metal dish with its own heating unit, used in China to warm or cook food at the table.

The regular fire pot, which is only used to warm food, is a one-piece dish with a heating unit at the bottom, a short "belly" through which the heat passes, and a round pot, surrounding the belly, in which the food is placed. A separate cover is placed over the container to keep food warm. Smokeless charcoal is placed in the bottom, and cooked food, such as Shantung cabbage, shrimp balls, meat balls, abalone and ham slices, or other combinations, is placed in the pot. When ready to serve, boiling chicken stock is poured in and the pot covered. The fire pot is then placed on the table and its contents served as a last course, since they stay warm throughout the meal. Such casseroles are frequently served in winter.

The chrysanthemum pot has five parts: a base, a cup for fuel (liquid alcohol), a wide metal frame with ventilated sides and a pot to sit inside, and a cover for the pot. Boiling soup is placed in this pot, too, but the alcohol fire cooks food, not merely warms it. Foods like sliced chicken, liver, beef, and shrimp are arranged on platters on the table. Each diner helps himself, first dipping his meat into the broth to cook it, and then into a mixture of beaten egg and soy sauce to cool and flavor it before eating. When everyone has eaten enough meat, cut-up greens and soaked cellophane noodles are placed in the broth. The pot is covered and its contents allowed to cook a few minutes. Then the soup is served to the diners, along with boiled rice, as a final course.

The Mongolian fire pot is much rarer than the other two. Mongolia is on the outer fringes of China, so most Chinese have never seen a Mongolian fire pot. It looks like the regular fire pot, but the belly is much enlarged. Charcoal is also used in this fire pot, but here it is used for cooking. The only meat used in a Mongolian fire pot is lamb. Boiling water—never stock—is placed in the pot, and a many-ingredient spicy sauce is used for dipping the cooked lamb.

It is not necessary to buy a fire pot, although they are decorative. The chrysanthemum pot, for instance, gets its name from the flowerlike designs formed by the flame through the copper perforations on its sides. An electric saucepan or a heavy pot placed on a hot plate is an effective substitute. Be sure the heating unit used keeps the liquid boiling strongly enough to cook meat (chicken, livers, sliced beef, or shrimp). If pork is included, use only precooked roast pork. When everyone has eaten enough meat, add cut-up greens and soaked cellophane noodles to the pot. The soup, which is considered a great delicacy, can then be served to the guests.

Q: *How many kinds of cleavers are there? Should I buy one? Should I buy more?*

A: There are two basic kinds of cleavers, the choppers and the slicers. Unless you plan to do a substantial amount of Chinese cooking, one, a slicer, is enough. An American meat cleaver or a poultry shears can be used in place of a chopper for cutting through bones. Too, your butcher will often cut meat to your specifications.

Q: *Do the Chinese eat from flat plates or bowls?*

A: Bowls are more important than plates. The standard Chinese place setting consists of a rice bowl, a flat salad- or dessert-sized plate, a porcelain soup spoon, a pair of chopsticks, and usually a bowl for soup.

Contrary to the American practice of placing some of each food on the dinner plate at the start of the main course, the Chinese place small spoonfuls of one dish on their rice or sometimes on the plate. They then eat that food with their rice before helping themselves to the next dish. The plate is often used simply as a receptacle for bones.

Soup is served with every meal. The ancient custom was for everyone in the family to share the center soup bowl. Now, however, small, individual soup bowls are used, and these are refilled from the large soup tureen many times during the meal. Porcelain soup spoons are used because they do not conduct heat.

Q: *What are chopsticks made of?*

A: Chopsticks can be made out of many different materials, including gold, silver, ivory, jade, coral, bone, plastic, wood, and bamboo. I have a chopstick collection that includes all of these. The average Chinese uses bamboo chopsticks for cooking and eating. There are two kinds of bamboo chopsticks: those made from small pieces, planed into shape, and those manufactured by slicing the large bamboo into several smaller sticks. The latter are often left rounded on two sides and squared off on the other two. These are used for cooking as well as for eating.

Wood absorbs the color and flavor of food too readily; therefore, wood is lacquered before it is used for chopsticks. Lacquered chopsticks cannot be used for cooking and do not last too long in any case, as heat and use cause the lacquer to peel.

Today gold chopsticks are only museum pieces, but once they were used by the Imperial Court for banquets. Silver chopsticks are part of many brides' and grooms' dowries, but they are not often used for eating, as silver conducts heat. Ivory chopsticks are used for banquets; they are more elegant than bamboo but also clean and practical. Jade, although sometimes used, is actually too fragile to make practical chopsticks.

Q: *How should I wash my chopsticks after use? Can I put them in the dishwasher?*

A: A dishwasher is excellent for washing bamboo chopsticks, providing precautions are taken to prevent them from falling through and getting into the machinery. Punch holes in the bottom of a metal can and place this can with the chopsticks in it in the silverware section of the dishwasher, or tie the chopsticks with an elastic band and lay them down in the top section.

Do not wash plastic or ivory chopsticks in a dishwasher, as the water is too hot and will warp or crack the plastic and discolor the ivory.

If you do not have a dishwasher and want to be sure your bamboo chopsticks are well sterilized, boil water in a pan and stand the washed bamboo chopsticks, eating end down, in the water for 5 minutes.

Q: *Does the use of chopsticks for eating help in enjoying Chinese food?*

A: This is hard to answer. To Chinese and Japanese people, of course, the problem never arises. They eat with chopsticks automatically, having been trained from birth.

Many Americans who have learned to eat with chopsticks feel it improves the flavor of the food. For those to whom the use of chopsticks comes easily, it is certainly more fun than eating with a fork. However, the food is more important than the utensil used, and if you just can't manage chopsticks, it is better to eat with a fork than not to eat. I don't put forks on the table for my students, but if someone asks for one, I will give it to him. Mastering the use of chopsticks may give a more psychological than real enhancement to flavor.

INGREDIENTS

Q: *What staples should I keep on hand if I intend to do a reasonable amount of Chinese cooking? Do I have to order these all from Chinese stores?*

A: Not all Chinese staples must be ordered from Chinese stores. Some are universal or can be found in the Chinese food department of most grocery stores or supermarkets. Universal staples include sugar, salt (preferably coarse or kosher), soy sauce (imported), dry sherry, cornstarch, and scallions. Oriental sesame seed oil is becoming increasingly available in health food departments.

Fresh ginger can sometimes be found in greengrocers' shops and Spanish-American markets in large cities, as well as in Chinese markets. Rock candy is often purchasable in candy stores.

Staples that must be purchased or ordered from Chinese grocery stores include dried fermented black beans, dried black mushrooms, dried tree (cloud) ears, cellophane noodles (bean thread), *hoisin* sauce, oyster sauce, and plum sauce.

Q: What different kinds of rice are there, and how does the manner in which they are cooked differ?

A: There are five different kinds of rice: long-grain, regular, short-grain, natural (brown), and glutinous.

Longer-grain rice absorbs more water and yields more cooked rice as a result. The following table gives the amount of water needed to cook 1 cup of each variety of rice and the amount of cooked rice that results:

1 Cup Rice	*Water (Cups)*	*Yield (Cups)*
Long-grain	1¾	3
Regular	1½	2½
Short-grain	1¼	2+
Natural (brown)	1¾	2½
Glutinous	1	2

Different parts of China produce different kinds of rice. Most farmers eat natural or unbleached rice, regardless of what district they live in.

Glutinous rice, also called "sweet" or "sticky" rice, is in a class by itself. It is not sweet, although many Chinese refer to it by that name, but it is often used in making desserts. This is the rice used in making *congee*, or rice gruel, which is eaten for breakfast or by invalids, and it is also the primary ingredient in stuffings for chickens, ducks, and other poultry.

Q: Why does long-grain rice not come out well if more than 1 cup is cooked at a time?

A: Often, the cook does not realize that the ratio of water to rice decreases slightly as the quantity of rice to be cooked increases. The following table shows the ratio of rice to water:

1 cup long-grain rice	1¾ cups cold water
2 cups long-grain rice	3¼ cups cold water
3 cups long-grain rice	4 cups cold water
4 cups long-grain rice	5 cups cold water
10 cups long-grain rice	11 cups cold water

The cooking time must also be adjusted.

One cup of rice takes 4 to 5 minutes to reach the boiling point. Then the heat is turned down to simmer, the pot is covered, and the rice cooked for 20 minutes. The flame is then turned off and the rice allowed to relax, off the stove, for another 20 minutes without the lid being opened to let steam escape.

When more than 1 cup of rice is cooked at the same time, the time taken to reach the boiling point varies, but the simmering and relaxing time remain the same.

Q: *In "Ways of Cooking Rice" you never mention brown rice. Why not?*

A: About 85 percent of the Chinese are farmers who must eat their rice as they get it from the farm, before it is milled or polished, that is, natural or brown rice. Therefore, most Chinese prefer the polished white rice, which only city people can afford to eat. Attempts to explain the nutritional advantages of brown rice usually fail. For the same reason, Chinese never add soy sauce to fried rice, feeling that it spoils the white color.

Brown rice is much higher in food value than white. If you wish to eat it with your Chinese meal, just prepare it according to directions on the package.

Q: *What is "sizzling rice"?*

A: The name "sizzling rice" was created in America, because when the dish the Chinese call "deep-fried rice crust" is dropped into hot soup, it makes a sizzling sound. "Deep-fried rice crust" is authentically Chinese, and can be made with either glutinous or long-grain rice.

During World War II, anti-Japanese feeling in China affected the name of this dish. It was considered a patriotic act to order "Bomb Tokyo, with chicken" or "Bomb Tokyo, with shrimp." Both smoke and noise are created when the rice sizzles, and the effect is not unlike that of a bomb dropping on a city.

Q: *Are potatoes ever used in Chinese cooking?*

A: Potatoes are not native to China, and are not used in any traditional dishes.

In modern China, however, potatoes are now cultivated and are used in stews and curries, dishes that originated in other countries and are now incorporated into the Chinese cuisine.

Q: *Is Chinese chicken broth different from American chicken broth?*

A: Many of my students ask this question, and the answer is yes. The cooking procedures are essentially the same, but the vegetables and seasonings used differ. While Americans generally include a variety of vegetables in their "soup greens," Chinese chicken broth consists only of chicken, water, 2 slices of fresh gingerroot, and 1 scallion. Salt is not used during cooking, but is added just before serving. A basic recipe for Chinese chicken broth follows:

INGREDIENTS

1 whole chicken (2 ½ to 3 pounds), cut up, or 2 ½ to 3 pounds backs, wings, necks, or other parts
2 slices fresh gingerroot
1 scallion, green part and all, cut into 2-inch lengths

COOKING PROCEDURE

Place the chicken pieces in a large saucepan and cover with water to a depth of about 1 inch over the top of the chicken. Add the gingerroot and scallion and bring to a boil, then turn down the heat, cover, and simmer for 40 minutes. Turn off the flame and allow the chicken to cool in the broth. When cool, strain the broth into a large container. Cover and refrigerate overnight. Skim off the fat before using, and add salt as specified in each recipe in which broth is used.

Q: *Can I eat Chinese food without eating pork?*

A: Yes, you can. Pork is the principal meat of most Asian countries, as well as of the South Sea Islands. However, Americans who cannot eat pork, or who do not like it, can substitute veal, chicken, or even shrimp in pork dishes. Don't deprive yourself of the pleasure of eating Chinese food because you don't eat pork.

Q: *Do egg rolls have egg in them?*

A: Yes, though there may be only one egg in many pounds of the dough used to make egg-roll wrappers. However, the dough is principally a flour-and-water dough, and the filling seldom if ever contains any eggs. What Americans know as egg rolls are often really "spring rolls."

In China, spring rolls and egg rolls are quite different. Spring rolls use "Shanghai wrappers," which are not machine made like egg-roll wrappers but individually hand rolled out of flour and water. Traditionally, they are only served on Chinese New Year, the first day of spring in the Chinese calendar. According to ancient custom, this was the only holiday allowed many domestic servants. Spring rolls could be made in advance by the kitchen help and reheated as an appetizer for the many guests who came to call.

Spring rolls are only one appetizer served at New Year's time. Each appetizer has its own meaning; spring rolls, because of their golden color and oblong shape, are thought to resemble gold bars. Guests, invited to eat them, know that their host wishes them wealth in the New Year. They are made in great quantities because they taste good and keep well.

A recipe for spring rolls is given in *The Pleasures of Chinese Cooking*, page 68, where they are called Shrimp Egg Rolls.

Q: *Are lichee nuts really nuts?*

A: No. Lichee nuts are to fresh lichees exactly what raisins are to grapes. Dried lichee fruits came into the United States and gained popularity very early, along with chop suey and egg rolls. Although it is not a nut, the dried fruit does have a nutlike flavor and texture, so Americans called it "lichee nut."

Q: *What is a winter melon? Can any American vegetable be used in place of it in a dish like winter melon soup?*

A: Winter melon is a white squash that ripens in winter. When it is whole, it looks like a very large, oversized football, covered with white powder. As long as it is not cut, the powdery substance preserves it for six months or more. Once cut, however, the pieces must be used fairly rapidly or they will spoil.

Winter melons are full of water and are prized more for texture than for taste. There is really no substitute for winter melon. Zucchini could be used, but it has an entirely different texture. Winter melon is primarily used for soup.

Q: *Why do Chinese vegetables taste so good? Are the vegetables different from ours, or are they differently prepared?*

A: Some Chinese vegetables are different from those native to the United States—*bok choy* and snow peas, for instance. However, many more are exactly the same or quite similar to American vegetables.

The manner of preparation makes the big difference. Chinese vegetables are cut into small pieces and stir fried quickly over high heat for a short time. They are seldom cooked covered, and are never overcooked; therefore, they do not become soggy or lose flavor. Also, since they are cooked in small quantities of oil and little or no water, no flavor is thrown out with the cooking liquid.

Tubular vegetables such as broccoli (see Broccoli Florets with Water Chestnuts, page 206) must be cooked longer than other vegetables. These are stir fried for an initial period; then the heat is lowered and the vegetable covered for an extra few minutes of cooking. Stir frying causes all the seasonings to mix well with the vegetable and to permeate the entire dish.

Q: *Is there a difference between the supermarket variety of celery cabbage and that sold in Chinese markets?*

A: The so-called Chinese cabbage that used to be the only variety sold in American supermarkets is Tientsin cabbage. It is long and shaped like a bunch of celery, green on one end and white on the other.

Recently, some supermarkets and greengrocers have begun to stock another variety, Shantung cabbage, formerly sold in Chinese markets only. This is entirely white in color, shorter, and thicker than the Tientsin cabbage. It has more flavor and is juicier, crunchier, and more tender.

Q: *How do snow peas differ from regular green peas?*

A: Snow peas are not simply immature green peas. Even when green peas are very young, the pods are not tender and edible like snow pea pods. Snow peas, or sugar peas, are a special variety of the common pea (*Pisum sativum*) with a tender pod and no parchment lining. The French call them *mange tout* because the pod is eaten as well as the peas. Snow peas are best when picked young, before the peas inside have been allowed to mature.

Q: *When do you use scallion green, and when do you use both green and white?*

A: In dishes like fried rice or soup, in which the scallion is added as a garnish just before serving, we use only the green. When the scallion is used for its flavor and cooked in the oil at the start of the cooking process, we use both green and white.

Q: *I notice many of your recipes call for vegetable oil. Is that the kind of oil you would use in China?*

A: Yes, most ordinary Chinese recipes do use vegetable oil.

Exotic or banquet dishes often require chicken fat, duck fat, or lard because they taste better and have a rich sheen. Butter is never used in China because there is not enough pastureland to support cattle raising on any major scale.

Q: *What oils do you include when you specify "vegetable oil" in a recipe?*

A: As I use the term, vegetable oil means any nonanimal oil. Corn oil, peanut oil, soybean oil, safflower oil, nonroasted sesame seed oil—all these fit my description. The Chinese seldom use olive oil. However, only butter, lard, and duck or chicken fat are absolutely excluded by the term "vegetable oil."

Q: *What is the difference between Oriental and Middle Eastern sesame seed oil? How is the Oriental oil used?*

A: Middle Eastern sesame seed oil is made from unroasted sesame seeds, and is therefore clear in color and flavorless. It is used as a cooking oil, like peanut or vegetable oil.

Oriental sesame seed oil is made from roasted seeds and has a pronounced, nutty flavor. Some of my students find it difficult to like at first, but if they keep sampling it in small quantities, they soon like the taste very much.

The Oriental oil is not normally used for stir frying. It is used in "cold-mix" or salad dishes, or added on top of the soup at the last minute for flavor. A dash of this oil can be added to vegetable dishes for extra flavor, too, but be sure that it is always added at the last minute. If allowed to cook with the food, the flavor will evaporate.

Sometimes students confuse Oriental sesame seed paste with tahini, a Middle Eastern paste made from untoasted seeds. The Oriental paste, like the oil, is always made from toasted sesame seeds, and has an exotic flavor and a texture similar to peanut butter.

Q: *Dry sherry is an ingredient in many of your recipes. Is it used instead of a native Chinese wine? If so, what is that wine and from what is it made?*

A: Dry sherry is used in place of Shaohsing wine, which is named after the place where it is made. Shaohsing wine is made from rice, as is Japanese sake, but it takes much longer to mature and is smoother in taste than sake. In China, there are many varieties and quality levels of Shaohsing wine, but the type most often used in cooking is very similar to dry sherry.

Q: *Is MSG a synthetic substance or is it found in nature, like sodium chloride (table salt)? If it is manufactured, how long have the Chinese been making and using it?*

A: Monosodium glutamate is synthetic. The Chinese manufacture it from soybean essence and other chemicals and have been making and using it for at least one hundred years.

Q: *Is there any difference between light and dark soy sauce besides appearance?*

A: Appearance is the least important difference between light and dark soy sauce. Actually, they should be named "light" and "heavy," or "thin" and "thick," but someone began calling them "light" and "dark" and the names stuck. The distinction is somewhat similar to that between dry and sweet wine. Dry wine is a liquid and therefore not dry; it is simply the opposite of sweet.

Dark soy sauce contains more molasses than light, making it thicker. Most Chinese cook with dark soy and use the light sauce for dipping, but the Cantonese cook with both varieties. Light soy sauce is thought to have a somewhat finer flavor.

Q: *If I cannot get dark soy sauce, how can I make my Chinese dishes dark brown in color?*

A: In the supermarket, in the Chinese food section, you can buy "bead molasses," which comes in a small jar. One-quarter teaspoon of this, mixed with the amount of soy sauce needed in your recipe, makes a good substitute for dark soy sauce.

Soy jam, available in Chinese markets, gives the same result, but if you can get to a Chinese market, you may as well buy dark soy sauce, which is no harder to find than soy jam.

Q: *Is arrowroot an acceptable substitute for cornstarch as a thickener? If so, do I substitute the same quantity? What is the thickener used in China?*

A: Arrowroot is a good substitute for cornstarch, and is often used by people allergic to corn or corn products. The same quantities should be used.

In China, water chestnut flour and lotus root flour are used as thickeners. Corn is not native to China; cornstarch would be as expensive there as water chestnut flour is here.

Q: *Most dishes in many Chinese restaurants have thick sauces. Is that true of the food the Chinese eat at home?*

A: No, most Chinese food is served with the natural juices formed in cooking, occasionally moistened with a little water or chicken broth. Restaurants often thicken their sauces for easier handling and because the sauce helps food to stay warm longer.

Q: *Do the Chinese serve duck sauce, soy sauce, and hot mustard for dipping with every meal at home as Chinese restaurants in America do?*

A: Absolutely not. In China, no condiments are placed on the table, not even soy sauce. The chef has the responsibility for making certain dishes salty and others bland. Normally, expensive dishes such as meat and chicken should be more salty, so that the diners will eat smaller quantities and consume more rice. Vegetable dishes are bland, permitting the eating of larger portions.

If deep-fried dishes are served, however, condiments for dipping do accompany them. Soy sauce and vinegar are used for dipping egg rolls, *kuo-tih,* and other deep-fried foods. The Cantonese use hot mustard and plum sauce for dipping. Duck sauce was invented in the United States and does not exist in China at all.

Q: *Are any foodstuffs used in Chinese cooking imported into China instead of being home grown or manufactured?*

A: The Chinese do not import any item for daily consumption as the Americans import coffee or tea.

Originally, many vegetables, such as potatoes, carrots, tomatoes, sweet bell peppers, beets, and corn were imported from the West. These, however, were soon cultivated in China and are now raised there.

Q: *Which Chinese vegetables grow well in the United States?*

A: The United States and China are in the Temperate Zone, and their climates are quite similar. Therefore, there is no reason why vegetables grown in China could not be cultivated in the United States.

Growing of Chinese vegetables here is governed by the law of supply and demand. In recent years, as Americans have come to know and ask for many Chinese vegetables, farmers have begun to raise them. The greater the demand is, the more plentiful the supply will become.

Among Chinese vegetables now grown in the United States are *bok choy*, mustard greens, winter melon, snow peas, icicle radish, celery cabbage, kohlrabi, and taro (often sold in Spanish-American markets). Scallions, ginger, spinach, broccoli, watercress, and many others are shared by both cultures.

Usually, when Chinese vegetables are not sold in a section of the United States, it is because they are not popular enough in the area. If you don't see your favorite Chinese vegetable in your grocery store, ask for it. If enough people ask, you may get it, and if you have a garden, write to seed suppliers in the meantime so that you can grow your own.

BEVERAGES

Q: *What do the Chinese drink during the day? Is much liquid drunk between meals?*

A: As I have stated in another answer, soup, rather than tea, is drunk with meals. Before and after meals, and all during the day, the Chinese drink tea. When the weather is warm, they drink even more tea—and always warm, never iced.

To conserve fuel, tea is made in concentrated form in the mornings, and hot water is poured into thermos bottles and kept warm for long periods of time to add to this concentrate when desired. Often, when the water in a family's thermos grows cold or is used up, or when unexpected guests arrive between meals, boiling water is purchased from large public caldrons, present in every neighborhood. This method of securing hot water is much cheaper than using fuel to heat more water, especially if it is not mealtime.

Q: *How can I tell what kind of tea to serve with a Chinese meal?*

A: It's up to you. There is no set rule about what kind of tea to serve. In China, people usually drink locally grown teas. Green tea, for instance, is served in Hangchow, where it is raised. The Cantonese favor black tea. The weather, too, may have something to do with which tea is served, different teas being more popular at different seasons of the year.

Choice of tea is entirely a matter of individual preference. You may want to experiment with different kinds of tea or to remain faithful to one favorite. Either method is perfectly correct.

Remember, however, that tea is not served with the meal at all in China. It is served immediately before and immediately after eating, but never during the meal itself.

Q: *Do the Chinese use sugar in tea? Why or why not?*

A: The Chinese almost never put sugar in their tea, nor do they add lemon or cream. They have become accustomed to eating

79

very little sugar in any form and do not, therefore, like any food sweet, in part because sugar is scarce and expensive. I sometimes add sugar in small quantities to food, but this custom is unique to the eastern section of China, from which I come.

In China, since tea is made in large quantities at the beginning of the day, constantly replenished, and drunk all day long, drinking a large quantity of sweet tea would be unrefreshing and cloying, so no sugar is added. True coffee lovers drink coffee black; the Chinese, being tea lovers, do the same.

There is one exception to this rule. When tea that includes dried chrysanthemum flowers is served, it is accompanied by raw rock sugar, and each diner puts a small lump of the sugar into his chrysanthemum tea.

Q: *What is green tea?*

A: Green tea is unfermented tea. Only the choicest part of the tea plant, the young buds, can be used. These are then wilted slightly and dried, while the remaining parts of the plant are saved for making other kinds of tea.

Green tea is the most expensive tea available. It has a pure bouquet and is very light in color. Never try to make this tea dark, as it will become bitter and unpleasant to drink.

Q: *Why are flowers used in tea?*

A: Flowers are an integral part of Chinese cooking. They are used, not only in tea, but also in preserving, decorating, and cooking.

Flowers added to tea make it more interesting, exotic, and fragrant. Probably the best-known flower-scented tea in America is jasmine tea, part of the green tea plant to which dried jasmine flowers have been added. Another example is rosebud tea, fully fermented, or "black," tea into which dried rosebuds are mixed.

Q: *Do the Chinese drink wine and hard liquor? What kinds do they drink? At what times do they drink?*

A: The Chinese are not, by and large, a drinking nation. We only drink on special occasions. At banquets, for instance, we do not want to discuss politics or gossip about our neighbors, so we may drink and play "finger games" similar to those played by the Italians. The difference is that, in China, the loser of the game, rather than the winner, drinks.

Shaohsing wine, made from rice, is the most common Chinese wine. There are several kinds of hard liquor, *mao-tai* liquor being perhaps the best known at present, though none is drunk by a significant proportion of the population. Neither wine nor hard spirits are ever consumed on an empty stomach, as the little drinking that takes place is only at mealtimes.

Ginger root

Chinese parsley or Cilantro

Dried Shrimp

Chinese chives

Sea bass

Bean curd

Szechuan pepper

Cleaver

Water chestnuts

Dried tiger-lily buds

Snow peas

Scallion

THE RECIPES

Soup

The Chinese never serve soup as a first course. Soup is considered a beverage rather than a food; therefore, it is served throughout the meal. In China cold liquids are never served, and tea is served either before or after meals. So soup is often the only dinner beverage.

In some areas a large bowl of soup is placed on the table at the beginning of each meal, because the diners are thirsty at the start. The family drinks soup while meat, vegetables, and large quantities of rice are eaten. At the end of the meal, what is left of the soup is reheated and served again to satisfy the thirst created by eating.

At banquets in China, soup is served at the very end. According to some schools of cooking, especially the Fukien school, two or three different soups are served between banquet courses to whet and rekindle the appetite. Such soups might include shark's fin soup, a seafood soup, or even a sweet soup such as Silver Fungus in Syrup (page 231)—a dessert in soup form, not unlike the fruit soups of middle European cuisine.

At Chinese banquets in the United States, soup is served at or near the beginning. Usually, I ask that soup be served after a cold appetizer and the first four stir-fry dishes. This practice preserves some of the authentic Chinese tradition, while making a small concession to American tastes.

Bok Choy and Bean Curd Soup

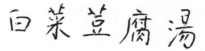

6 SERVINGS

Here is a typical example of Chinese "home cooking." This soup is simple, nourishing, and delicious, and is served, with little variation, all over China.

INGREDIENTS

1 pound *bok choy* (Chinese green)

6 medium-sized dried Chinese mushrooms

2 small squares, or one large, fresh bean curd

4 cups chicken broth, fresh or canned

2 teaspoons salt, only if fresh broth is used

3 tablespoons oil

PREPARATION

Soak *bok choy* in cold water for 10 minutes. Rinse well until no sand remains. Cut into ½-inch pieces.

Wash mushrooms in cold water. Then soak at least 20 minutes in warm water. Cut each mushroom into 4 pieces, discarding stems.

Slice bean curd into pieces about 1 x 1 x ¼ inches.

COOKING PROCEDURES

Heat broth, adding salt if broth is fresh.

Stir-fry *bok choy* in oil for about 3 minutes. Add to the boiling soup.

Add bean curd and mushrooms to soup. Bring soup to boil again. Cover and let simmer for about 7 minutes. Serve immediately.

TIPS

Bok choy and fresh bean curd are available in Oriental markets.

Watercress, spinach, or celery cabbage can be substituted for *bok choy*.

When using canned broth, chill in refrigerator to solidify fat. Then open can with beer-can opener, making a larger hole on one side and a small puncture on the other. Pour soup through puncture so fat remains in can.

Chicken Watercress Soup

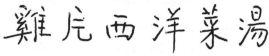

6 SERVINGS

Watercress grows abundantly in southern China. It is often used in soups such as this clear one, which is very light and tasty.

INGREDIENTS

1 whole chicken breast
½ egg white (beat 1 egg white lightly, then divide in half)
1 bunch watercress
6 cups chicken broth, fresh or canned
1 tablespoon salt, if fresh broth is used
½ cup water chestnut slices
⅛ teaspoon white pepper

PREPARATION

Bone and skin chicken breast. Put it in the freezer until it is hard enough to slice thin. Slant-slice chicken breast into pieces about 1 x 1 x ⅛ inches. Mix with half of an egg white.

Wash watercress and cut into inch-long pieces.

COOKING PROCEDURES

Heat broth in a large saucepan until boiling. Add salt (if used) and stir a few times.

Add water chestnuts and watercress. When the broth boils again, add the chicken mixture, stirring immediately with chopsticks to prevent the pieces from sticking to each other. As soon as the soup boils again, turn off flame. Sprinkle with white pepper and serve.

TIPS

Avoid overcooking, as it makes the chicken tough.

Clam and Icicle Radish Soup

蛤 蜊 蘿 蔔 絲 湯

6 SERVINGS

The Chinese who live in or near seaports are very fond of fresh clams and other seafood. Clams are often used in soups, such as this one with icicle, or white, radishes. It is a clear soup, with a taste and texture unusual yet pleasing to American palates.

INGREDIENTS

16 to 18 littleneck clams (about 2 pounds)
1 teaspoon vegetable oil
2 slices fresh ginger
1 tablespoon dry sherry
2 teaspoons salt
3 cups icicle radish shreds, peeled first
1 stalk scallion in 2-inch pieces
1 teaspoon sesame seed oil

PREPARATION

Clean each clam carefully with a vegetable brush. To remove sand, soak in enough water to cover, to which 1 teaspoon of vegetable oil has been added, for 2 to 3 hours.

Boil 3 cups of water in a saucepan. Add 3 or 4 clams, bring to boil again. Keep boiling until clams begin to open. As soon as a clam opens, pick it out and add another clam. Continue until all clams are opened and picked out. Take clam meat out of all shells except 6. Leave these clams in a bowl for later use.

Let the water clams were cooked in settle and then pour the clearer portion into a measuring cup. Discard sediment. Add cold water until there are 4 cups in all.

COOKING PROCEDURES

Boil the 4 cups of liquid in a saucepan. Add ginger, sherry, and salt. Then add radish shreds and bring to a boil. Cover, turn flame to medium, and cook for 10 minutes. When ready to serve, add scallions and clams and cook for just a few seconds until clams are warm. Pour into large soup tureen and add sesame oil as topping. (Each serving gets one clam in the shell as a garnish.)

TIPS
To avoid the meat being chewy, be sure the clams are not overcooked.

Icicle radishes are the long white radishes often available at green-grocers' in the United States, especially in the spring. If not generally available, they can be found in Chinese grocery stores. Substitute red radishes if necessary, peeling off red skin, and cut in slices.

Dried Lotus Root and Sparerib Soup

排骨藕乾湯

8 SERVINGS

In Canton, soups like this one are brewed daily in most restaurants. Yet they are such favorites that they are doled out only to well-known regular customers.

Slow simmering gives Cantonese soups their typical rich flavor and nourishing quality. This one, for instance, takes 5 hours to cook. Its unique flavor comes from ingredients like lotus root and tangerine peel, as well as from length of cooking time.

INGREDIENTS
8 to 10 pieces dried lotus root
4 cups fresh spareribs, each piece cut into about 1½-inch size
4 slices *Wei-san* spice
20 seeds *chi-tzu* spice

2 pieces dried tangerine peel, about the size of fifty-cent coins
1½ tablespoons salt

PREPARATION
Soak dried lotus roots overnight in 1 cup cold water. Drain and cut into inch-size pieces. Bring 2 quarts water to a boil and add the spareribs. Bring to boil again and boil for 5 minutes. Drain spareribs and wash off scum.

COOKING PROCEDURES
Put 4 quarts of cold water in a 6-quart saucepan. Add lotus roots and bring to boil. Simmer for 1 hour. Add spareribs and again bring to boil. Simmer for another hour. Add the *Wei-san, chi-tzu,* and tangerine

peel and simmer for a third hour. Add salt and continue simmering for 2 more hours. (The soup can be served reheated as well.)

TIPS

Wei-san is the root of a plant that grows in the district of the Wei River in Honan.

Chi-tzu is the berry of the Chinese matrimony vine, which grows in the United States as well as in China. The young plant can be eaten as a vegetable.

Tangerine peel gives a pleasant flavor to any dish, and it, as well as the other two spices, can be purchased in Chinese grocery stores in large cities in the United States. Dried lotus roots can also be found there. They come in boxes or in bags and keep a long time on the shelf.

Fish Maw and Shrimp Ball Soup

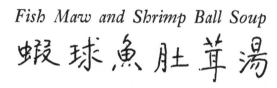

6 SERVINGS

Anyone who has been in a Chinese grocery store may have wondered about the white, puffy objects encased in plastic and shaped like little clouds, which hang from racks. These are pieces of fish maw, a Chinese delicacy. I must confess that fish maw is the cured stomach of various kinds of fish, but I hope my readers will try it anyway. The taste is a pleasant surprise, light and delicate, without a trace of "fishy" smell.

INGREDIENTS

½ ounce dried fish maw
6 cups chicken broth, fresh or canned
1 tablespoon salt, only if fresh broth is used
½ cup minced water chestnuts

15 shrimp balls (about 5 ounces)
¼ cup cornstarch dissolved in ¼ cup water
2 egg whites, beaten until frothy
1 tablespoon finely chopped cooked Smithfield ham

PREPARATION

Soak fish maw in 2 cups very hot water for 10 minutes. When cooled to touch, squeeze out all the water. Shred and then mince it.

COOKING PROCEDURES

Bring chicken broth to a boil. If fresh broth is used, add the salt. Add fish maw and boil for 3 minutes.

Add minced water chestnuts and shrimp balls. Mix and again bring to boil.

Thicken with predissolved cornstarch (stirred again to make sure the cornstarch and water are thoroughly mixed).

Add beaten egg whites. Stir and turn off flame. Pour into a tureen, sprinkle chopped ham on top, and serve.

TIPS

Shrimp balls are available ready made in Chinese grocery stores, but a recipe for preparing them at home is given on page 206 of *The Pleasures of Chinese Cooking*.

Laver and "Egg Flower" Soup

6 SERVINGS

Laver is only one of many types of seaweed, rich in iodine, used in Oriental cooking. Once Americans adjust to the idea of eating it, they find that it has an interesting, if a bit "fishy," taste. Seaweeds like laver are added to soups, to cold-mix dishes, and to chicken or meat courses. They may also be used as side dishes. Easy to prepare, this soup is different from egg drop soup because it is not thickened with cornstarch. The eggs will form clusters and look like flowers. Egg drop soup is a variation of the egg flower soup so popular around the Shanghai district.

INGREDIENTS

3 sheets dried laver (seaweed)

2 eggs

1 to 2 stalks scallion, green part only

6 cups chicken broth, fresh or canned

1 tablespoon salt, only if fresh broth is used

⅛ teaspoon white pepper

1 tablespoon Oriental sesame seed oil

PREPARATION

Tear laver sheets by hand into 1-inch pieces.

Beat eggs until white and yolk are thoroughly mixed.

Cut scallion green into ¼-inch pieces, to make ¼ cup.

COOKING PROCEDURES

Bring chicken broth to boil. Add salt, if needed, scallion, and laver and stir a few times, then add eggs.

As soon as the soup boils, turn off the flame. Stir briefly with chopsticks or fork, then sprinkle with white pepper and float sesame seed oil on top. Pour into soup tureen and serve hot.

Peanut and Hog's Maw Soup

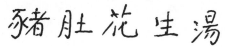

6 SERVINGS

Americans are so accustomed to thinking of peanuts as a snack that they may forget that they are rich in protein and therefore a nourishing food. To the Chinese, no nourishing, tasty, available foodstuff would be degraded to the status of an "extra." Here, peanuts are combined with hog's maw and spices to produce an unusual and inexpensive soup. Cantonese tree ears are a different variety from those used elsewhere in the book. The common tree ears (Cantonese call them "cloud ears," and this is how we will refer to them) become soft when soaked, but the Cantonese tree ears remain crunchy.

INGREDIENTS

1 tablespoon dried Cantonese tree ears (optional)

½ cup dried "first layer" bean curd

1 cup raw peanuts, shelled and skinned

1 precooked hog's maw

1 piece dried tangerine peel, the size of a fifty-cent piece

1 tablespoon salt

¼ teaspoon monosodium glutamate

PREPARATION

If used, soak Cantonese tree ears in ½ cup warm water for 20 minutes.

Soak the "first layer" bean curd in lukewarm water for 30 minutes. Drain. Cut into 2-inch lengths.

Cut maw into ½ x 1½-inch pieces. Place in cold water, bring to boil, and boil for 10 minutes. Drain and discard liquid.

COOKING PROCEDURES
Combine all the ingredients in a large soup kettle. Add 2 quarts of cold water, bring to boil, and cook over high flame for 10 minutes, then turn flame to very low and simmer for 2 hours. Pour into a tureen and serve.

TIPS
Precooked hog's maw is recommended because cleaning and cooking a hog's maw is very unpleasant work. Precooked maws are available in any Chinese food store that sells roast pork or cooked duck. They are very inexpensive.

Dried Cantonese tree ears are sold in some Chinese food stores, but may be difficult to find. There is no acceptable substitute, so if you cannot find them, it is better to omit them.

Dried tangerine peel is a spice which can be bought in Chinese grocery stores.

"First layer" is the top layer of bean curd, which is skimmed off during processing. It can be purchased dried, in packaged form, in Chinese grocery stores.

Peking Sour and Peppery Soup

北京酸辣湯

6 SERVINGS
This soup comes from Peking, where the climate gets colder than in other parts of China. Therefore, this is a particularly popular soup for winter meals.

The use of either black or white pepper earmarks any dish as belonging to the northern school of Chinese cooking.

93

INGREDIENTS

¼ pound fresh lean pork	½ teaspoon sugar
¼ cup dried Chinese mushrooms	2 tablespoons light soy sauce
12 tiger-lily buds	2½ tablespoons wine vinegar
1 tablespoon dried cloud ears	⅛ teaspoon black pepper
1 cake fresh bean curd	2½ tablespoons cornstarch, dis-
1 egg	solved in 2 tablespoons of
5 cups chicken or pork broth	cold water
¼ cup bamboo shoots in shreds	1 tablespoon Oriental sesame
1 tablespoon salt	seed oil

PREPARATION

Cut the pork into matchstick-sized shreds.

Soak Chinese mushrooms, lily buds, and cloud ears in 1 cup of hot water for 20 minutes. Rinse, drain, and shred the mushrooms and cloud ears. Cut the tiger-lily buds into 1-inch lengths.

Cut fresh bean curd into shreds.

Beat the whole egg until white and yolk are thoroughly mixed.

COOKING PROCEDURES

Heat broth in a large saucepan until boiling. Add pork strips and mix a few times with two chopsticks. Keep the soup boiling as you add bean curd, bamboo shoots, mushrooms, lily buds, and cloud ears. Add salt, sugar, soy sauce, wine vinegar, and black pepper. Boil for 2 more minutes; stir a few times with chopsticks. Thicken with predissolved cornstarch first stirring to recombine. Pour in egg. Turn off flame immediately. Stir gently a few times with chopsticks. Dish into casserole and sprinkle sesame seed oil on top. Serve hot.

TIPS

Partially freeze the pork, then slice it first before cutting into shreds.

Chinese mushrooms, cloud ears, lily buds, and bean curd can be bought in Chinese and Oriental stores. Certain gourmet stores also carry some of these ingredients.

The cooking takes a very short while, and preparation, as always, can be done ahead of time.

In China beef broth is not used, but if desired, it can be substituted. Veal shreds can also be used in place of pork shreds, but the genuine ingredients are always the tastiest.

Pork, Cellophane Noodle, and Szechuan Preserved Kohlrabi Soup

榨菜肉絲湯

4 SERVINGS

This is a tasty Szechuan soup.

Kohlrabi is grown in several provinces, but only in Szechuan is it preserved, using the famous Szechuan peppercorns as well as other spices. Preserved kohlrabi is very salty and spicy, but if used sparingly, it gives a unique, delicious flavor to dishes like this one.

INGREDIENTS

¼ pound fresh, lean pork butt
¼ cup dried Chinese mushrooms
2 ounces dried cellophane noodles
¼ cup Szechuan preserved kohlrabi

1 scallion, green part only
4 cups water
½ teaspoon salt

PREPARATION

Cut the pork, half frozen or half thawed, into matchstick-sized shreds, to make about ½ cup.

Soak the Chinese mushrooms in warm water for 20 minutes, then drain and remove the stems. Cut into fine shreds.

Soak cellophane noodles in hot water for 15 minutes. Drain and cut into 2-inch lengths.

Wash Szechuan preserved kohlrabi and cut into fine shreds.

Wash and cut scallion green into ⅛-inch pieces.

COOKING PROCEDURES

Bring to boil 4 cups of water. Add pork shreds and stir a few times with chopstick or fork. Then add mushrooms, kohlrabi, and salt. Cook for 2 minutes. Add cellophane noodles. As soon as the soup boils again, add the scallion. Remove from the heat, pour into a tureen, and serve hot.

Tɪᴘs
Szechuan preserved kohlrabi comes in cans. Once the can has been opened, store unused kohlrabi in a wide-mouthed jar in the refrigerator. It will keep for several months. See the index for the other recipes calling for Szechuan kohlrabi in this book.

Shark's Fin Soup

4 SERVINGS

Shark's fin is the caviar of China, the most elegant and expensive single item of food in the cuisine. Except for a handful of the very rich or sophisticated, most Chinese have never eaten it.

So-called shark's fin is the dried cartilage taken from fins of a particular species of shark. The skin, sand, and fishy odor must be carefully removed, a process which takes many days and is too difficult for any but the bravest housewife. Now, however, canned shark's fin is available, and the American housewife can serve a banquet dish formerly eaten only by the Chinese gourmet.

Iɴɢʀᴇᴅɪᴇɴᴛs
½ chicken breast
¼ cup dried Chinese mushrooms
4 cups chicken broth, fresh or canned
1 tablespoon salt, only if fresh broth is used
1 tablespoon shredded ginger
¼ cup shredded cooked Smithfield ham

2 tablespoons chopped scallion green
¼ cup French-style cut fresh or frozen snow peas
2 cans shark's fins (net weight 10 ounces each)
¼ cup cornstarch, dissolved in ¼ cup cold water
⅛ teaspoon white pepper

Pʀᴇᴘᴀʀᴀᴛɪᴏɴ
Bring 1 cup of water to rapid boil and add chicken breast. Boil 10 minutes. Set pan aside and allow the chicken to cool in the broth for 20 minutes. Skin and bone chicken and shred the meat.

Soak Chinese mushrooms in ½ cup of warm water for 20 minutes. Drain. Cut off stems and shred, to make ¼ cup.

COOKING PROCEDURES

Heat broth until boiling, adding the salt if fresh broth is used. Add mushrooms, ginger, ham, chicken, and scallion. Cook for 2 minutes. Add shark's fin, juice and all. Mix a few times, then add the snow pea shreds. Bring to boil and thicken with the predissolved cornstarch (stirred once more so the water and cornstarch are evenly mixed).

Sprinkle white pepper on top of soup. Serve hot.

TIPS

If Smithfield ham is not available, boiled ham in shreds may be substituted.

Winter Melon–Fish Maw Soup

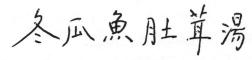

6 SERVINGS

Winter melon is a staple of Chinese restaurants, popular with Americans. This variation may seem somewhat formidable to those unfamiliar with it. However, it is a typical Cantonese soup, quite mild, and a welcome change from the more common winter melon soup.

INGREDIENTS

1 pound winter melon
2 ounces dried fish maw
6 cups chicken broth, fresh or canned
1 tablespoon salt, only if fresh broth is used

¼ cup cornstarch, dissolved in ¼ cup cold water
1 tablespoon minced cooked Smithfield ham

PREPARATION

Peel a 1-pound piece of winter melon and cut it into 3 or 4 pieces. Place pieces in a saucepan with enough water to cover, bring to a boil and boil for 10 minutes. Leave the melon in water to cool for 10 minutes, then remove it and cut it first into slices, then shreds, and finally into small dice. There should be about 2 cups.

Soak fish maw in warm water for 1 hour, then drain and squeeze out the water. Cut the maw into ½-inch shreds and then into ½-inch dice.

COOKING PROCEDURES
Put the chicken broth and diced fish maw in saucepan and bring to a boil. Boil for 10 minutes, adding salt if necessary, then add the diced winter melon and bring to a boil again. Thicken with the predissolved cornstarch (stirred once more so the cornstarch and water are evenly mixed) and pour into large tureen. Sprinkle minced ham over the top and serve.

TIPS
Dried fish maw is sold in Chinese grocery stores, usually in 4-ounce packages. After using 2 ounces for this recipe, keep the remaining 2 ounces, still dried, in the freezer. It will keep many months.

Prosciutto ham may be substituted for the Smithfield, if necessary.

Salads

The dishes listed under "salads" are not real salads in the American sense. The Chinese are not accustomed to eating raw vegetables, because vegetables in China are fertilized by methods which make it dangerous to eat them raw. Therefore, vegetables used in Chinese salads are usually parboiled and cooled before being mixed with dressing. If used in salads uncooked, vegetables like tomatoes, cucumbers, broccoli stems, kohlrabi must be peeled carefully.

Another category included in this section are "cold mix" dishes, such as Szechuan Peppercorn Chicken (page 161). These are pre-cooked meat, or meat and vegetable, dishes, served at room temperature, which can either be included in a Chinese dinner or served as the main dish for a summer luncheon.

Should any salad be served at a banquet, it would include meat or seafood along with a vegetable. Plain vegetable salad, like a plain hot vegetable, is considered too ordinary for a banquet.

Celery and Soy Sauce–Pressed Bean Curd Salad

凉拌芹菜乾絲

6 SERVINGS

Bean curd is a soybean product. When pressed and seasoned with soy sauce, its high protein content is intensified and its taste improved. Combining soy sauce–pressed bean curd with Pascal celery results in a pleasant contrast of the ordinary with the exotic and of textures and flavors.

INGREDIENTS

1 medium-sized head Pascal celery

2 squares soy sauce-pressed bean curd

Sauce:

2½ tablespoons light soy sauce

2½ tablespoons Oriental sesame seed oil

1 teaspoon wine vinegar

½ teaspoon salt

½ teaspoon sugar

¼ teaspoon Chinese hot pepper oil

PREPARATION

Remove strings from outer skin of celery and cut stem into 1-inch pieces. Cut each piece lengthwise into ¼-inch strips. This should yield about 2½ cups. Drop the celery strips into 1 quart boiling water and boil for about 2 minutes, then drain and soak in cold water for 5 minutes. Drain.

Cut each bean curd square in half and split each half into two pieces. Then cut into 1½ x ¼ x ¼-inch pieces.

Mix all the sauce, ingredients together. Combine the celery and bean curd. Add the sauce and mix well.

Arrange on plate and leave in refrigerator. Serve cold.

TIPS

In large cities, soy sauce–pressed bean curd can be bought commercially made in Oriental food shops. Otherwise, it is quite simple to make it yourself (see Glossary, page 290).

100

Abalone and Agar-Agar Salad

凉拌洋菜鲍鱼

4 SERVINGS

To many Californians, fresh abalone steak is a familiar treat. However, the meat of this large mollusk is too perishable to be shipped without some kind of preservation.

Cured, prepared abalone, sold water-packed in cans, is even more tender and flavorful than fresh. The meat has many uses, as in this colorful, tasty, exotic salad. In China abalone is too expensive for general use except at banquets. However, only a small quantity of abalone is required in this salad, which is easy to make and ideal for summer parties.

INGREDIENTS

½ ounce dried agar-agar
½ can abalone, preferably Cal-
mex brand
1 egg
¼ teaspoon salt
1 teaspoon vegetable oil
1 tablespoon cooked Smithfield
ham in fine shreds

Sauce:
1 tablespoon light soy sauce
2 tablespoons Oriental sesame
seed oil
½ teaspoon sugar
¼ teaspoon Chinese hot pepper
oil

PREPARATION

Soak agar-agar in 2 cups *cold* water for 10 minutes. Drain and cut into 2-inch pieces.

Cut the abalone into matchstick-sized shreds.

Beat egg until white and yolk are thoroughly blended, then add the salt and beat a few more times. In a 12-inch frying pan, heat the vegetable oil until hot. Turn off flame and pour in egg. Tip pan quickly so the egg covers the entire surface, forming a large, thin pancake. When the egg has set and is cool enough to handle, slice it into julienne strips. Dish into a small bowl.

Combine the soy sauce, sesame seed oil, sugar, and hot pepper oil and set aside until serving time.

Combine the agar-agar, abalone, egg strips, and ham strips in a bowl. Immediately before serving, pour the sauce over the mixture.

TIPS

Agar-agar is a form of seaweed. It must be soaked in *cold* water, since it will melt in hot. It is used by the Chinese as a coagulating agent for jelly.

For a hotter, spicier dish, increase the hot pepper oil to ½ teaspoon.

Broccoli Stem Salad

4 SERVINGS

There are more ways to serve broccoli florets than there are for the stems. Therefore, the thrifty and ingenious Chinese invented uses for broccoli stems. This is a delicious salad in which only broccoli stems are used.

INGREDIENTS

2 cups broccoli stems	2 tablespoons Oriental sesame
1 teaspoon salt	seed oil
Sauce:	½ teaspoon sugar
2 tablespoons light soy sauce	

PREPARATION

Peel stems very carefully; remove all the tough outer skin. Slant-slice stems until there are 2 cups of broccoli pieces about 1 x ½ x ¼ inches. Sprinkle pieces with salt; shake and let stand for about ½ hour. When ready to mix with the sauce, wash and drain off liquid.

Mix light soy sauce, sesame seed oil, and sugar, then pour over broccoli and mix well. Serve cold as a salad.

TIPS

Be sure to use only Oriental sesame seed oil, which is dark brown in color. This will give a nutty flavor to the salad.

Use only stems of broccoli. If you have not already cooked the florets, save them and cook them plain as a vegetable or in combination with meat. A recipe for Broccoli Florets with Water Chestnuts is given on page 206 of this book.

Cellophane Noodles and Chicken Salad

凉拌芝蔴醬粉絲

4 SERVINGS

There are three "cold mix" chicken salad recipes in this book. However, they are quite different in taste and texture. In this recipe, chicken and cucumbers are shredded very fine and mixed with a sauce heavily flavored with toasted sesame seed products. The result is subtle, and very different from any Western "chicken salad."

INGREDIENTS

2 ounces dried cellophane noodles	Sauce:
1 cucumber	3 tablespoons Oriental sesame seed paste
½ cup cooked chicken, in shreds	2 tablespoons Oriental sesame seed oil
2 tablespoons Smithfield ham shreds	1 tablespoon salt
	1 tablespoon dry mustard

PREPARATION

Soak cellophane noodles in warm water for 20 minutes. Drain and cut into 2-inch lengths. Cook for 2 minutes in 1 cup boiling water. Drain.

Peel, seed, and shred 1 cup of cucumber.

Combine the sesame seed paste, sesame seed oil, salt, and dry mustard with 6 tablespoons cold water. Combine the cellophane noodles with the cucumber, chicken, and ham, then pour the sauce over, mix well, and serve.

TIPS

Oriental sesame seed paste and Oriental sesame seed oil are made from toasted sesame seeds. Both are available in Oriental food stores, and the oil is also available in health food stores and departments.

One tablespoon of dry mustard may seem like a large quantity, but it becomes absorbed in the sauce and has a surprisingly subtle taste. If you wish a distinct mustard flavor, you may want to use a teaspoonful more. Taste the salad first, using the recommended quantity, before deciding to add mustard.

Chicken Shreds with Green Bean Paste Salad

凉拌雞絲粉皮

4 SERVINGS

Dried green bean paste sheets look like thin panes of wavy, light green stained glass. They are rarely obtainable in fresh form here, but the dried sheets are sold in most Chinese markets in large American cities. The "green" beans from which this paste is commercially manufactured are mung beans, pale green in color, not American string beans.

INGREDIENTS

½ raw chicken breast
 3 sheets dried green bean paste
   (about 3 ounces)
Sauce:
 3 tablespoons peanut butter
 3 tablespoons Oriental sesame
   seed paste

3 tablespoons Oriental sesame
  seed oil
4 tablespoons water
2 tablespoons light soy sauce
2 tablespoons Chinese hot
  pepper oil

PREPARATION

Plunge the chicken breast into 1 cup boiling water and boil rapidly for 10 minutes. Allow chicken to cool in its own broth approximately 20 minutes, then drain, saving the broth for another purpose. Remove skin and bones and shred chicken.

Soak green bean paste in boiling water for half an hour. (Water *must* be hot. Use enough to submerge the sheets totally.) Drain and cut into coarse shreds, about 2 x ½ inches in size.

Mix shredded green bean paste with chicken.

Combine all the sauce ingredients, mixing until a smooth paste is formed. Add sauce to chicken mixture and blend well. Refrigerate until serving time and serve cold.

TIPS
Sesame seed paste is made in China, and comes in either jars or cans. Like sesame seed oil, it is made of the roasted seeds, and the resulting smoky taste is very tantalizing.

Chicken and Agar-Agar Salad

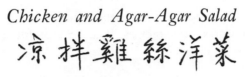

4 SERVINGS

Agar-agar is a seaweed product that the Chinese use both in salad and as a coagulating agent in making jelly and aspic. It comes in dried strips resembling transparent noodles. When soaked in boiling water, it dissolves completely and will become firm after it gets cold again. Therefore, to be used in salad, it must be soaked only in cold water.

INGREDIENTS

1 egg	1 teaspoon sesame seeds
¼ teaspoon salt	Sauce:
1 teaspoon vegetable oil	1 tablespoon light soy sauce
½ ounce dried agar-agar	2 tablespoons Oriental sesame
1 whole chicken breast	seed oil
10 scallions, green part only	½ teaspoon sugar

PREPARATION
Beat egg until white and yolk are thoroughly mixed. Add salt and beat a few more times. In a 12-inch frying pan, heat vegetable oil until hot. Turn flame off and pour in egg. Swirl pan quickly so the egg covers the entire surface, forming a large, thin pancake. When the egg has set and is cool enough to touch, slice it into julienne strips. Dish into a small bowl.

Soak agar-agar in 2 cups of *cold* water for 10 minutes. Drain. Cut into 1½-inch pieces.

Boil 2 cups water and add chicken breast. Bring to boil again. Turn flame to medium, cover the pan and cook for 15 minutes. Cool the chicken in the broth until it can be touched, then drain. Discard skin and bones. Shred the breast into strips by hand.

Cut the green part of the scallions into ¼-inch pieces.

Combine sauce ingredients and set aside.

Mix agar-agar with chicken, egg and scallion. Then mix with sauce. Top with sesame seeds. Serve.

TIPS

Agar-agar may be purchased in Oriental stores. It is very light and 4 ounces will last for several recipes. It also keeps for a long time and needs no refrigeration.

Fresh Bean Curd Salad

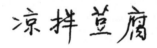

凉拌荳腐

6 SERVINGS

We often think of rice as the most important food in China. Actually, bean curd is just as essential because of its high protein content.

Hundreds of millions of Chinese have little or no meat to eat, and therefore no animal protein in their diet. Vegetable protein from the soybean and its various products is essential to their health. Bean curd is the most common and well-liked of all soybean products. It is eaten uncooked in salads, and is also cooked with other vegetables or meat and fish.

INGREDIENTS

4 squares fresh bean curd
½ cup chopped scallion, green part only

Sauce:
3 tablespoons light soy sauce

3 tablespoons Oriental sesame seed oil
½ teaspoon sugar
2 teaspoons minced fresh ginger

PREPARATION

Cut bean curd into small dice and sprinkle with chopped scallion.

Combine sauce ingredients in a bowl. When ready to serve, pour the sauce over the bean curd.

TIPS

To make it more tasty, I prefer to mash the bean curd with a serving spoon just before serving.

Bean curd can be stored in the refrigerator for a week. Submerge it in cold water in a covered container with a little salt added to the water.

Mung Bean Sprout Salad with Egg Strips

8 SERVINGS

There are two kinds of bean sprouts in the Chinese markets. This variety, grown from the mung bean, is the kind we commonly call "bean sprouts."

Mung beans, sometimes called "mung peas," are like small, dried peas and green in color. Although the yellow soybean sprouts have more nutritional value, they must be cooked for at least 6 minutes to enhance the flavor and are therefore not as widely used as the mung bean sprouts.

INGREDIENTS

1 pound fresh mung bean sprouts (about 4½ cups)
1 egg
1 teaspoon vegetable oil
¼ cup chopped scallion, green part only
Sauce:
¼ cup wine vinegar

2 tablespoons light soy sauce
2 tablespoons vegetable oil
2 tablespoons Oriental sesame seed oil
½ teaspoon sugar
½ teaspoon Chinese hot pepper oil

PREPARATION

Float bean sprouts in a large basin of cold water. Stir with hands. Let the green skin of the bean float off. Drain.

Beat the egg until the white and the yolk are thoroughly mixed. Heat the teaspoon of vegetable oil in a 10 to 12-inch frying pan, then turn off the flame and add egg. Swirl the pan quickly so the egg covers the entire surface, forming a large, thin pancake. As soon as the egg sets and is cool enough to handle, slice it into julienne strips. Set aside in a small bowl.

Combine sauce ingredients and refrigerate until ready to serve.

Combine the bean sprouts with the egg strips and scallion.

About 5 minutes before serving, stir the sauce with chopsticks and pour over the bean sprout mixture. Mix well and serve cold.

TIPS

The Orientals, who prefer not to eat bean sprouts raw, make this salad by first boiling 2 quarts of water and plunging in the bean sprouts. They then turn off the flame and leave the sprouts in the water for 2 minutes, then they drain the sprouts and soak them in cold water to retain their crispness. I prefer this method, but it is purely a matter of personal preference.

Chinese hot pepper oil can be purchased in Chinese grocery stores. It is made from chili pepper flakes and vegetable oil. Red Hot Devil sauce in the same amount may be substituted.

Jellyfish and Icicle Radish Salad

凉拌海蜇蘿蔔絲

8 SERVINGS

Most Americans feel hesitant about eating jellyfish, but those who have tried have found their bravery rewarded with a new and delightful taste experience—for jellyfish makes a pleasant, crunching sound and tastes remarkably good.

INGREDIENTS

1½ tablespoons light soy sauce
2 tablespoons Oriental sesame seed oil

½ teaspoon sugar
½ teaspoon Chinese hot pepper oil (optional)

1 medium-sized icicle radish, more if necessary	½ cup chopped scallions, green part only
1 teaspoon salt	2 ounces soaked, drained, and shredded jellyfish

PREPARATION

Combine the soy sauce, sesame seed oil, sugar, and hot pepper oil, if used, and refrigerate until serving time.

Peel icicle radish and cut into fine shreds. Measure 1½ cups of shreds, using more radishes if needed. Sprinkle salt over the radish and let stand for 25 to 30 minutes. Rinse and drain.

Mix jellyfish, radish, and chopped scallion in a salad bowl. Just before serving, pour sauce over salad. Serve cold.

TIPS

Icicle radishes are available in Chinese and Japanese grocery stores and in many greengrocers' stores as well. Seed catalogs list icicle, or white, radish seeds for sale; so the home gardener can raise them.

Dried, preserved jellyfish, imported from China and Japan, requires advance preparation if it is to be used in this or other dishes. Immediately after purchasing, wash the jellyfish many times in cold water, then place it in a jar with cold water and keep it until needed, at least several days. Just before using, drain and rinse again.

If the jellyfish is bought in large sheets, wash and shred the whole sheet first and then wash it again before soaking. The shreds will keep for several weeks in water in the refrigerator.

Lotus Root Salad

凉拌甜酸藕

4 SERVINGS

Lotus root is plentiful in the areas around Hangchow, Soochow, and Shanghai, where this sweet-sour salad has become a favorite. The red color of the wine vinegar and the lacy design of the lotus root combine to make this salad attractive as well as appetizing.

For would-be lotus eaters who cannot go to China, canned lotus root, exported to the United States and sold in Chinese markets here, substitutes very well for the fresh.

INGREDIENTS

1 twelve-ounce can sliced
  lotus root
1 cup wine vinegar

1 cup sugar
½ teaspoon salt

PREPARATION

Slice each slice of lotus root into two pieces. The resulting slices should be about ⅛ inch thick.

Warm the vinegar in a saucepan and dissolve the sugar and salt in it, then marinate the lotus root in the sauce for 24 hours in the refrigerator. Drain and serve cold.

TIPS

Note that this salad must be made at least a day in advance, as it takes 24 hours to marinate.

Steamed Eggplant Salad

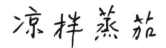

4 SERVINGS

Eggplant is often cooked this way in Soochow, Shanghai, and Hang-chow. Cooks in these regions discovered that it was economical and easy to place several small eggplants on the rack of a steamer while it was being used to steam other food.

INGREDIENTS

3 tablespoons light soy sauce
3 tablespoons Oriental sesame
  seed oil

1 pound eggplant

PREPARATION

Combine the soy sauce and sesame seed oil. Reserve to use as sauce. Wash the eggplant, then remove the green stem.

COOKING PROCEDURES

Place the eggplant, whole, on the rack of a steamer and steam for 10 minutes. Cool thoroughly, then tear with your hands into strips 3 x ¾ inches. Mix with sauce and serve.

TIPS

Long, tubular eggplants are more suitable for this salad than the roundish, as they are easier to tear into strips with the hands.

String Bean Salad with Sesame Seed Paste

4 SERVINGS

This salad is an example of the northern Chinese cooking style recently introduced to the United States. It has a distinctive flavor, strange to those unfamiliar with Chinese food; indeed, some may not like it. For those who like northern Chinese cooking, this dish will be a real treat, especially in summer.

INGREDIENTS

1 pound fresh string beans
¼ cup Oriental sesame seed paste
2 squares preserved bean curd
1 tablespoon preserved bean curd liquid
1 tablespoon light corn syrup
3 tablespoons Oriental sesame seed oil
¼ teaspoon Chinese hot pepper oil

PREPARATION

Wash string beans and break into 2-inch lengths. Bring 2 quarts water to a boil. Drop beans into boiling water and bring to boil again. Cook, uncovered, for 8 minutes. Drain and rinse in cold water until cold, drain again and leave in refrigerator to chill.

Combine the sesame seed paste with the preserved bean curd and the bean curd liquid. Add the corn syrup and mix well, then add the sesame seed oil and hot pepper oil and blend into a smooth paste.

Mix the paste with the chilled beans, tossing thoroughly to blend. Serve cold.

Tips

In China, pole beans would be used here instead of string beans. If available, they should be substituted for string beans to add authenticity.

Preserved bean curd, known as "bean cake," comes in jars. Since it is salty, it should not be overused. It keeps well in the refrigerator.

Water Chestnut and Broccoli Salad

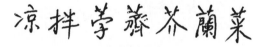

6 SERVINGS

This salad is colorful as well as tasty. Because chopped frozen broccoli is used, it can be served at any season of the year.

Ingredients

10 water chestnuts
 2 ten-ounce packages frozen chopped broccoli
 1 square soy sauce–pressed bean curd, finely chopped (optional)
 1 tablespoon finely minced preserved red ginger (optional)

Sauce:
 2 tablespoons light soy sauce
 2 tablespoons Oriental sesame seed oil
 ½ teaspoon sugar
 ½ teaspoon salt
 ¼ teaspoon Chinese hot pepper oil

Preparation

Finely chop the water chestnuts.

Thaw and drain broccoli. Chop a few more times to make it fine, then mix with minced water chestnuts and bean curd, if using. Set aside.

Combine the soy sauce, sesame seed oil, sugar, salt, and hot pepper oil, and 10 minutes before serving, mix sauce with broccoli. Sprinkle red ginger, if using, on top. Chill, and toss once more before serving.

TIPS

Oriental sesame seed oil can be purchased in Oriental stores and in some supermarkets, especially those with health food sections. It keeps well on the shelf and is rich in vitamin A.

Soy sauce–pressed bean curd can be bought in some Chinese grocery stores. If you prefer to make it yourself, see page 240.

Preserved red ginger comes in a bottle, and keeps well for several months without refrigeration. Caution: Buy only the kind sold in Chinese grocery stores, as the kind imported from other Oriental countries does not taste sweet and cannot be used in this recipe.

Fresh broccoli may be used. Parboil before chopping.

Meat

In China, other areas of the Orient, and the South Seas, pork is so much more common than any other meat that the words "meat" and "pork" are used synonymously. Other meats—beef, veal, and so on—must be identified specifically. To most Chinese, lamb is an unfamiliar and distasteful meat. Only in Mongolia, where nomadic tribes move around to seek pasture lands for sheep, is lamb eaten. Most Chinese do not attempt to cook lamb; they are concerned that its strong odor will linger and flavor their woks or cooking utensils.

There are two principal kinds of meat dishes: those made primarily of meat in relatively large pieces, and those in which ground, shredded, sliced, or cubed meat is stir fried with vegetables. The first kind includes red-cooked and roasted whole meats. Often the large whole meat, once cooked, is cut into small pieces and reheated in combination with vegetables. More often, however, the meat is stir fried, combined with vegetables, from the start. Although the prevalence of combination dishes had its origin in necessity—shortage of fuel and livestock dictating that a little meat be cooked quickly with a larger quantity of cheaper foodstuffs—by now the Chinese prefer meat cooked this way, because of the endless variety thus possible.

Pork is the food of every day, so it is never served at banquets. Beef, veal, and lamb are seldom served at authentic banquets either, because they are not highly regarded by the Chinese. The only meat dish sometimes served at a banquet is bear's paw, which is considered a delicacy.

Curry Beef

咖 喱 牛 肉

8 SERVINGS

Although curry is not native to China, curried dishes have been incorporated into Chinese cooking for at least fifty years. Adapted and modified, these curries are now quite different from those of other countries.

INGREDIENTS

2 pounds shank beef, boned	4 tablespoons curry paste
½ pound onions	2 tablespoons dry sherry
1 pound potatoes	2 tablespoons light soy sauce
2 cloves garlic	1 teaspoon salt
4 tablespoons vegetable oil	1½ teaspoons sugar

PREPARATION

Cut the shank beef into 1-inch cubes.

Peel the onions and cut into 1 x 1-inch pieces.

Peel the potatoes and cut them obliquely into pieces almost 1 inch long, then soak in cold water until ready to use. Drain before using.

Mince the garlic by first crushing with the broad side of the cleaver and then chopping fine.

COOKING PROCEDURES

Heat 2 tablespoons of the vegetable oil in a wok. Add garlic and stir a few times. Add onion and mix well. Transfer into a large saucepan.

Heat the remaining 2 tablespoons of vegetable oil in the same wok.

Add curry paste and mix a few times. Add beef and mix well. Transfer beef to the large saucepan with the onion. Turn flame to high.

Add dry sherry, soy sauce, salt, and sugar. Mix a few times.

Add 1 cup cold water. Bring to boil. Cover, turn flame down to medium, and cook for 40 minutes, stirring from time to time.

Place potatoes on top of beef without mixing. Cover. Continue cooking over medium-low flame for 20 minutes more. Mix thoroughly and serve.

Tips

Curry beef tastes even better when reheated, but rather than heating it in the oven, be sure to heat on top of range over low flame for about 25 minutes. It is a dish that can be prepared beforehand with excellent results. It can also be frozen, thawed to room temperature and heated as above.

Flank Steak Shreds with Rice Sticks

牛肉絲炒米粉

4 SERVINGS

Recently, Chinese restaurants have begun to serve transparent white shreds which look like cocoanut, as a garnish. These are fried "rice sticks," noodles made with rice flour instead of wheat flour.

Rice sticks are especially popular in the provinces of Canton and Fukien. In this version the noodles are not deep fried, but are soaked and then stir fried with meat and vegetables.

Ingredients

8 ounces rice sticks (½ package)	¼ cup dried Chinese mushrooms, soaked and shredded
½ pound flank steak (1 cup)	4 cups *bok choy* leaves or
1 tablespoon dry sherry	celery cabbage leaves,
1½ tablespoons oyster sauce	shredded
2 teaspoons cornstarch	1 teaspoon salt
4 tablespoons vegetable oil	½ teaspoon sugar

2 teaspoons light soy sauce	1 cup chicken broth, fresh or
2 cups fresh bean sprouts	canned
(½ pound)	

PREPARATION
Rinse the rice sticks in hot water for 1 minute, then drain and soak in cold water for 10 minutes. Drain again before using.

Slice the steak, half frozen or half thawed, very thin, then shred. Combine the shreds with the sherry, oyster sauce, and cornstarch.

COOKING PROCEDURES
Stir fry the steak in 2 tablespoons of the oil in a wok or skillet for 2 minutes. Set aside.

Heat the remaining 2 tablespoons oil in a clean wok or skillet, then add the mushrooms and stir. Add the *bok choy* shreds and stir, then add the salt, sugar, and light soy sauce. Stir once more, then add the bean sprouts. Add the rice sticks and broth and stir until the liquid is almost all absorbed. Add the stir-fried steak, mix thoroughly, and serve.

TIPS
Veal, pork, or lamb shreds can be substituted to make an entirely different-tasting dish. Prepare in exactly the same way.

Flank Steak with Preserved Mustard Greens

酸菜牛肉片

4 SERVINGS

Broad-leafed Chinese mustard greens are grown abundantly in the Canton region. Here, preserved greens, rather than fresh ones, are used to give the familiar "steak with oyster sauce" a new and exciting taste.

INGREDIENTS
| ½ cup preserved mustard greens | 1 teaspoon sugar |
| ½ pound flank steak (1 cup) | 3 tablespoons vegetable oil |

2 teaspoons dry sherry	1 tablespoon cornstarch
1 tablespoon oyster sauce	½ cup water chestnut slices

PREPARATION
Wash mustard greens and drain. Cut into 1 x 1 x ¼-inch slices.

Slice half-thawed or half-frozen flank steak into pieces the same size as the greens, then combine with ½ teaspoon of the sugar, 1 teaspoon oil, sherry, oyster sauce, and cornstarch.

COOKING PROCEDURES
Heat 2 more teaspoons oil in wok or skillet. Stir fry mustard greens for a minute, add the remaining ½ teaspoon sugar and mix well. Set aside.

In the same wok or skillet, heat the remaining oil and stir fry flank steak for about 2 minutes. Add water chestnut slices and mix well. Return the mustard greens to the wok and stir. Serve.

TIPS
Preserved mustard greens can be bought canned or bottled. If canned mustard greens are used store the unused part with its liquid and refrigerate.

The Chinese, however, like to preserve their own because they are more hygienic and taste better. A recipe for preserving mustard greens follows:

2 pounds fresh Chinese mustard greens	¼ cup coarse (kosher) salt

Wash and dry mustard greens. Spread on paper towel. Let them wilt in room temperature. In a large container (about 3-quart size), alternate layers of ½ pound of greens and 1 tablespoon salt. Continue until greens and salt are used up.

Let stand at room temperature for 2 hours. Cover and weigh down with a 1-pound weight (heavy object, stone, or bowl of water) overnight.

The next day, remove greens from container, store in a jar, and refrigerate. The preserved greens can be stored in refrigerator for several weeks.

Steak Slices with Onion

洋葱炒牛肉片

4 SERVINGS

The Chinese way of preparing steak requires only a small quantity of meat, and therefore it is much more economical than the American method. This dish is a close cousin to "Beef with Oyster Sauce" found on Chinese restaurant menus. The onion slices are a pleasant addition and change the whole appearance and taste.

1 pound sliced flank steak (2 cups)	¼ cup vegetable oil
	3 to 4 sliced onions
1 tablespoon dry sherry	1 teaspoon sugar
3 tablespoons oyster sauce	1 teaspoon salt
1 tablespoon cornstarch	

PREPARATION
Marinate steak in dry sherry, oyster sauce, and cornstarch for about 10 minutes.

COOKING PROCEDURES
Heat 1 tablespoon oil in a work or skillet and add onion. Stir fry the onion for 3 minutes, or until wilted. Add sugar and salt. Mix well. Remove onion from the wok and set aside.

Heat 3 tablespoons oil in the same skillet or wok and stir fry the steak, stirring rapidly, until it turns grayish, about 3 to 4 minutes. Return the onion to the wok and mix well with the steak. Dish and serve at once.

TIPS
All cuts of beef can be used for steak slices except round steak, which is too lean and therefore too tough for this type of cooking. Veal can also be substituted for beef in this recipe.

Szechuan Shredded Beef

乾燒牛肉絲

4 SERVINGS

This Szechuan dish is rapidly gaining great popularity with Americans. It is pleasantly spicy and relatively hot when compared with other dishes in this book. This version has been toned down slightly so you can enjoy its flavor and still prepare it as often as you wish with no fear of adverse consequences.

INGREDIENTS

1 ounce dried cellophane noodles	1 teaspoon cornstarch
1 cup vegetable oil	½ cup bamboo shoot shreds
¾ pound flank steak (1½ cups)	½ cup carrot shreds
1 tablespoon dry sherry	½ cup snow pea shreds
1 tablespoon soy sauce	1 teaspoon salt
2 tablespoons *hoisin* sauce	1 tablespoon ginger shreds
	½ teaspoon chili pepper flakes

PREPARATION

Deep fry cellophane noodles in the oil at 350° for a few seconds. Drain on a paper towel, reserving oil. Set the noodles aside.

Slice the beef, half frozen or half thawed, very thin, then shred the slices. Combine the beef shreds, sherry, soy sauce, *hoisin* sauce and cornstarch.

COOKING PROCEDURES

Heat 2 tablespoons of reserved oil in a wok or skillet and stir fry bamboo shoots, carrots, and snow peas for 1 minute. Add salt, then stir, and set aside.

In same wok or skillet, heat 6 more tablespoons oil and add ginger. Stir a few times. Add beef mixture and stir fry for 2 minutes. Add chili pepper flakes and mix well. (Drain off excess oil if necessary.)

Return cooked vegetables to wok and stir well, then remove contents of wok to a platter.

Arrange cellophane noodles over and around beef mixture and serve hot.

TIPS

Be sure not to soak the cellophane noodles for this dish; they must be *dry* for deep frying.

Hoisin sauce is found at Chinese grocery stores. After opening can, transfer contents to a glass jar, seal, and store in refrigerator. It will keep for many months.

Tricolored Meat Platter (Chicken, Steak, Watercress)

炒 三 絲

4 SERVINGS

This platter is unusually pretty and tastes very good. Served with boiled rice, it is a whole meal in one dish.

INGREDIENTS AND PREPARATION

1 ½ cups chicken breast in shreds (1 whole chicken breast, about
 ¾ pound)

Mix chicken shreds with:　1　egg white, unbeaten

　1　teaspoon salt

　½　teaspoon sugar

　1　teaspoon minced fresh ginger

　2　tablespoons oil for stir-frying chicken

1 ½ cups steak shreds (about 12 ounces)

Mix steak shreds with:　1　tablespoon dark soy sauce

　2　teaspoons *hoisin* sauce

　1　teaspoon sugar

　1　teaspoon cornstarch

　1　tablespoon dry sherry

　2　tablespoons oil for stir frying steak

2 bunches watercress; wash, discard 1 inch from the stems and then cut remaining watercress in half

> 1 tablespoon vegetable oil for stir-frying watercress
> ½ teaspoon salt
> ⅛ teaspoon monosodium glutamate

COOKING PROCEDURES

Stir fry the watercress in 1 tablespoon of the oil. Add ½ teaspoon salt and the monosodium glutamate. Stir well. Cook for about 2 minutes over high flame without covering. Using slotted spoon, remove the cress and place it in center of a platter. Be sure there is no liquid on platter.

Heat 2 tablespoons of the oil. Add the chicken mixture and stir quickly over high flame for about 2 minutes. When the chicken turns white, remove it to one end of the platter.

Heat 2 tablespoons of the oil over high flame. Add steak mixture and stir fry for about 2 minutes or until steak loses its redness. Remove it and place on the other end of the platter. Serve immediately.

TIPS

It is important to have three distinctly different colors and tastes, but actual foods used to give this effect can be varied. For instance, chicken can be substituted for beef and mixed with *hoisin* sauce to give a reddish-brown color. Spinach can be used in place of watercress and cooked in the same manner.

Lamb Shreds with Scallions

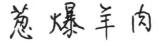

4 SERVINGS

While sheep are not common to most of China, and the great majority of Chinese have never tasted lamb, sheep raising is a principal activity of Mongolia. Therefore, lamb dishes in the Chinese cuisine are usually Mongolian in origin. This dish is included because it is tasty and be-

cause it will give Americans an opportunity to use lamb in Chinese cooking.

INGREDIENTS

10 ounces boneless lamb
2 to 3 bunches scallions, green part and all
2 tablespoons dry sherry
1 tablespoon light soy sauce
1 tablespoon cornstarch
¼ cup vegetable oil
1½ teaspoons salt
½ teaspoon sugar
⅛ teaspoon monosodium glutamate

PREPARATION

Cut the lamb, half frozen or half thawed, into shreds 1½ x ¼ x ¼ inches, to make 1 cup.

Wash scallions and cut into 2-inch lengths, to make 5 cups.

Marinate lamb shreds in sherry, light soy sauce, and cornstarch for 10 minutes.

COOKING PROCEDURES

Stir fry the scallions in 2 tablespoons of the oil in a wok or skillet until they wilt. Add salt, sugar, and monosodium glutamate and stir well, then remove from the wok and set aside.

Add the remaining oil to skillet or wok. Stir fry the lamb shreds about 3 minutes, or until no red color remains. Return scallions to the skillet or wok and mix well. Dish and serve immediately.

TIPS

Any reasonably tender cut of lamb can be used. If you prefer, beef or pork shreds may be substituted for the lamb.

The monosodium glutamate may be omitted if you are sensitive to it. Otherwise the quantity used here is small enough to enhance the taste without causing difficulty.

Fresh and Salt Pork Casserole
with Summer Bamboo and Thinly Pressed Bean Curd

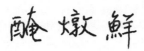

4 SERVINGS

Casseroles are very popular in China in the winter. China has very little central heating, and food remains warm longer in a casserole. Chinese casseroles have a high liquid content, somewhat like "chicken in the pot." During cold months, it is customary for Chinese families to eat one casserole dish with each meal.

INGREDIENTS

½ pound salt pork
1 pound fresh pork (½ pound fresh side and ½ pound lean butt)
7 sheets thinly pressed bean curd (*pai-yeh*)

½ teaspoon baking soda
1 cup summer bamboo shoots in oblique pieces (½ can)
2 teaspoons salt

PREPARATION

Boil salt and fresh pork in 2 quarts water for 5 to 6 minutes. Rinse in cold water until thoroughly cold. Drain. Cut into pieces 1 x 1 x ½ inches.

Cut each sheet of thinly pressed bean curd into two pieces. Tie into knots as shown in sketch. Soak in hot water, to which baking soda has

Cut thin pressed bean curd into 2 pieces

Make a long, loose roll and then twist

Start to roll loosely

Tie into a loose knot

been added, for 10 minutes. Rinse carefully several times in cold water, until water is clear and no trace of soda remains.

COOKING PROCEDURES

Put 2½ quarts water in a large flameproof casserole. Add the salt pork and fresh pork and bring to a boil. Turn the flame down to medium and cook for 35 minutes. Add bamboo shoots and cook for another 20 minutes. Add salt. Mix a few times. Add bean curd knots and cook over low flame another 15 to 20 minutes. Serve in casserole.

TIPS

This dish is even better if prepared ahead of time and reheated.

If fresh sides and butts are not available, any combination of half fat, half lean pork can be used.

Summer bamboo shoots are long and narrow, like white asparagus tips. They are sold in cans in Japanese or Chinese grocery stores.

Baking soda must be added to soften the bean curd. Be sure all soda is rinsed off before cooking.

Cassia Pork (Kwei-Hwa Ro)

4 SERVINGS

Pork is prepared in this manner in northern China, especially Peking. It is called Cassia Pork because the eggs added are firmly scrambled and broken into bits resembling the Chinese cassia flower. This dish is similar to the Mo-Shu-Ru Pork often served in Chinese restaurants. It contains tiger-lily buds, which, because they are orange and pointed before opening, are called "golden needles." In August they can be gathered in the morning dew from roadside clumps of tiger lilies and dried in the sun or in a warm, turned-off oven.

The dish is often served with "doilies" or thin pancakes, a recipe for which is included on page 128.

INGREDIENTS

½ pound fresh lean pork butt
¼ cup dried cloud ears (tree ears)
24 dried tiger-lily buds
¼ cup dried Chinese mushrooms
½ cup canned bamboo shoots
4 eggs
3 tablespoons vegetable oil

1 tablespoon dry sherry
1 tablespoon light soy sauce
1 teaspoon salt
1 teaspoon sugar
1 teaspoon Oriental sesame
seed oil

PREPARATION

Cut the pork, half frozen or half thawed, into matchstick-sized shreds, to make 1 cup. Set aside to allow shreds to reach room temperature before cooking.

Soak the cloud ears, tiger-lily buds, and mushrooms in 1 cup warm water for 30 minutes. Rinse and drain. Cut each tiger-lily bud into 1-inch pieces and the mushrooms and cloud ears into shreds, first removing the stems from the mushrooms.

Beat eggs. Scramble in 1 tablespoon oil for 3 minutes, tossing with spoon and breaking the eggs into little pieces. Remove from the skillet and set aside.

COOKING PROCEDURES

Heat the remaining vegetable oil in a wok or frying pan. Add pork and stir fry quickly for about 3 minutes, or until all pork strips turn grayish. Add dry sherry, soy sauce, salt, and sugar. Mix well. Add the tiger-lily buds, mushrooms, cloud ears, and bamboo shoots. Stir and cook for a minute. Add scrambled eggs. Mix for a few seconds longer. Add sesame seed oil, stir and remove to a serving platter. The dish may be eaten as is or served with doilies.

TIPS

Although it is fun to gather fresh tiger-lily buds, it is time consuming to dry them at home. It is preferable to buy them already dried at Chinese food stores. They are inexpensive and can be kept for many months on the shelf. The taste is as good as freshly gathered ones.

Oriental sesame seed oil is made from toasted sesame seeds. Dark in color and nutty in flavor, it is sold in Oriental and health food stores.

All Chinese, except the Cantonese, refer to "tree ears," rather than "cloud ears." However, in a *Cantonese* grocery, if you ask for "tree ears," you will get something quite different. As most Chinese groceries in this country are Cantonese, we indicate "cloud ears" when we want this specific type of tree ear.

Important: The eggs must be scrambled until dry and flaky.

DOILIES FOR CASSIA PORK

MAKES ABOUT 16 DOILIES

INGREDIENTS

2 cups sifted all-purpose flour
⅘ cup boiling water

2 tablespoons vegetable oil

PREPARATION

Place sifted flour in a mixing bowl. Gradually stir in the boiling water with chopsticks or wooden spoon. When cool enough to touch, knead with your hands until smooth and silky, about 8 minutes. Add 1 tablespoon oil and knead for another minute. Cover with a damp cloth and let sit for 15 minutes.

Knead the dough for another 2 minutes. Roll out evenly on a lightly floured board until a large sheet about ¼ inch in thickness is formed. Using a cookie cutter or glass about 2½ to 3 inches in diameter, cut the dough into rounds. Brush one side of each round with a little oil. With oiled sides facing, lay one round over another. Slowly roll out from the center, to about 5 to 6 inches in diameter.

COOKING PROCEDURES

Heat an ungreased heavy skillet or griddle on top of stove. Cook one pair of doilies over low flame for about 2 minutes, or until bubbles form. Turn over and cook other side, then remove from the pan and pull the two pieces apart. Continue until all are cooked, piling them up and covering them to keep warm.

TIPS

These pancakes are really quite easy to make. However, allow plenty of time to make them the first time you try. They can be made ahead of time and frozen. When ready to use, keep them at room temperature for an hour. Then wet steam for 3 to 5 minutes, or until soft.

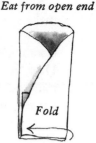
Eat from open end

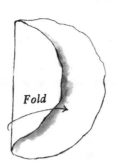
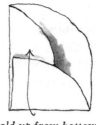
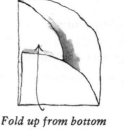

Fold

Fold up from bottom

Fold

Put pork in middle
of doily

To eat with the pork dish, spread a doily on a clean plate. Scoop up a rounded spoonful of the pork mixture and place on the doily. Fold one side over and then fold the right side over at a 90-degree angle. Roll up the doily and eat with your fingers, keeping open side of doily up.

Chinese Roast Pork with Snow Peas

雪荳乂燒

4 SERVINGS

The Chinese seldom carve and eat a large cut of meat, such as a pork roast, in the American manner. Chinese roast pork is made in strips similar to spareribs. These strips are then further divided into slices, shreds, or cubes, and reheated with a sauce or in combination with a vegetable. The following is an example:

INGREDIENTS

¾ pound snow peas
¼ pound Chinese roast pork
2 tablespoons vegetable oil

1½ teaspoons salt
½ teaspoon sugar

PREPARATION

String and wash the snow peas and slant-cut into 1-inch pieces.

Slice the roast pork into pieces the same size as the snow peas, to make ½ cup.

COOKING PROCEDURES

Heat vegetable oil in skillet or wok. Stir fry the snow peas for 2 minutes. Add salt and sugar. Mix well. Add roast pork slices and mix a few times. Serve immediately.

TIPS

Chinese roast pork may be bought frozen in some American supermarkets, or freshly roasted in Chinese grocery stores. If you wish to roast your own, the recipe may be found on page 131 of *The Pleasures of Chinese Cooking*. An illustration of the way to attach the pork strips to the shelf of your oven is on page 67 of that book.

Dried Bean Curd with Pork Slices

二 竹 肉 片

6 SERVINGS

One of the many products of the soybean is dried bean curd. This is skimmed from the top as the fresh bean curd is being made and then dried. After drying, it is deep-fried in vegetable oil to prevent spoilage.

INGREDIENTS

¼ pound dried "second layer" bean curd (*r-cho*)
2 tablespoons dried cloud ears (tree ears)
¼ cup dried Chinese mushrooms
½ pound fresh pork
¼ cup bamboo shoots

¼ cup water chestnuts
3 tablespoons vegetable oil
1 tablespoon dry sherry
2 tablespoons dark soy sauce
1 teaspoon salt
½ teaspoon sugar
½ cup broth

PREPARATION

Soak dried bean curd in 2 cups very hot water for 20 minutes. Rinse

Cut thin bean curd into 2" squares

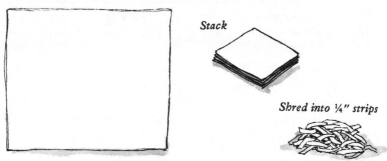

Stack

Shred into ¼" strips

repeatedly, changing water until water runs clear. Drain and cut into ¼-inch pieces.

Soak cloud ears in ½ cup warm water for 15 minutes, then rinse and drain.

Soak dried Chinese mushrooms in ½ cup warm water for 15 minutes, then drain. Remove the stems, and cut each mushroom into 2 to 4 pieces.

Cut the pork, half frozen or half thawed, into 1 x 1 x ⅛-inch slices, to make 1 cup.

Cut bamboo shoots into pieces the same size as the pork.

Slice the water chestnuts in thin rounds.

COOKING PROCEDURES

Heat oil in a wok or skillet over high flame and stir fry pork slices for about 3 minutes or until they all turn grayish. Add sherry, soy sauce, salt, and sugar and mix well, then add mushroom pieces, bamboo shoots, water chestnuts, and cloud ears; mix well.

Add the sliced bean curd and stir for about a minute. Add broth and bring to a boil.

Cover, turn the flame to medium, and cook for about 6 minutes. Serve immediately.

TIPS

Here is the secret of producing both this and other good-tasting Chinese dishes: have everything ready and then work fast over high flame.

Whenever further cooking is needed, the food can be covered and the flame reduced.

All Chinese grocery stores carry tree ears, or cloud ears, as they are called by the Cantonese. They are light, and a few ounces will last a long time, as no dish uses a great deal. Since they are dried, they do not need refrigeration, but will keep for many months on the shelf.

Dried "second layer" bean curd may be purchased in ½-pound packages in Chinese grocery stores. Before being added to the dish, the dried "second layer" bean curd must be soaked in hot water and rinsed many times so all excess grease is removed and the texture of the bean curd is restored. Once prepared, it is good when reheated.

Ground Fresh Pork with Cellophane Noodles

碎 肉 粉 絲

4 SERVINGS

Cellophane or bean thread noodles are made from mung bean flour. Translucent when cooked, they have no flavor of their own, but absorb the flavor of pork, beef, or chicken. They are interesting in texture and in appearance and greatly enhance any dish.

INGREDIENTS

2 ounces cellophane noodles (1 small package)
½ pound ground fresh pork (1 cup)
3 tablespoons vegetable oil
2 tablespoons dry sherry
2 tablespoons dark soy sauce
1 teaspoon salt
½ teaspoon sugar
½ cup water chestnuts, finely minced
½ cup chicken broth, fresh or canned

PREPARATION

Soak cellophane noodles in warm water for about 20 minutes, or until very soft and transparent, then drain and cut into 2-inch pieces.

COOKING PROCEDURES

Stir fry pork in oil for 2 minutes. (Make sure that all pork turns grayish.) Add sherry, soy sauce, salt, and sugar. Mix well.

Add minced water chestnuts and stir. (Some of the liquid will be absorbed.)

Add cellophane noodles and stir a few more times. Add broth. Cook without cover over medium flame until the broth is almost all absorbed, about 2 to 3 minutes.

TIPS

Be sure that the pork is thoroughly cooked before adding any of the other ingredients. If any pink is left in the pork, it is not cooked.

Veal may be substituted for pork, but the flavor will not be as good.

Lion's Head (Giant Pork Patties)

獅 子 頭

4 SERVINGS

"Lion's Head" is a name given to a ground pork and cabbage dish made especially in Yangchow, in eastern China. Traditionally it is served on the New Year, although it can be served at other times of the year. If Lion's Head is to be eaten on New Year's Day, the meat must be shaped into four patties to signify the four blessings of happiness, prosperity, longevity, and health.

INGREDIENTS

1 pound coarsely ground lean pork (2 cups)
1 tablespoon dry sherry
¼ cup dark soy sauce
1 teaspoon sugar
2 tablespoons cornstarch
¾ cup cold water
2 pounds Chinese (celery) cabbage
¼ cup vegetable oil
½ teaspoon salt

PREPARATION

Mix pork with sherry, soy sauce, and sugar. Gradually mix in cornstarch with a little of the water at a time, until all the cornstarch and most of the water have been used up.

Rinse and drain the cabbage, then cut into 1-inch pieces.

COOKING PROCEDURES
Heat oil in wok or skillet. Using a half-cup measuring cup as a scoop, scoop a level cupful of the meat mixture and gently drop it in hot oil. Turn after a minute, flattening slightly into a thick patty. Both sides should be browned. Continue making patties until all pork is used up.

Place all cabbage pieces in a flameproof casserole on a burner. Sprinkle the salt over the cabbage, then place the pork patties on top. Cover. Turn flame to low and slowly bring to boil. Continue cooking on low heat for 1 hour. Serve in the casserole.

TIPS
Lion's Head can be made several hours before serving and simply reheated on top of the stove.

Brussels sprouts, cut in half, can be substituted for the celery cabbage, but use ¼ cup water to add moisture.

Pork, Bamboo Shoots, and Szechuan Preserved Kohlrabi Shreds

4 SERVINGS

Since preserved kohlrabi is a Szechuan specialty, any dish in which it is featured is bound to be typical of that province's cooking. However, this combination of pork and bamboo shoots with Szechuan preserved kohlrabi is lively and spicy without being overly peppery, and is therefore especially popular.

INGREDIENTS
½ pound fresh lean pork butt	¼ cup bamboo shoots
¼ cup dried Chinese mushrooms	1 to 2 sweet peppers

1 cup fresh bean sprouts	1 tablespoon dry sherry
¼ cup Szechuan preserved kohlrabi	1 tablespoon dark soy sauce
	1 tablespoon sugar
2 tablespoons vegetable oil	2 tablespoons cold water

PREPARATION

Cut the pork, half frozen or half thawed, into matchstick-sized shreds, to make 1 cup.

Soak the mushrooms in warm water for 20 minutes. Drain, remove the stems, and shred.

Cut the bamboo shoots into similar shreds.

Cut sweet peppers in half and clean out the seeds and the soft part from the center. Cut lengthwise into 2 x ¼-inch strips, to make 1 cup.

Wash bean sprouts and drain.

Shred the preserved kohlrabi.

COOKING PROCEDURES

Heat oil in a wok or frying pan. Add pork and stir fry for 3 minutes, then add sherry, soy sauce, and sugar and mix well. Add mushrooms, bamboo shoots, and kohlrabi shreds. Stir and cook for 1 minute, then add sweet pepper. Stir and add 2 tablespoons cold water. Cover, turn flame to medium, and cook for 2 to 3 minutes.

Add bean sprouts, mix thoroughly, and serve.

TIPS

Veal shreds can be substituted for pork. However, the cooking time will then be only 2 minutes for the veal.

Fresh kohlrabi cannot be substituted for the Szechuan preserved kohlrabi, which comes in cans available in Chinese grocery stores. Once opened, remove the kohlrabi from the can and store in a jar. If kept in refrigerator, it will be good for months.

Pork Shreds with Pressed Bean Curd and Chinese Chives

韮菜肉絲

4 SERVINGS

Chinese chives are a seasonal vegetable, particularly well liked by natives of China's east coast. Their flavor is stronger than that of scallions and not as pungent as garlic. Many Chinese who will not eat garlic enjoy Chinese chives.

INGREDIENTS

½ pound fresh pork (1 cup)
¼ cup dried Chinese mushrooms
½ cup bamboo shoots
1 cup Chinese chives
1 cup fresh bean sprouts
1 square pressed bean curd

2 tablespoons vegetable oil
1 tablespoon dry sherry
1 tablespoon dark soy sauce
1 teaspoon salt
½ teaspoon granulated sugar

PREPARATION

Cut the pork, half frozen or half thawed, into matchstick-sized shreds.

Soak the mushrooms in warm water for 20 minutes, then drain, remove the stems and shred.

Cut the Chinese chives into 1½-inch lengths.

Wash and drain the bean sprouts.

Shred the bamboo shoots.

Cut the bean curd into fine shreds.

COOKING PROCEDURES

Stir fry pork shreds in oil for 3 minutes. Add sherry, soy sauce, salt, and sugar and mix well. Add mushrooms, bamboo shoots, Chinese chives, and bean curd shreds. Mix thoroughly again, then add ¼ cup water and cook for 2 minutes. Mix in bean sprouts, mix again, and serve.

TIPS

Pork shreds prepared this way can be served with steamed Shanghai spring-roll wrappers and wrapped as is Cassia Pork (page 129). If the pork mixture is thoroughly chilled, it can be used as a filling for Shanghai spring rolls.

Buy Chinese chives in small quantities, since they keep only a few days in the vegetable compartment of the refrigerator. If you do have some left over, chop them very fine and add them to scrambled eggs.

This recipe calls for white pressed bean curd (sold fresh in the refrigerator cases of Chinese grocery stores), not the kind to which soy sauce has been added.

Pork with Icicle Radish

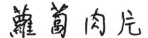

4 SERVINGS

The Chinese know more than two hundred ways to cook pork, but that does not mean that two hundred pork dishes can be served in any one region or at all seasons of the year. This dish, for instance, can only be prepared when icicle radishes are in season, and the season is brief. Icicle radishes out of season have a woody texture and lack taste.

INGREDIENTS

¼ pound fresh pork (½ cup)
3 cups icicle radish, peeled and sliced
2 tablespoons vegetable oil

1 tablespoon dry sherry
1 tablespoon dark soy sauce
½ teaspoon salt
½ teaspoon sugar

PREPARATION

Cut the pork, half frozen or half thawed, into slices 1 x 1 x ¼ inches. Icicle radishes should be sliced approximately the same size as the pork slices. Parboil radish slices in 2 cups of boiling water for 3 minutes. Drain.

COOKING PROCEDURES

Heat oil in a wok or skillet. Add pork and stir fry for 3 minutes. Add sherry. Mix. Then add soy sauce, salt, and sugar. Mix well. Add icicle radish slices and mix some more. Cover and cook for 4 to 5 minutes over medium flame. (If mixture seems dry, add 2 tablespoons cold water before covering.) Remove to a platter and serve.

TIPS

Icicle radishes are found in Japanese and Chinese supermarkets. They are much bigger than American white radishes, and seem like a cross between a turnip and a radish. They can also be grown in home gardens, and seeds are available through major seed catalogs.

This dish can be made ahead of time and reheated before serving. The flavor improves with reheating, so don't hesitate to make this the day before a party and keep in the refrigerator overnight.

Red-Cooked Pork Cubes with Braised Bamboo Shoots

油燜筍燒肉

4 SERVINGS

"Red-cooked" dishes are popular around the districts of eastern China. The phrase "red-cooked" describes the reddish-brown color of the meat after it has been cooked in a large amount of dark soy sauce. Red cooking done in Shanghai and Soochow almost always uses some sugar, which makes it distinctive of these regions.

INGREDIENTS

2 pounds lean fresh pork butt
1 scallion
2 tablespoons vegetable oil
2 slices fresh ginger, each about 1 inch in diameter and ⅛ inch thick

½ cup dry sherry
3 tablespoons dark soy sauce
1 tablespoon sugar
1 can braised bamboo shoots (16 ounces)

PREPARATION

Cut pork butt into 1-inch cubes.

Wash and cut scallion into 2-inch pieces.

COOKING PROCEDURES

Heat oil in a 3-quart saucepan and add ginger and scallion. Mix a few times. Add pork cubes and mix until all pork cubes are coated with oil. Add sherry, dark soy sauce, and sugar. Mix again. Add 1 cup cold water. Bring to boil, cover and cook over medium flame for 30 minutes. Uncover and add the braised bamboo shoots. Stir briefly, then turn the flame to low and continue cooking for another 15 minutes.

TIPS

This dish can be kept warm in the oven at 140 degrees for about half an hour. It can also be prepared ahead and reheated in the same saucepan on top of the range. Simply bring it back to boiling point.

Braised bamboo shoots, which are available in cans in Chinese grocery or specialty stores, are quite salty and are very different in taste from plain bamboo shoots.

Red-Cooked Whole Shoulder of Pork

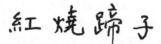

紅 燒 蹄 子

8 SERVINGS

"Red-cooked" dishes, which are especially popular in the districts of Shanghai and Soochow, have the great advantage of being even better as leftovers, either hot or cold.

Pork is the most important meat in China. In the American sense, pork can be considered the "main dish," regardless of how many additional dishes are served. Cooked this way, it should be tender and juicy, and able to be eaten without the use of a knife. Just push the meat away from the bone with chopsticks.

INGREDIENTS

1 fresh shoulder of pork (about 5 to 6 pounds), skin left on	30 dried tiger-lily buds ½ cup dried cloud ears

½ cup dried Chinese mushrooms 4 slices fresh ginger
½ cup dry sherry 2 scallions, cut into 2-inch pieces
½ cup dark soy sauce ¼ cup rock candy
1 teaspoon salt

PREPARATION

Wash the pork shoulder in cold water. Meanwhile, bring about 4 quarts of water to boil in a large saucepan. Submerge shoulder, again bring to boil, and boil for 10 minutes. Wash and rinse shoulder in cold water to get rid of scum.

Soak the tiger-lily buds and cloud ears in 1 cup warm water for 20 minutes, then drain and tie one knot in each lily bud.

Rinse the cloud ears and drain.

Soak mushrooms in 1 cup warm water for 20 minutes. Cut off stems and leave each mushroom whole.

COOKING PROCEDURES

Place a bamboo rack or 2 chopsticks on the bottom of a 6-quart pan. Lay the pork shoulder on top of rack or chopsticks, then turn on the flame to high and add sherry, soy sauce, salt, ginger slices, and scallion. Add 6 cups cold water and bring to boil. Cover, turn flame to medium low and simmer for 4 hours, basting and checking once every hour. Add mushrooms, cloud ears, and tiger-lily buds and cook for 30 minutes longer. Add rock candy to liquid and baste the meat a few times. Cover and cook for another 30 minutes. If there is more than ½ cup of liquid left, remove the cover and cook another 10 minutes, or until only ½ cup liquid remains. Serve meat on platter with remaining sauce poured over.

TIPS

This is a dish that can serve 8 to 10 persons at one meal, or be served to a smaller group and then reheated and used for another meal. It is also good served cold. After one meal, take out the large bones and flatten the meat in a dish. Chill it and then slice cold.

The skin must be cooked with the shoulder to give flavor. It can then be discarded, but many people have learned to enjoy eating the skin after it has been cooked in this way.

Light brown sugar, in same quantity, can be substituted for rock candy.

Soybean Sprouts, Puffed Bean Curd, and Pork Shreds

黄荳芽肉片

4 SERVINGS

Anyone with even a nodding acquaintance with Chinese food has eaten "bean sprouts," or at least seen them listed on a menu. The bean sprouts commonly used come from the Asian mung beans, but soybeans also produce a sprout, one that is even more nutritious and better tasting than the more common mung bean sprout. Many Chinese chefs hesitate to use soybean sprouts because their roots must be removed one by one and they take longer to cook than mung bean sprouts. Once the cleaning and cooking have taken place, however, the result is well worth the extra effort.

INGREDIENTS

6 medium-sized puffed bean curds (optional)
½ teaspoon baking soda
1½ pounds soybean sprouts
½ pound lean fresh pork butt
3 tablespoons peanut oil

1 tablespoon dry sherry
1½ tablespoons dark soy sauce
½ teaspoon salt
½ teaspoon sugar
1 scallion, cut into 2-inch lengths

PREPARATION

Soak the 6 puffed bean curds in 2 cups very hot water, with the baking soda, for about 10 minutes. Rinse several times and squeeze out excess water, then cut into ¼-inch slices.

Clean the soybean sprouts and pick off each root. Wash and drain.

Cut the pork, half frozen or half thawed, into slices, then shred, to make 1 cup.

COOKING PROCEDURES

Stir fry the pork shreds in oil for about 3 minutes, then add the sherry and stir. Add soy sauce, salt, sugar, and scallion and mix well. Add puffed bean curd slices and stir, then add the bean sprouts and mix thoroughly. Add ½ cup cold water and bring to boil. Turn flame to medium, cover, and cook for about 10 minutes. Mix a few times, then cover once more and cook for another 2 to 3 minutes. Can be eaten hot or at room temperature.

TIPS

Baking soda must be used here to soften the puffed, fried bean curd and remove excess oil. It has no effect on the taste of the food or on its nutritional value. However, be sure to rinse the puffed bean curd several times so that no baking soda taste remains.

Steamed Ground Pork with Water Chestnuts

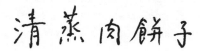

清蒸肉餅子

4 SERVINGS

Steaming is an often-used method of food preparation in China. It grew out of the necessity of conserving fuel, but it has other advantages as well. Steaming preserves flavors, allowing them to blend subtly, and since natural juices are retained, little food value is lost during the cooking process. Here is a steamed dish which presents a delightful combination of textures and flavors.

INGREDIENTS

- 1 one-inch-square piece Szechuan preserved kohlrabi
- 1 pound ground fresh pork (2 cups)
- 1 tablespoon dry sherry
- 1 tablespoon soy sauce
- ½ teaspoon salt
- ½ teaspoon sugar
- 1 teaspoon vegetable oil
- ½ cup minced water chestnuts

PREPARATION

Wash the piece of Szechuan preserved kohlrabi. Slice off enough for 1 tablespoon. Shred and mince.

Combine the ground pork with sherry, soy sauce, salt, sugar, and oil. Add minced water chestnuts and mix well, then sprinkle with the kohlrabi.

COOKING PROCEDURES

Bring water to boil in the bottom section of a steamer.

Put the pork mixture in an ovenproof dish. Place dish on a rack in the upper portion of the steamer, then cover and steam over high heat for 20 minutes. Remove from steamer and serve.

TIPS

Szechuan preserved kohlrabi comes in cans, available in Chinese grocery stores. Once the can has been opened, the remaining kohlrabi will keep many months in a covered jar in the refrigerator.

For wet steaming, it is best to use a Chinese steamer. If none is available, place a dish on a rack over a coffee or similar can (4 inches in diameter and 3 inches high, with both top and bottom removed) that has been placed in a large kettle or saucepan. Add water to a depth of 1½ inches, cover, bring to high boil. Steam for desired length of time.

Steamed Salted Eggs and Fresh Eggs with Ground Fresh Pork

肉餅子燉蛋

4 SERVINGS

Finding salted duck eggs is the only part of this recipe which is at all difficult. They are available in any large city with a Chinatown.

Salted and fresh eggs with ground fresh pork is a luncheon dish popular in eastern China. It is easy, both to prepare and to eat, and is an appropriate addition to a summer menu.

INGREDIENTS

½ pound ground fresh pork (1 cup)
1 teaspoon dry sherry
1 teaspoon light soy sauce
½ teaspoon sugar
2 tablespoons minced water chestnuts

2 fresh eggs
2 preserved salted duck eggs
1 scallion, cut into 2-inch lengths

143

PREPARATION

Combine the pork with sherry, soy sauce, and sugar in an ovenproof dish.

Add the water chestnuts and mix well, then even the surface of the pork with a spoon.

Break each of the 2 fresh eggs on opposite corners of the pork.

Break each of the 2 salted eggs on the remaining corners.

Lay scallion pieces over all.

COOKING PROCEDURES

Wet steam in 2 quarts of boiling water over a high flame for 20 minutes. Serve in the ovenproof dish.

TIPS

The fresh eggs can be either chicken or duck eggs, according to availability. If possible, use duck eggs, as the yolks are redder and more attractive looking.

Be sure you don't use a double boiler when you steam; the steam must circulate all around the ovenproof dish inside the covered cooking pot or steamer.

Wu-Sih Pork

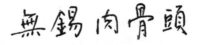

無錫肉骨頭

6 SERVINGS

This dish is the most famous product of Wu-Sih, a city near Shanghai. Bamboo baskets of Wu-Sih Pork are sold at the railway station, and passengers whose trains stop at that station often rush out to buy several baskets to take home to their families as a specialty dish. The Chinese are practical people: this custom proves more rewarding than sending picture postcards or buying models of the Statue of Liberty.

INGREDIENTS

1 rack of spareribs (about 2 pounds)	2 slices fresh ginger
	2 scallions, green part and all

3 tablespoons wine vinegar	1 small piece cinnamon bark
3 tablespoons dark soy sauce	¼ cup sugar

PREPARATION

Cut the rack of ribs into 4 pieces lengthwise, then cut into smaller pieces along every rib. In a large saucepan, bring 2 quarts water to a boil. Drop in spareribs; bring to boil again. Drain and rinse in cold water 2 or 3 times.

COOKING PROCEDURES

Place ginger and scallion in a 6-quart pan. Turn flame to high and add ribs. Add vinegar, soy sauce, cinnamon bark, and sugar. Bring to boil. Add 1 cup cold water. When the mixture boils again, turn flame to medium low and cover. Cook for 1 hour, then remove the ribs from the pan and pour the liquid into a container. Keep both in refrigerator overnight. On the next day, skim off all fat from liquid and pour it over ribs again. Just before serving, reheat by cooking for 15 minutes on top of the range.

TIPS

This is an excellent buffet dish, because it must be made at least the day before, and can even be made several days before it is needed.

The best kind of spareribs to use are those called "country spareribs," which have more meat and more taste than ordinary ribs.

Poultry

Chicken is both the most common and most honored poultry in China. To impress a visitor with how highly he is esteemed, the Chinese hostess says, "I have killed a chicken to honor you," much as Americans speak of "killing the fatted calf." For family consumption, the whole chicken is usually cut up and cooked in any of a number of ways. Chicken parts are more commonly served at restaurants, where many chickens are bought at once so that they can be cut up and different parts used in different dishes. Whole chicken is a banquet dish, because the average Chinese home has neither the fuel nor the oven for roasting a chicken whole. There are well over a hundred chicken dishes in the Chinese repertoire.

Duck cooked in the Chinese manner has become very popular in the United States. In China, however, while Peking Duck and other duck dishes are served at banquets, they are far from the main attraction. The price of a banquet is determined by whether bear's paw, shark's fin, bird's nest, or sea cucumber is to be served. Peking Duck is a greater favorite of Americans than of the Chinese, and the ever-popular "pressed duck" does not even exist in China in the form served in the United States. Because of their popularity,

I have included several duck dishes in both this book and *The Pleasures of Chinese Cooking*.

Squab, roasted, red cooked, or minced, is exclusively served at banquets. Squabs are expensive, and their preparation is too time consuming and difficult for the average Chinese home cook to attempt.

Chicken Breasts with Mung Bean Sprouts and Pickled Cucumber Shreds

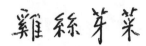

4 SERVINGS

This is a banquet dish, not because of ingredients used but because an inordinate amount of time is consumed in its preparation. If the proper taste and texture are to be produced, each bean sprout must be cleaned by hand to remove the roots. This process, however, though time consuming, is well worth the effort.

INGREDIENTS

1 large whole chicken breast	½ red or green bell pepper
1 teaspoon dry sherry	½ pound mung bean sprouts
¼ teaspoon salt	(2 cups)
1 teaspoon cornstarch	2 tablespoons vegetable oil
2 slices fresh ginger	¼ cup pickled cucumber slices

PREPARATION

Skin and bone the chicken breast, half frozen or half thawed, and cut into matchstick-sized shreds. Combine the chicken shreds and the sherry, then add the salt and cornstarch and mix again.

Shred the ginger.

Slice the bell pepper, to make ½ cup.

Pick roots off mung bean sprouts. Wash and rinse. Drain.

COOKING PROCEDURES

Heat oil and add ginger shreds. Add chicken and stir fry quickly for 2 minutes. Add cucumber slices. Mix. Add green pepper shreds and stir. Then add bean sprouts. Mix thoroughly and dish.

TIPS

This dish is not only tasty but extremely pleasing to the eye. The last-minute cooking is simple. Only be sure to allot plenty of time for cleaning the bean sprouts.

Chinese pickled cucumbers, packed in 6-ounce cans and sold in Chinese grocery stores, differ from American pickles in that they are preserved in salt rather than vinegar. They can be used in small quantities in a variety of different ways. For another recipe for them in this book, see Chicken with Chinese Pickled Cucumber Cubes on the following page.

Chicken with Chinese Pickled Cucumber Cubes

4 SERVINGS

Many non-Chinese have the misconception that every Chinese dish requires a great variety of fresh vegetables. I used this chicken dish because chicken is well liked, inexpensive, and nutritious and because I wanted to demonstrate that only one vegetable need be used. Water chestnuts are the vegetable; the pickles are added strictly for flavoring.

INGREDIENTS

2 whole chicken breasts	½ cup Chinese pickled cucumber
1 tablespoon dry sherry	1 cup water chestnuts
1 teaspoon salt	3 tablespoons vegetable oil
1 teaspoon cornstarch	1 teaspoon sugar

PREPARATION

Skin and bone chicken. Cut into 1-inch cubes. Mix with sherry, salt and cornstarch.

Cut the pickled cucumber into ¼-inch cubes.
Dice the water chestnuts.

Cooking Procedures

Heat oil in skillet or wok. Add chicken cubes and stir fry until all chicken pieces have turned white. Add pickled cucumbers. Mix thoroughly. Add sugar. Mix again. Add water chestnuts. Mix a few more times. Dish.

Tips

Chinese pickled cucumbers are sold in Chinese grocery stores in 6-ounce cans. They are entirely different from the American variety. Use only a very small quantity of the Chinese pickled cucumbers; they are very salty. Any left over can be stored in a jar in the refrigerator, where they will keep for weeks. They can also be minced and sprinkled sparsely over tossed salad in place of bacon bits or anchovies.

Chicken with Chestnuts

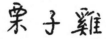

栗 子 雞

4 SERVINGS

Although Westerners may think of duck as the typical Chinese poultry, chicken, too, is a favorite food in China. There are well over a hundred different chicken recipes in the Chinese cuisine.

This chicken dish originated in the district around Shanghai, and is still very popular there. Be sure to allow time for the chestnuts to soak overnight.

Ingredients

1 cup dried shelled chestnuts
2 large whole chicken breasts
2 large chicken legs (drumsticks and thighs)

½ cup bamboo shoots
¼ cup dried Chinese mushrooms
2 tablespoons vegetable oil
2 slices fresh ginger

1 scallion, cut into 2-inch lengths
2 tablespoons dry sherry
2 tablespoons dark soy sauce

2 teaspoons sugar
1 cup chicken broth, fresh or
  canned
2 tablespoons *hoisin* sauce

PREPARATION

Cut chicken breasts and legs into 1-inch pieces, including skin and bones, with meat cleaver or kitchen shears.

Cut bamboo shoots into 1-inch pieces.

Soak dried chestnuts overnight in 2 cups cold water; chestnuts will expand to absorb most of the water. The next day, put them in a saucepan and add 2 cups cold water. Bring to a boil. Turn flame to medium, cover, and cook for 20 minutes. Drain. Set aside.

Soak the dried Chinese mushrooms in ½ cup warm water for 20 minutes, then drain and remove the stems, but leave whole.

COOKING PROCEDURES

Heat oil in wok or frying pan. Add ginger and scallion. Add chicken and mix thoroughly. Transfer to a 3-quart saucepan. Add sherry, soy sauce, and sugar and mix well. Add bamboo shoots and mushrooms. Mix well again. Add chestnuts and stir a few more times.

Add chicken broth and bring to a boil. Cover, turn flame down to medium low and cook for 25 minutes. Uncover and mix. Turn flame down to low and cook for another 15 minutes. Stir in *hoisin* sauce and cook for another minute uncovered.

TIPS

This is a dish which tastes even better and has a better texture when prepared ahead of time. It can be cooked a day or so in advance and refrigerated, or several weeks ahead and frozen. When ready to use, thaw and heat on top of the range.

Dried, shelled chestnuts are available in Chinese grocery stores. If fresh chestnuts are in season, substitute 1 cup raw, shelled.

Soy Sauce Whole Chicken

豉 油 雞

4 SERVINGS

We tend to think of Chinese chicken dishes as consisting of cut-up chicken mixed with vegetables. In this dish, a Cantonese specialty, the chicken is cooked whole, and no vegetable is added during cooking.

INGREDIENTS

1 fresh-killed whole chicken (3 to 4 pounds)
1½ cups dark soy sauce
1½ cups dry sherry
½ cup sugar
2 whole star anise

1 1 x ½-inch piece cinnamon bark
1 tablespoon Oriental sesame seed oil
8 to 10 lettuce leaves

PREPARATION

Remove neck and giblets from chicken and set aside for another use. Clean chicken well; wash and dry it.

COOKING PROCEDURES

Combine the soy sauce, sherry, sugar, star anise, cinnamon bark with ½ cup cold water in a large wok with a cover or a large saucepan. Bring all ingredients to boil, then add the chicken, breast side down, bring to boil again. Cover, turn flame to medium, and cook for 5 minutes. Turn chicken to one side, a quarter turn, and again cover and cook for 5 minutes. Repeat this procedure twice more until chicken has been cooked on all sides (20 minutes in all).

Turn off flame, but leave the cover on the pan and let the chicken sit in the hot sauce for 15 additional minutes. At end of that time, uncover pan and lift out chicken with a fork. Place chicken on plate and paint all over with sesame seed oil. Cool thoroughly in the refrigerator.

To serve: Cut chicken into bite-sized pieces, skin and bones included. Arrange 8 to 10 lettuce leaves on platter and place chicken pieces on top. If desired, spoon 2 to 3 tablespoons of sauce over chicken. Reserve rest of sauce for another use.

TIPS

Soy sauce chicken can be served warm, but then it must be carved and not chopped. If the chicken is chopped when warm, the sauce will spatter and the pieces will be uneven in size.

This is one main dish that is even better if prepared the day before, since it is easier to cut when very cold.

It is very important that a fresh-killed chicken be used for Soy Sauce Chicken to insure the proper taste and a uniform dark-brown color.

Steamed Ham with Chicken and Chinese Mustard Greens

玉 樹 雞

6 SERVINGS

Eye appeal is as important as taste appeal in Chinese cooking. This attractive combination of greens, pink ham, and white chicken has the added advantage of excellent flavor. Large-leafed mustard is more abundant in Canton than in other parts of China, and this dish is a Cantonese specialty.

INGREDIENTS

3 whole chicken breasts
½ pound boneless Smithfield ham
2 teaspoons sugar
3 cups fresh Chinese mustard green stems, in 1-inch pieces

2 tablespoons vegetable oil
1 teaspoon salt
1 tablespoon cornstarch dissolved in 1 tablespoon water

PREPARATION

Place chicken breasts and ham in a deep ovenproof bowl and place on a rack in the upper part of a steamer. Steam, covered, for 20 minutes. Cool, reserving at least ¼ cup juice for later use. Skin and bone the chicken breasts and cut the meat into bite-sized cubes. Cut the ham into 1 x 1 x ¼-inch slices. Alternate ham slices and chicken cubes attractively on a platter and keep warm.

Boil 2 cups of water, to which sugar has been added. Add mustard greens. Boil for 2 minutes. Drain and soak in cold water. When ready to proceed, drain again.

COOKING PROCEDURES

Heat the oil in a wok or skillet and stir fry the mustard greens for 2 minutes. Add salt and mix well. Remove the greens from the wok and arrange all around the chicken and ham on the platter. Heat the reserved juice from the chicken and ham to boiling. Thicken with the dissolved cornstarch (stirred again so the water and cornstarch are thoroughly mixed) and pour over all the chicken, ham, and mustard greens. Serve immediately.

TIPS

Ham and chicken can be steamed an hour before, if necessary. Prearrange them on ovenproof serving platter and reheat in the oven at 200 degrees for 10 minutes. Stir fry mustard greens and make sauce just before serving. Take the dish out of the oven, arrange drained mustard greens, and pour sauce over all.

Chinese mustard greens are not to be confused with the American variety. They are available only in Chinese grocery stores.

Stir-Fry Chicken Liver

4 SERVINGS

In China, chicken for ordinary family consumption can only be purchased whole, so chicken liver is considered a delicacy as a main dish. Only restaurants, which serve many chickens a day, can collect enough chicken livers to make dishes with them. This method of preparing the livers comes from Shanghai.

INGREDIENTS

1 pound chicken livers	½ cup dried Chinese mushrooms
¼ pound fresh snow peas	5 tablespoons vegetable oil

1 cup bamboo shoots, sliced	2 slices fresh ginger
½ teaspoon salt	1 tablespoon dry sherry
½ teaspoon sugar	1½ tablespoon light soy sauce

PREPARATION
Wash chicken livers and cut each into 2 to 3 pieces. String snow peas and cut into 1-inch pieces, to make 1 cup. Soak the mushrooms in 1 cup warm water for 20 minutes, then drain; cut off the stems, and cut mushrooms into wedges.

COOKING PROCEDURES
Heat 2 tablespoons of the oil in a wok or skillet. Stir fry the mushrooms for a minute, then add the bamboo shoots and snow peas. After stirring a few times, add salt and sugar and remove the vegetables to a bowl.

Heat remaining oil in the wok and add ginger slices. Stir fry the livers over a high flame for 2 minutes. Add sherry and light soy sauce and mix well. Cook for 3 to 4 minutes. Return bamboo-shoot mixture to the wok. Mix thoroughly and serve.

TIPS
This is a good dish for either company or family, since none of the ingredients is hard to obtain. Either order the mushrooms by mail or buy them from any Oriental food store, but be sure to get a large quantity (half a pound), as they keep well and are used in many different dishes.

Stuffed Boneless Chicken

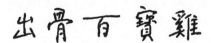

出骨百寶雞

6 SERVINGS

Because of the cost of some of the stuffing ingredients and the time required in preparation, stuffed chicken is usually considered a banquet dish. Chickens are boned and stuffed in many parts of China, but the items used in the stuffing vary according to the place of origin of each recipe. This method is typically Cantonese.

155

INGREDIENTS

1 whole chicken (3 to 4 pounds)
2 slices fresh ginger
2 scallions, cut into 2-inch lengths
½ cup dry sherry

¼ cup dark soy sauce
1 tablespoon sugar
2 cups chicken broth, fresh or canned

STUFFING

1 cup raw glutinous rice
2 links Chinese sausage
¼ cup dried Chinese mushrooms
¼ cup water chestnuts, cut in small dice

1 teaspoon salt
2 tablespoons light soy sauce
½ cup canned gingko nuts
Cooked chicken meat, diced (from chicken above)

PREPARATION

Combine the glutinous rice and 1½ cups cold water in saucepan. Bring to boil. Cover, turn flame to low and cook for 10 minutes. Turn off flame and let the rice relax for 15 minutes.

Steam the Chinese sausages in a double boiler for 15 minutes. When cool to touch, cut into ¼-inch dice.

Soak the Chinese mushrooms in warm water for 20 minutes, then drain, remove the stems, and dice.

Cut water chestnuts into small dice.

Skin the whole chicken by starting from the neck end, using a small knife. Disjoint each wing and gradually work down after loosening wings from the rest of the body. Keep all meat attached to the bones and loosen skin carefully, being especially careful when detaching the skin at the back not to break it. When most of the chicken has been worked over, cut at the joint of the legs and remove the body of the entire chicken with meat attached. The wings and the drumsticks should be attached to the skin. Leave the skin in the refrigerator until ready for stuffing.

1. *Cut through wing joint to separate the wing from the body, being careful not to break the skin. Repeat on other wing. They should hang loose from the body*

2. *Loosen membrane with your hand and roll back the skin of the breast. The skin and meat are not attached at this part of the chicken*

3. *Turn bird over and begin cutting the skin away from the carcass, cutting toward the bone so as not to break the skin*

4. *Cut along the side of the breast on both sides*

5. *Peel skin back on the leg to expose the joint, and sever. Repeat wtih the other leg*

6. *Make four slits in each drumstick and pull skin back over each leg*

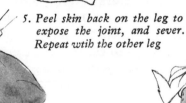

7. *Chicken skin is now inside out. Sever tail from the body. You now have the whole skin with drumsticks, wings and tail*

8. *Sew neck opening before stuffing and then sew tail part after stuffing*

Boil the chicken meat with bones in 2 cups of water, or enough to cover the chicken, for 15 minutes. Allow meat to cool in liquid until cool enough to touch, then debone the chicken and cut meat into small dice.

Combine the cooked rice, salt, and light soy sauce. Then add prepared sausages, water chestnuts, mushrooms, and gingko nuts. Mix thoroughly with 2 chopsticks, and stir in the chicken meat last.

Truss the neck end of the chicken skin and stuff the chicken from the other end, then truss the other end and push the stuffed skin into the shape of a chicken.

COOKING PROCEDURES

To keep meat from sticking, place 2 chopsticks at the bottom of a large casserole. Place the chicken, breast side up, on the chopsticks. Add the ginger and scallions, then add the sherry, dark soy sauce, and sugar. Place casserole on a burner, turn the flame on to high, and bring to a boil. Add the chicken broth and return to a boil. Cover, turn the flame down to medium low, and cook for 15 minutes, basting occasionally. Continue cooking for another 8 to 10 minutes.

Serve from the casserole. Use a knife to cut the whole chicken, first in half lengthwise and then into 6 servings. Spoon some of the sauce over each serving.

TIPS

This dish takes time to prepare, but it can either be cooked early and warmed or cooked ahead of time and frozen. On the day of serving, thaw and reheat.

If the casserole is too small for chopsticks, break chopsticks to size.

Glutinous rice is the correct translation, but some storekeepers may call it "sweet" or "sticky" rice.

Skin the chicken earlier and cook the meat so that it is cool enough to dice when you are ready to stuff it.

Chinese sausages come in links of two and are sold by weight (1 pound or ½ pound) in Chinese grocery stores. If kept in the refrigerator they will be good for weeks, but if frozen they can be kept for months.

Sliced steamed Chinese sausages could be served as a side dish.

Stuffed Chicken Wings

三絲翅膀

4 SERVINGS

American readers, seeing the title of this dish, may not believe their eyes. The idea of stuffing anything as tiny as a chicken wing appears not only difficult, but hardly worth the effort. Actually, the dish is a tribute to Chinese thrift and ingenuity. Once tried, it proves easy to make and delightful to taste.

INGREDIENTS

16 chicken wings

16 strips of bamboo shoots,
1½ x ¼ x ¼ inches

16 strips of Smithfield ham,
1½ x ¼ x ¼ inches

16 strips of Chinese mushrooms,
(soaked before cutting),
1½ x ¼ x. ¼ inches

2 scallions, in 2-inch lengths

1½ tablespoons light soy sauce

1 teaspoon salt

3 tablespoons vegetable oil

¼ cup Chinese mushrooms,
soaked and cut in wedges

½ cup bamboo shoots, in thin
slices

2 ounces snow peas or ¼ cup
green bell pepper, cut in
1-inch squares

½ teaspoon sugar

2 teaspoons cornstarch, dissolved in 1 tablespoon water

PREPARATION

Cut the wings apart at both joints. You will use only the middle section. (Save other parts for soup).

*1. Middle section of wing
Cut off ends of joint with cleaver*

2. After boiling, bones will stick out

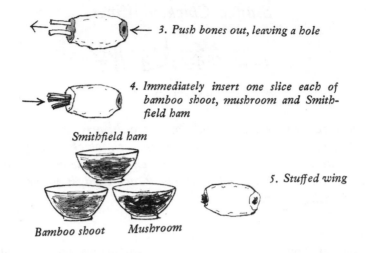

← 3. *Push bones out, leaving a hole*

4. *Immediately insert one slice each of bamboo shoot, mushroom and Smithfield ham*

Smithfield ham

5. *Stuffed wing*

Bamboo shoot　*Mushroom*

Bring 2 cups of water to a boil. Add chicken and boil 4 minutes. Remove from pan and cool till meat is touchable. Save broth. Sever the tendon at both ends of each piece, about ½ inch from end. Gently, with your fingers, push out the bones inside each piece. Immediately, in the cavity left by removing the bones, place 1 strip each of bamboo shoot, ham, and mushroom. Repeat with all the wings. Marinate in 1 tablespoon of the soy sauce and ½ teaspoon of the salt for 20 minutes.

COOKING PROCEDURES
Heat the oil in a wok or skillet and fry the wings for 2 to 3 minutes, then turn over gently and cook for another minute. Add the scallions, mushroom wedges, the ½ cup sliced bamboo shoots, and the snow peas or peppers. Add the remaining soy sauce and salt and the sugar and stir a few times, then add ½ cup of reserved broth and cook for 2 minutes. Thicken with the predissolved cornstarch (stirred again to make sure the water and cornstarch are thoroughly mixed), then serve.

TIPS
The chicken wings can be stuffed in advance and kept in the refrigerator. Mushrooms, bamboo shoots, and snow peas can be sliced before cooking. This way, the final cooking takes very little time.

If you have trouble boning the chicken wing as directed, split the wing lengthwise, bone it, and put in the three strips of stuffing. Then tie the stuffed wing with a scallion green previously dipped in hot water until pliable.

Szechuan Peppercorn Chicken

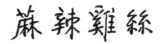

4 SERVINGS

This is a chicken dish, prepared in the Szechuan style that is especially good when served for luncheon. I suppose Americans would call this "Szechuan chicken salad."

INGREDIENTS

2 whole chicken breasts	¼ cup vegetable oil
4 scallions, green part and all	¼ teaspoon crushed red pepper flakes
4 slices fresh ginger	
1 head iceberg or romaine lettuce	1 tablespoon dark corn syrup
	1 tablespoon *hoisin* sauce
1 teaspoon Szechuan pepper-corns, crushed	1 tablespoon dark soy sauce
	2 cloves garlic, finely minced

PREPARATION

Wash and drain the chicken breasts. Cut one of the scallions into 2-inch lengths. Chop the others to make ¼ cup. Bring 2 quarts of water to a boil in a saucepan along with 1 slice ginger and the 2-inch scallion pieces. Then add the chicken breasts and again bring to a boil. Cover. Turn the flame down to medium, and cook for 15 minutes. Turn off the flame and let the chicken cool in its own liquid for at least 20 minutes. Then skin and bone the chicken, pulling the meat away from the bones. Tear the meat into coarse shreds with your fingers.

Mince the remaining ginger slices to make 1 tablespoon.

Shred the lettuce to make 4 cups.

COOKING PROCEDURES

Combine the crushed peppercorns, vegetable oil, chopped scallion, minced ginger and chili pepper flakes in a small saucepan and boil for 1 minute.

Combine the corn syrup, *hoisin* sauce, and soy sauce and garlic in a bowl. Add the hot mixture to the mixture in the bowl and mix with chopsticks.

Combine the chicken with the lettuce shreds. Just before serving, pour hot sauce over and mix well. Serve.

TIPS

A few Szechuan peppercorns will go a long way, but there is no substitute for their exotic flavor. If you prefer a more peppery taste, use ½ teaspoon of red pepper flakes.

Velvet Chicken

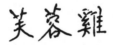

4 SERVINGS

This elegant dish proves that the Chinese consider every possible way in which food can appeal to the senses. Velvet chicken excels not only in taste and appearance, but in texture. The contrast between the smoothness of the chicken mixture and the crunchy snow peas and bamboo shoots makes this a dish for the gourmet, whatever his country of origin.

INGREDIENTS

1 whole chicken breast	1 pound lard or vegetable shortening
8 egg whites	
½ cup bamboo shoots	2 tablespoons vegetable oil
3 ounces Smithfield ham	2 ounces snow peas
1 teaspoon salt	1 tablespoon dry sherry
2½ tablespoons cornstarch	2 scallions, cut into ¼-inch pieces
½ cup chicken broth, fresh or canned	

PREPARATION

Slice the chicken breast, half frozen or half thawed, into paper-thin slices, 1 x 1 x ¼ inches.

Beat egg whites with electric or hand beater until stiff.

Slice the bamboo shoots into 1 x 1 x ¼-inch pieces.

Cut the ham into pieces the same size as the bamboo shoots.

COOKING PROCEDURES

Combine the chicken slices with the beaten egg whites, ½ teaspoon of the salt, the cornstarch, and chicken broth, and set aside. Heat the lard or shortening until very hot, then remove from the heat and allow to cool for 1 minute.

Pour chicken mixture into lard or shortening and turn slowly with a spatula. Return to a hot flame and cook for a few seconds or until chicken is opaque. Dish chicken mixture and pour off shortening.

Heat the 2 tablespoons oil in a wok or skillet. Add snow peas, bamboo shoots, and ham squares. Stir a few times until heated through, then add the remaining ½ teaspoon salt, stir again, and remove from the wok.

Without adding oil, put the chicken mixture in the wok. Add sherry. Return vegetable mixture. Mix a few times. Add scallions. Dish and serve hot.

TIPS

Snow peas, available in any large city with a Chinatown, also come frozen, but the frozen variety are not very crisp. If only frozen snow peas are available, thaw at room temperature, rinse with cold water, and drain, then add them to the dish at the last minute. Or you may defrost them by submerging in boiling water and immediately removing and rinsing with cold water.

Smithfield ham is the best ham to use in Chinese cooking, as it is nearest in taste to the Chinese King Hwa ham. To keep ham for future use, clean away the skin and fat, then wash, dry, and boil in water for 20 minutes. Store in the refrigerator and use in all Chinese recipes calling for ham.

White-Cut Chicken

白 切 雞

4 SERVINGS

Few Americans have tasted "white-cut chicken." However, this is the easiest and most popular method by which the Chinese prepare chicken, universal throughout China. It is misleading to call this dish "boiled chicken," because the chicken is not boiled to make soup but for its firm, flavorful meat. This is an excellent introduction to Chinese food for those who feel timid about eating anything "far out."

INGREDIENTS

1 roasting chicken (3 to 4 pounds)
1 teaspoon salt

1 scallion, cut into 2-inch lengths
1 slice ginger, 1 x 1 x 1/8 inches

PREPARATION

Remove the giblets and neck from inside chicken. Reserve these for another purpose. Clean the chicken thoroughly. Wash and drain.

COOKING PROCEDURES

Bring 2 quarts of water to a boil in a 4-quart saucepan. Add salt, scallion, and ginger. Submerge the chicken in the boiling water. Bring to a boil again. Cover and cook on medium-high heat for 15 minutes. Turn off flame, but do not remove cover. Allow chicken to rest in liquid for 20 minutes.

After 20 minutes, lift chicken out of broth with a fork and chill thoroughly in the refrigerator. When cold, cut the chicken, with skin and bones, into 1 x 2-inch pieces. Arrange the pieces on a platter and serve with either soy sauce or *hoisin* sauce as a dip.

TIPS

Fresh-killed chicken must be used to give this dish the proper flavor.

If the chicken is too large to be eaten at one sitting, save half the chicken uncut and freeze it. To serve, simply thaw and chop.

The stock may be saved and used as a base for chicken soup. Add the reserved neck and giblets, plus additional chicken parts, and soup greens and salt if desired. Simmer for 1 hour.

Orange-Spiced Duck

4 SERVINGS

In this Cantonese recipe, duck is cooked spiced with tangerine peel. I have added fresh oranges to enhance the flavor, although oranges are not used in China because they are available only at certain seasons. This dish is such a favorite that the Chinese prefer to use only spices so they can cook it all year round.

INGREDIENTS

1 Long Island duckling (5 to 5½ pounds), frozen
1 teaspoon salt
2 large leeks
2 oranges
½ cup dry sherry
¼ cup dark soy sauce
1 piece dried tangerine peel, the size of a fifty-cent piece

1 whole star anise or 8 pods
2 tablespoons dark corn syrup or honey
1 tablespoon cornstarch dissolved in 1 tablespoon cold water

PREPARATION
Thaw and clean duck. Sprinkle with salt.

Wash leeks. Slice each leek in half and carefully rinse off all sand between the leaves. Cut into 2-inch pieces, to make 2 cups.

Peel the oranges and cut them in half, then cut each half into slices.

COOKING PROCEDURES
Preheat the oven to 350 degrees. Place the duck, breast side up, on a rack in a roasting pan, with 1 inch of water beneath the rack, and

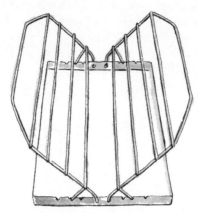

Adjustable rack to fit in your roasting pan

roast for 1 hour. When the hour is almost over, prick duck with fork to let out fat. Remove from pan.

Put ½ cup of the leeks on the bottom of a small roasting pan with a cover and lay the duck, breast side up, on the leeks. Stuff another ½ cup leeks inside the duck's cavity and lay the remaining 1 cup around the duck. Place the pan on a burner and turn the flame on to high. Add the sherry and soy sauce and bring to a boil, then add 2½ cups cold water and bring to a boil again. Turn the flame down to low, and simmer for 30 minutes. Baste a few times, then cook for another 30 minutes.

Add the tangerine peel and star anise to the liquid and pour the corn syrup over the duck. Cover and continue to cook for 1 hour longer, then baste again, turn the flame to medium, and cook, uncovered, for 10 minutes. (There should be about ½ cup of liquid left.)

Place the duck on a platter and arrange the orange slices over and around it. Thicken the leftover ½ cup sauce with the predissolved cornstarch (stirred again to make sure the water and cornstarch are thoroughly mixed) and pour over the duck. Serve hot.

TIPS

It takes 3 hours to cook this duck, but the first hour of roasting can be done a day ahead, and the remaining two can be done several hours in advance. Just before serving, heat the duck in the roaster and cook for the last 10 minutes.

Tangerine peel and star anise, used here, are available in Chinese grocery stores. They are expensive, but a little goes a long way, and like all spices, they keep.

Pressed Duck with Almonds

西湖鴨

4 SERVINGS

This dish, served especially in Cantonese restaurants, has long been a favorite of Americans. It cannot be found in exactly this form in China, but has been adapted from several similar Chinese dishes. Pressed duck is an excellent and popular way of serving duck. There are two cooking stages, and the first must begin the night before you plan to serve the dish.

INGREDIENTS

1 Long Island duckling (5 pounds), frozen
1 tablespoon salt
1 piece dried tangerine peel, 1 x 1 inches
1 egg white, lightly beaten
¼ cup water chestnut flour, dissolved in 3 tablespoons cold water to make batter
2 cups vegetable oil for deep frying

2 cups lettuce shreds
4 tablespoons chopped almonds
Sauce:
2 cups chicken broth, fresh or canned
1 tablespoon soy sauce
1 teaspoon salt (omit if canned broth is used)
3 tablespoons cornstarch, dissolved in 3 tablespoons water

PREPARATION

Thaw duck thoroughly, then wash and wipe dry with paper toweling, both inside and out. Cut off the wing tips and tail. Rub 1 tablespoon of the salt all over duck, inside and out, then place the piece of

167

tangerine peel inside the cavity. Leave the duck in the refrigerator overnight.

Bring 2 quarts water in the bottom of a large steamer to a full boil. Place the duck in the top section of the steamer, without a plate, so that the duck fat will drip into the water during steaming. Steam over high flame for 1 hour. When the duck is cool enough to touch, cut in half lengthwise through the back. Spread out flat and remove all bones, being very careful to keep the skin intact. Place the boned duck in a square pan, approximately 7 x 7 x 2 inches. Press evenly and firmly with your hands until the whole square is about ¾ inches thick. Coat one side with half the egg white and half of the water chestnut batter. Turn over and coat the other side in the same manner. Cut into 4 smaller squares. (At this point, all or some of the duck thus prepared can be frozen, or be refrigerated if used within 2 days.)

COOKING PROCEDURES

Deep fry each piece of duck in oil at 375 degrees for about 3 to 4 minutes. (If the duck was frozen, it should be thawed to room temperature before frying.) Drain on a paper towel.

Meanwhile, bring the chicken broth to a boil, adding the soy sauce, and remaining 1 teaspoon salt if fresh broth is used. Add the cornstarch predissolved in water (stirring again to make sure water and cornstarch are thoroughly mixed), and stir until smooth and thick.

To serve, cut each square into uniform pieces, 1 x 2 inches. Place on a bed of lettuce shreds, pour the sauce over, and sprinkle with chopped almonds. Serve immediately.

TIPS

This is a long procedure, but not really a difficult one. Since the duck can be pressed ahead of time and frozen, it is best to do well in advance. Frying the duck and making the sauce will not be too much work.

If water chestnut flour is not available, cornstarch can be substituted.

Roasted Stuffed Boneless Duck

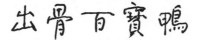

4 TO 6 SERVINGS

In many parts of China, duck is often boned before it is stuffed. The technique of boning and stuffing is the same throughout China, but the stuffings used differ from region to region. The recipe given here is Cantonese in origin.

INGREDIENTS

1 Long Island duckling (5 pounds), frozen
½ cup dried Chinese mushrooms
2 cups raw glutinous rice
4 links Chinese sausage

2 tablespoons vegetable oil
4 teaspoons salt
1 slice fresh ginger, about ½ inch thick

PREPARATION

Thaw and clean the duck. Save the gizzard and liver for another purpose.

Soak the dried mushrooms in 1 cup warm water for 20 minutes. Drain and cut off stems. Cut each mushroom into dice.

Using a 2-quart saucepan, cook the glutinous rice in 3 cups cold water. First bring to a boil, then cover and simmer for 10 minutes. Turn off the flame, without uncovering or otherwise disturbing the rice, and let the rice rest for 20 minutes.

Boil the Chinese sausages in 1 cup water for 6 minutes. Discard water. Cool and then cut into little dice.

Stir fry the mushrooms in oil for 1 minute. Add sausages and mix. Then add the cooked rice and mix well. Add 2 teaspoons salt and mix again.

Remove bones of duck, leaving meat and skin intact, as shown here. Turn the duck inside out and rub with ginger. Then sprinkle the remaining 2 teaspoons salt all over the inside. Turn the duck right side out. Truss the neck opening before stuffing. Stuff, using up all the stuffing, then truss the other end. (*See next page for detail.*)

1. Cut neck skin off to 1 inch from the body. Begin pulling back skin at neck. Then sever both wings at the joint, working inside the skin, and being careful not to tear skin

2. With small cuts, scrape away the meat from the bone, rolling the meat back as you work

3. Separate thigh from carcass, cutting through the joint at the body. Scrape down meat from the thigh bone toward the drumstick and remove thigh bone

4. Roll skin back and make four slits in the drumstick meat.

Inside out

5. Duck is now inside out. Cut through tail bone leaving meat and skin in one piece

6. *When duck has again been turned right side out, sew neck skin down*

7. *Stuffed and sewn, ready to roast*

Cooking Procedures

Cover a cake rack with foil, then cut slits in the foil for air circulation.

Preheat oven to 375 degrees. Pour cold water to a depth of 1½ inches in the bottom of a roasting pan. Place the duck on the rack above the water and roast for 1½ hours.

To serve, cut with knife or metal spoon into 6 even pieces.

Tips

The stuffing may be slightly changed to suit individual taste, but all the items used must be precooked and mixed well before using.

The whole stuffed duck can be prepared and frozen for days. When ready for use, thaw the duck for 8 to 10 hours and proceed to roast.

Spiced Roast Duck

4 SERVINGS

Here is a duck recipe that will be very welcome to Americans. The duck is oven roasted, a process relatively rare in China where few ovens exist, but much easier than braising or deep-frying a whole duck. The skin is crisp, the inside tender and juicy, and the flavor uniquely Chinese.

INGREDIENTS

1 Long Island duckling (5 pounds or a little more), frozen
2 tablespoons salt
2 tablespoons dry sherry
2 tablespoons *hoisin* sauce
1 teaspoon five spices powder
2 tablespoons dark corn syrup
1 tablespoon ground brown bean sauce

PREPARATION

Thaw and clean the duck, then dry thoroughly with paper towels. Rub the duck with the salt, both inside and out. Leave in refrigerator for 8 hours, preferably overnight.

Mix sherry, *hoisin* sauce, five spices powder, corn syrup, and ground brown bean sauce in a bowl. Using your hands, rub the sauce all over duck, both inside and out, until all the sauce is used up. Let sit at room temperature for 2 to 3 hours.

COOKING PROCEDURES

Preheat oven to 300 degrees. Pour water to a depth of 1 inch into a roasting pan, then place the duck, breast side up, on a rack above the water. Roast for 1 hour, then turn the duck over, breast side down, and roast for another hour. Increase the heat to 350 degrees and again turn the duck over, breast side up, for 30 minutes. Remove from oven and let cool. When ready to serve, cut into bite-sized pieces, hot or cold, and arrange on a platter.

TIPS

This duck tastes equally good hot or cold, though it is easier to handle when cold. Cook it the day before and serve it cold, or reheat it, or prepare it well in advance and freeze it, well wrapped in foil. To serve after freezing, thaw and reheat in its foil wrapping in a 300-degree oven for 30 minutes.

Five spices powder, like the *hoisin* sauce and ground brown bean sauce, can be purchased at Oriental grocery stores. It will keep indefinitely on the shelf. Both sauces should be transferred to glass jars after opening and stored in the refrigerator. They, too, keep a long time.

Taro Duck

芋 頭 鴨

4 SERVINGS

Duck cooked with taro is a holiday dish, traditionally served on the Moon Festival. This autumn feast falls on the fifteenth day of the eighth moon, and was thought to be the birthday of the moon goddess, the night on which the moon is at its brightest. Duck with taro is served then because it is a well-liked dish, and taro is plentiful at that time of year.

INGREDIENTS

1 Long Island duckling (about 5 pounds), frozen
1 teaspoon salt
1 scallion
2 slices fresh ginger
½ cup sherry
¼ cup dark soy sauce
2 tablespoons sugar
1 can taro, drained and each piece cut in half

PREPARATION

Thaw and clean duck. Sprinkle with salt. Roast as for Orange-Spiced Duck (page 165), in a preheated oven at 375 degrees for 1 hour. Discard excess fat.

COOKING PROCEDURES

Put a small roaster (with a cover) on a burner. Place a bamboo rack on the bottom of the roaster, then place the duck on the rack, breast side up, and turn on the flame to high. Add scallion and ginger. Add sherry and soy sauce, and bring to a boil. Add 2½ cups cold water and again bring to a boil. Cover, turn the flame down to medium low, and simmer for 1 hour, basting occasionally, then add the sugar and cook for another 30 minutes.

Add drained taro pieces, making sure all are submerged in the liquid. Baste again and continue cooking for another 30 minutes. (At the end of this period, if more than ½ cup of liquid remains, turn the flame to high and cook, uncovered, for 7 to 10 minutes.) When only ½ cup liquid remains, remove the duck to a platter. Cut into bite-sized pieces, surround with the taro, and pour gravy over all. Serve immediately.

TIPS

If a bamboo rack is unavailable, lay 2 chopsticks parallel to each other on the bottom of the roaster and place the duck on them. This will keep the duck from sticking to the pan.

An oval, enameled, cast-iron pot can be substituted for the roasting pan.

Most of the cooking can be done beforehand. Prepare, up to the point of adding the taro, and when ready, warm duck over the range, add taro and proceed from there.

Minced Squab

4 SERVINGS

Squab, prepared in this Cantonese fashion, is definitely a banquet dish, both because of its cost and the amount of work involved. All the ingredients used are available in American markets, but the result is uniquely Chinese. If you can afford both the time and the money, the result will be worth the effort and expenditure.

INGREDIENTS

1 head Boston lettuce
1 squab (1½ pounds)
½ cup cooked chicken livers
    (4 ounces)
1 slice ginger
½ teaspoon salt
½ pound ground fresh pork
    (1 cup)

¼ cup vegetable oil
1 tablespoon dry sherry
2 tablespoons light soy sauce
1 teaspoon sugar
½ cup minced water chestnuts
½ cup minced, soaked Chinese
    mushrooms

PREPARATION

Break off and wash whole lettuce leaves, arranging as cups on platter.

Skin and debone squab. Using only the meat from the breast and the second joint of the legs, mince fine, to make about ½ cup.

Cook the chicken livers in 2 tablespoons water with the ginger and salt for about 10 minutes. Cool and mince.

COOKING PROCEDURES

In a wok or skillet, stir fry the pork in 2 tablespoons of the oil for about 3 minutes, or until gray. Add sherry and 1 tablespoon of the soy sauce and mix well, then remove from the pan and set aside.

Heat the remaining oil and stir fry the minced squab. Add the remaining soy sauce and sugar and mix well; add the reserved pork to the squab. Stir, then add the water chestnuts and mushrooms and mix thoroughly. Add minced liver, stir again, and serve.

How to eat: Each person takes a cuplike lettuce leaf in his hand and adds a rounded tablespoon of the squab mixture. The lettuce is then folded over and the "package" eaten with the fingers.

TIPS

Ground pork is used as filler because in China it is a relatively inexpensive meat. In the United States, however, pork is quite expensive, and not all butchers will grind it, but it does give a pleasant variation in flavor.

This dish requires last-minute cooking, but a great deal of the preparation can be done earlier in the day. Prepare the squab, the chicken livers, and all the seasonings in the morning, and the actual cooking time will not be very long.

Fish and Seafood

Fish and seafood are abundant and popular in China, both as everyday and as banquet dishes. Because freshness is all important, only locally available seafoods are cooked and eaten in each area. For those living inland, lake and river shrimps and crabs are excellent substitutes for the salt-water variety. Lobster is generally found only near the sea. Canton is a port city—hence, Lobster Cantonese (page 190).

A word to the fisherman: If you have caught a fish yourself, it should be cleaned and scaled as soon as it is brought home, and then frozen for future use. The only exception to this rule is shad. The Chinese do not remove the scales from shad because the fat under the scales sweetens the fish during cooking. They feel that the flavor is so much better that it is worth the inconvenience of removing the scales while eating the shad.

Fish are usually cooked whole, either steamed or fried. Shrimp are cooked in the shell, even when stir fried with other foods. The Chinese feel that shrimp tastes better cooked this way, and do not mind removing shrimp shells at the table. However, since Americans may feel awkward shelling shrimp in company, I use shelled shrimp in my recipes.

Clams are a common and popular seafood throughout China. Chinese clams are smaller, more tender, and require less cooking than American clams. Recipes in this book are adapted for the American variety.

Such sea delicacies as shark's fin and sea cucumber, which are main attractions of any banquet at which they are served, are banquet foods because of expense and difficulty in preparation. Other seafoods are also served at banquets, prepared in an elaborate and complicated fashion. Chinese banquets conclude with the serving of a whole fish, usually deep fried. This could not be done at home; few families could spare enough oil to immerse a whole fish.

The Chinese feel that their methods of cooking seafoods are more delicate than Western methods, resulting in less "fishy" taste and aroma.

Red-Cooked Fish (Whiting)

紅燒魚

4 SERVINGS

The Chinese like to eat fish with almost every meal, and try to include a fish course as one of the three or four dishes served in every family dinner. Steaming and red cooking are the two most common ways of preparing fish. Here, whiting is used to illustrate the principle of red cooking fish.

INGREDIENTS

1 or 2 whole whiting (2½ pounds), cleaned and scaled but head and tail left on
2 tablespoons all-purpose flour
½ cup vegetable oil
4 slices fresh ginger

3 scallions, cut into 2-inch lengths
3 tablespoons dry sherry
4 tablespoons dark soy sauce
1 teaspoon salt
2 tablespoons sugar

PREPARATION

Wash and clean fish. Dry, both inside and out, with paper towels. Roll in the flour.

COOKING PROCEDURES

Heat oil in a wok, deep skillet or heavy saucepan. Add ginger and let sizzle. Fry fish on one side for 5 minutes. Turn over carefully with a spatula and fry another 4 minutes. Add the remaining ingredients and 1½ cups water and bring to a boil. Cover, turn flame to medium and cook for about 15 minutes. Scoop fish carefully out of the pan. Dish, pour sauce over and serve at once.

To serve, in order to make the fish more presentable, flake off small portions, dipped in sauce, as individual servings. Additional helpings can follow.

TIPS

Whiting is not the only fish that can be prepared by this method. Other fish that can be substituted are cod tail, butterfish, porgy, whitefish, carp, striped bass, and sea bass. Use the same quantity (2½ pounds).

Green Seaweed and Fillet of Sole

苔條麵拖魚

4 SERVINGS

Fillet of sole with seaweed originated in Ningpo, on the seacoast of China. Fish is the staple food of Ningpo, and green seaweed, gathered and dried in the area, is used as an herb to add flavor and color to many different foods.

INGREDIENTS

1 cup tempura flour
4 teaspoons powdered green seaweed
1 cup club soda
1 pound sole fillets

2 tablespoons all-purpose flour
2 cups vegetable oil for deep frying, approximately
Pieces of asparagus, string beans, etc. (optional)

PREPARATION

Make a batter by combining the tempura flour with the seaweed and then with the club soda. Cut each sole fillet into 1 x 2-inch rectangles. Wipe dry. Just before dipping in batter, sprinkle on both sides with regular flour.

COOKING PROCEDURES

Heat the oil to about 350 degrees. Dip pieces of sole in batter and deep fry, a few at a time, for 5 seconds each. Use leftover batter for dipping and frying vegetable pieces, if desired. When all fish is fried, serve with the following dip.

DIP

¼ cup sour cream

2 teaspoons *hoisin* sauce

2 teaspoons chili sauce

2 teaspoons tomato catsup

⅛ teaspoon garlic powder

1 red or green bell pepper

Combine all ingredients except pepper. Cut pepper in half and remove the seeds; use pepper as a container for the dip. Place the dip in the center of the platter and arrange the fried fish around it.

TIPS

Make dip well ahead of serving time. Prepare pepper and store in refrigerator until ready for use.

Green seaweed, packed in spice jars and sold in Oriental grocery stores, comes powdered and ready to use. The jars may be labeled "dried powdered seaweed."

Tempura flour, sold in Japanese stores, is recommended for convenience. A mixture of flour and baking powder could be substituted, but tempura flour is premixed in correct proportions and available at the same stores that sell green seaweed.

Red-Cooked Fish with Fresh Bean Curd

2 SERVINGS

Although some Americans find bean curd, the custardlike substance made from soybean "milk," strange-tasting at first, many become very fond of it. Rich in protein and versatile as well, it can be eaten uncooked in salad or cooked with meat or fish. Here is an example of its use with fish; it absorbs the flavor of the fish and sauce, and is very tasty.

INGREDIENTS

1 whole sea bass (about 1 pound), cleaned and scaled but head and tail left on
1 tablespoon all-purpose flour
2 squares fresh bean curd
¼ cup vegetable oil
2 slices fresh ginger

2 tablespoons dry sherry
1½ tablespoons dark soy sauce
½ teaspoon salt
½ teaspoon hot bean paste
2 whole scallions, in 2-inch lengths

PREPARATION

Wash the fish. Pat dry, both inside and out, with paper towels.
Roll fish in flour. Shake off excess flour.
Cut each square of bean curd into 8 pieces.

COOKING PROCEDURES

Heat vegetable oil in wok or large skillet. Add ginger slices, then the fish. Fry fish for 5 minutes. Turn over carefully and fry the other side for another 3 minutes.

Add sherry, soy sauce, salt, hot bean paste, and 1 cup water. Cover and cook over medium flame for 5 minutes, then uncover and place the bean curd in the sauce around the fish. Cover again and cook over a medium-low flame for another 5 minutes. Sprinkle scallions over fish. Spoon some sauce over scallions. Dish and serve.

TIPS

Other small whole fish of around one pound can be used instead of sea bass—flounder, striped bass, bluefish, porgy, or carp.

Hot bean paste comes in cans, and is available in Chinese grocery stores.

Boneless Sweet-Sour Pine Nut Fish

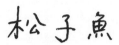

6 SERVINGS

In many Chinese restaurants, this is known as "Squirrel Fish." In Chinese phonetics the words "pine nut" and "squirrel" sound very similar. Since pine nuts are not native to China and are thus very expensive, some restaurants leave out pine nuts to save money. The cooked fish is curled back and looks somewhat like a baby squirrel, which gives rise to the name "Squirrel Fish." My students and I prefer calling it "Pine Nut Fish."

INGREDIENTS

3 pounds fillets of sea bass, striped bass, or yellow pike, skins left on
1½ teaspoons salt
½ cup all-purpose flour
2 cups vegetable oil for deep frying
2 tablespoons pine nuts
Sauce:
1½ cups chicken broth, fresh or canned

5 tablespoons wine vinegar
5 tablespoons sugar
1½ tablespoons light soy sauce
4 tablespoons tomato catsup
½ cup frozen peas and carrots
½ cup water chestnuts, diced
¼ cup dried Chinese mushrooms
2½ tablespoons cornstarch, dissolved in 3 tablespoons water

PREPARATION

Cut each fillet into 1 x 3-inch pieces. Deeply score each piece on the inside, then sprinkle that same side with salt. Roll in dry flour before deep frying, making sure that the flour gets into the deep score, and shaking off excess.

COOKING PROCEDURES

Heat oil to 375 degrees and deep fry 3 to 4 pieces of fish at a time until slightly brown and crunchy looking, then drain on paper toweling and keep warm. Continue in the same manner until all the pieces are cooked.

To make sauce: Heat broth in a saucepan with the vinegar, sugar, soy sauce, and catsup. When the mixture boils, add the peas and carrots, water chestnuts, and mushrooms and cook for a minute, then thicken with the predissolved cornstarch, stirring again to make sure the water and cornstarch are thoroughly mixed.

Place the fish on platter and pour sauce over just before serving. Sprinkle the pine nuts over the fish and serve hot.

TIPS

The fish can be deep fried about 10 to 15 minutes before serving, but sauce and fish must be combined at the last minute.

Poached Fish, Canton Style

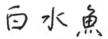

4 SERVINGS

Poached fish is a welcome addition to any Chinese meal. It is high in protein, low in calories, and quite easy to prepare. This Cantonese version utilizes "tea melon" to give the dish an unusual flavor.

INGREDIENTS

1 whole sea bass (about 2 pounds), cleaned and scaled but head and tail left on
4 slices fresh ginger
1 scallion
2 tablespoons "tea melon"

1 tablespoon dry sherry
1 tablespoon light soy sauce
1 tablespoon dark soy sauce
1 teaspoon salt
6 tablespoons vegetable oil

PREPARATION

Wash the fish and dry it, both inside and out, with a paper towel. Score twice on each side.

Shred the ginger, scallion, and "tea melon."

COOKING PROCEDURES

Bring 3 quarts water to a boil in a large saucepan. Drop in the fish, bring to a boil again, and boil for 10 minutes. Scoop up fish carefully and lay on a plate. Combine the sherry, light and dark soy sauce, and salt and pour over the fish, then sprinkle on the "tea melon" and scallion shreds. Heat oil until boiling, drop in ginger shreds, and cook 1 minute. Pour the boiling oil over fish and serve immediately.

To eat, make an incision along backbone of fish and lift meat off with spoons or chopsticks.

TIPS

If you have a fish poacher, by all means use it, as it will help immensely in lifting the fish out of the water.

Only very fresh fish can be used in this dish.

"Tea melon" comes in cans and is available at any Chinese grocery store. After opening can, put the contents in a jar and store in refrigerator.

Steamed Floured Carp

6 SERVINGS

This is a banquet dish from Soochow, in eastern China. The taste is delightfully subtle, a change from the black bean and garlic flavor Westerners have come to associate with so many Chinese fish dishes.

INGREDIENTS

1 fresh-killed whole carp (1 to 1½ pounds), cleaned and scaled but head and tail left on

½ cup rice flour or Cream of Rice

1 bunch Chinese parsley (cilantro) of which half is chopped for sauce	½ teaspoon sugar
	½ teaspoon salt
	1 tablespoon dry sherry
Sauce:	⅛ teaspoon ground chili pepper or cayenne
¼ cup vegetable oil or rendered chicken fat	
	¼ cup chopped cilantro (half of bunch above)
2 tablespoons dark soy sauce	
2 tablespoons light soy sauce	

PREPARATION

Pour water to a depth of 2 inches into the bottom section of 3-tiered steamer and bring to a boil.

Wash and dry the fish and score 3 times on each side. If fish is too large for bowl you intend to steam it in, cut it in half vertically, dividing it into a head section and a tail section. Smother the fish, both outside and inside, with the rice flour immediately before steaming. Put the fish into a fireproof bowl and place bowl on middle rack of steamer.

Combine sauce ingredients in another fireproof bowl. Place this bowl on the top rack of the same steamer as the fish.

COOKING PROCEDURES

Steam both fish and sauce over a high flame for 15 minutes. When done, remove the fish to a platter, and if it was cut apart, reshape it into a whole fish. Decorate it with the remaining sprigs of Chinese parsley, covering the break in the middle. Pour the sauce over the fish and serve at once.

TIPS

If you do not have a three-tiered steamer, steam the fish in the steamer you do have and prepare the sauce in a double boiler.

If the Cream of Rice is used as a substitute for rice flour, it should be dry roasted—that is, without oil—over a low flame in a hot wok or skillet for a few minutes, until just before it turns brown.

To keep Chinese parsley, wash it well, wrap in a dry paper towel, and store in the vegetable section of the refrigerator in a plastic bag. It will stay fresh for a week.

Only fresh-killed fish can be used for this dish. Pick out your own live carp in your fish store and have it killed and cleaned there.

Sweet-Pungent Whole Fish

甜酸全魚

6 SERVINGS

Sweet-pungent fish is often served as the finale of a Chinese banquet, because the Chinese word for "plentiful" or "complete" has the same sound, yu, as the Chinese word for "fish." The fish is served last but seldom eaten, or at least never finished. This is taken as a good omen, a sign that the banquet was successful and that there is food left over for future banquets.

INGREDIENTS

1 whole sea bass (about 1½ pounds), cleaned and scaled but head and tail left on
3 tablespoons cornstarch
3 tablespoons flour
3 tablespoons sherry
1 tablespoon dark soy sauce
1 teaspoon salt
¼ cup dried Chinese Mushrooms
¼ cup bamboo shoots, shredded
1 scallion, green part and all
¼ cup Chinese sweet mixed pickles
Vegetable oil for deep frying

Sweet-Pungent Sauce:
6 tablespoons sugar
1 tablespoon tomato sauce
¼ cup vinegar
1 tablespoon soy sauce
1½ tablespoons cornstarch, dissolved in ½ cup cold water
1 teaspoon salt

PREPARATION

Wash and clean fish. Pat dry with paper towels. Make 3 diagonal cuts on each side of the fish. Mix 3 tablespoons cornstarch, flour, sherry, 1 tablespoon soy sauce, and 1 teaspoon salt into a smooth paste. Rub this mixture into the surface of the fish, inside and out, until all the paste is used up.

Soak the Chinese mushrooms in ½ cup warm water for 20 minutes, then drain and remove the stems. Shred the mushrooms to make ¼ cup.

Shred the scallion to make 2 tablespoons.

Shred the Chinese sweet mixed pickles.

Combine the sweet-pungent sauce ingredients in a separate bowl. Set aside.

COOKING PROCEDURES

Heat oil in a deep fryer to 350 degrees. Put in fish and fry for about 15 minutes, then drain on a paper towel. Flatten the underbelly of the fish slightly while still warm so that the fish will stand up on a platter. Keep warm.

Heat 1 tablespoon oil in skillet or wok. Add mushrooms, bamboo shoots, and scallions and stir fry for 1 minute. Add sweet-pungent sauce mixture and cook until it thickens. Mix in Chinese pickles, then pour this sauce over the fish and serve at once.

TIPS

Even the Chinese regard Sweet-Pungent Whole Fish as a restaurant dish, and few would attempt it at home. However, the recipe is given here for the adventurous cook who owns a deep-fryer and is willing to take extra time and effort.

Chinese sweet mixed pickles are sold only in Chinese specialty stores.

Clams in Black Bean Sauce

豆 豉 蛤 蜊

4 SERVINGS

To most Americans, clams rank just below apple pie in any list of typically American foods, so it may come as a surprise to find that Chinese living in coastal areas, who have never heard of clam chowder, eat and enjoy clams. Here clams are cooked with black beans, a favorite Chinese accompaniment for seafood.

INGREDIENTS

18 to 20 littleneck clams (about 2½ pounds)

2 cups liquid, preferably the

juice of the clams

1 tablespoon vegetable oil

4 thin slices fresh ginger

2 cloves garlic, crushed	2½ tablespoons cornstarch, dissolved in 3 tablespoons water
2 tablespoons crushed fermented black beans	
2 tablespoons oyster sauce	2 tablespoons chopped scallion, green part

PREPARATION
Wash and clean clams. Soak in water for about 1 hour, then drain. Heat 2 quarts of water to a boil and add half the clams. As soon as each opens, remove it, then add the remaining clams and repeat the process. Pour cooking liquid into a container and let sand settle to the bottom. Measure out 2 cups of liquid for making sauce.

COOKING PROCEDURES
Heat oil in a saucepan. Add ginger, garlic, and fermented black beans. Let them sizzle in the oil for a minute. Add 2 cups clam liquid. Let it boil for 2 minutes. Discard ginger and garlic.

Add oyster sauce and mix a few times. Thicken with the predissolved cornstarch mixture (stirring again to make sure the water and cornstarch are thoroughly mixed).

Arrange clams on platter and sprinkle scallions on top.

Pour boiling sauce over clams. Serve immediately.

TIPS
Fermented black beans and oyster sauce, both staples that have many uses and keep well on the shelf, are available in Chinese grocery stores.

To crush the black beans, place them on a flat surface and hit hard with a heavy object, such as the flat side of a cleaver.

After the package of beans has been opened, place the remaining beans in a plastic bag, tied securely, or in a jar with a good lid.

Clams Steamed with Eggs

蛤蜊燉蛋

4 SERVINGS

Only at a banquet are courses served one at a time in China. However, this light dish is suitable for serving as a first course or as part of the main course, accompanied by a meat dish and a vegetable dish.

Chinese clam shells are thinner than the U.S. variety. However, even with American clams, preparing this dish is well worth the extra effort entailed.

INGREDIENTS
1 dozen littleneck clams ½ teaspoon salt
4 eggs

PREPARATION
Wash and scrub the clams thoroughly. Put them in 3 cups cold water and bring to a boil, cooking until shells begin to open just slightly. As soon as this happens, remove them and place them in a bowl. Save the liquid and let it cool, allowing the sand and dirt to settle to the bottom. When ready to use, pour off clear liquid and reserve it, discarding sand and dirt at the bottom.

Beat eggs until yolk and white are thoroughly mixed, then add ½ teaspoon salt and beat a few times more.

COOKING PROCEDURES
Place 8 of the best clams, in their shells, in a large Pyrex bowl (about 1½-quart size). Add meat of remaining clams. Pour eggs into the bowl. Mix with chopsticks. Add all the clam liquid, or enough to fill the bowl.

Bring 2 quarts water to a boil in the bottom of a large steamer. Put the bowl containing the clams and eggs on the steamer rack, then cover and steam for 15 minutes. Serve hot.

TIPS

Another way of preparing this dish is to boil the clams until they open fully. Pick out the meat and discard the shells. Let the liquid settle, then use 1½ cups of it, with the egg, to make clams steamed with eggs as in the master recipe. However, keeping the shells makes each clam into a little mound, an interesting-looking dish.

Lobster Cantonese

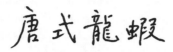

4 SERVINGS

Americans who have always found the Cantonese method of preparing lobster particularly appealing will be pleased to know that this dish can be prepared at home. The secret of its exciting taste is leaving the meat in the shell. Once the shells are removed, most of the flavor disappears.

INGREDIENTS

1 live lobster (about 1½ pounds)
2 tablespoons vegetable oil
2 teaspoons crushed fermented black beans
2 cloves garlic, finely minced
¼ pound ground fresh pork (½ cup)
1 tablespoon dry sherry
1 tablespoon dark soy sauce
½ teaspoon salt
½ teaspoon sugar
1 cup chicken broth, fresh or canned
1 tablespoon cornstarch, dissolved in 2 tablespoons cold water
2 scallions, cut into 2-inch lengths
1 egg, lightly beaten

PREPARATION

Wash lobster. Cut off claws and legs. Disjoint the claws and crack with cleaver. Discard small legs.

Cut the head off at the groove and split the lobster lengthwise, then remove and discard the gills, intestinal canal, and pouchlike stomach. Cut whole lobster—shell and all—into bite-sized pieces. Rinse and drain.

COOKING PROCEDURES

Heat oil in a wok or skillet, then add black beans and garlic and stir a few times. Add pork and stir fry for 2 minutes. Add lobster and stir until the shell turns pink.

Add sherry, soy sauce, salt, and sugar and stir. Add chicken broth and bring to a boil. Cover, turn the flame down to medium, and cook for 3 minutes, then thicken with the predissolved cornstarch (stirred again to make sure the water and cornstarch are thoroughly mixed), stirring a few times. Add the scallions, then turn off flame and pour in beaten egg. Stir a few times and serve hot.

TIPS

Avoid overuse of black beans and garlic. Use the exact amounts stated in the recipe, as it is very important to maintain the correct proportions.

Shrimp can be substituted for lobster and prepared in the same way.

If killing the lobster bothers you, have it cut up according to instructions above at the fish store. Be sure to use it immediately, however.

Shrimp and Kidney

炒 腰 蝦

4 SERVINGS

In China, kidneys are considered a greater delicacy than shrimp and are extremely expensive. For that reason, this is a banquet dish. It is a good example of national, as opposed to regional, Chinese cooking, and is served at banquets in all parts of China.

This dish may take a little extra advance preparation, but the small amount of last-minute work it needs is quickly done, and the taste is so good that the effort is well worthwhile.

INGREDIENTS

4 pork kidneys (about 1 pound)	¼ cup dry sherry
3 teaspoons salt	½ pound raw shrimp
2 slices ginger, 1 x 1½ inches	6 tablespoons vegetable oil

1 clove garlic, crushed
1 tablespoon dark soy sauce
½ teaspoon sugar
¼ cup Smithfield ham, sliced
¼ cup bamboo shoots, sliced

1 stalk scallion, in 2-inch lengths
1 tablespoon cornstarch, dissolved in 2 tablespoons cold water

PREPARATION

The day before cooking this dish, cut each kidney into halves lengthwise. Cut out all white veins and deep red spots. Score each kidney half, then cut into 1 x ½-inch pieces. Rinse several times in cold water. Drain, add 1 teaspoon salt and 1 slice ginger and let stand 10 minutes. Rinse and drain. Add 2 tablespoons sherry and let stand 10 minutes. Drain again. Add cold water to cover and soak in refrigerator overnight or at least 10 to 12 hours. Drain when ready to cook.

On the day of cooking, shell, devein, and wash shrimp. Add 1 teaspoon salt to a bowl of water and add shrimp. Stir or whip with chopsticks for about 2 minutes, then rinse and dry on paper towel.

COOKING PROCEDURES

Heat 2 tablespoons of the oil in a wok or skillet and stir fry shrimp for just a minute. Add 1 tablespoon of the sherry and the remaining teaspoon salt. Stir, then remove from the wok and set aside.

Let garlic sizzle in the remaining oil for a few seconds. Add drained kidney; stir quickly for just *30 seconds*. Add the remaining sherry, soy sauce, and sugar and stir, then add ham, bamboo shoots, remaining slice ginger, and scallion. Stir, then add the reserved shrimps and stir again. Thicken with the predissolved cornstarch (stirred again to make sure the water and cornstarch are thoroughly mixed) and serve immediately.

TIPS

Be sure to prepare the kidney the day before you plan to cook this dish. This method of soaking removes all unpleasant odors, and makes it possible to cook the kidney very quickly, leaving it tender and tasty.

Directions for preparing Smithfield ham can be found in the glossary.

Shrimp Susanna

煎蝦餅

8 SERVINGS

If "Shrimp Susanna" sounds like an unusual title for a Chinese recipe, there is a good reason for the name. My late sister, Susanna, adapted the recipe for these very tasty shrimp cakes from the difficult, traditional method to a more practical, modern style of cooking. They are excellent as an appetizer, and can be made ahead of time and reheated for serving.

INGREDIENTS

1 pound raw shrimp
2 strips bacon
¼ cup chopped scallion, green part only
1 teaspoon minced fresh ginger
¼ medium-sized cooking apple, peeled and cut into small dice
½ teaspoon salt
¼ teaspoon sugar
Pinch of white pepper
2 teaspoons cornstarch
1 teaspoon dry sherry
2 eggs, unbeaten
¼ cup vegetable oil
1 cup of lettuce shreds

PREPARATION

Shell and devein shrimp. Wash and drain. Cut into very small pieces.

Fry or broil the bacon until crisp, then drain on paper towelling and crumble into fine pieces.

Combine the shrimp, bacon, scallion, ginger, and apple dice, then add salt, sugar, pepper, cornstarch, and sherry; mix well. Add unbeaten eggs and mix again carefully.

COOKING PROCEDURES

Heat oil in a frying pan. When oil is hot, drop the shrimp mixture in tablespoonfuls into the pan. After cooking for about a minute, turn each over. When delicately brown, take out and lay on the bed of shredded lettuce. Serve immediately.

TIPS

If you wish, you can make shrimp cakes ahead of time, and simply reheat them on a cookie sheet in a preheated 400-degree oven. Heat for no longer than 5 minutes.

The cakes can also be cooked and then frozen. Be sure to thaw to room temperature before reheating.

Shrimp in Wine-Rice Sauce

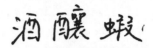

4 SERVINGS

Wine rice is a fermented rice made from glutinous rice, using wine yeast as the fermenting agent. The fermentation process takes 2 to 3 days. Once made, wine rice can be stored in a jar and left in the refrigerator for weeks.

In large cities in the United States, wine rice can be purchased in Chinese grocery stores. But you can do it yourself, with the right ingredients, several days ahead of the following recipe.

INGREDIENTS

1 pound raw shrimp	4 tablespoons vegetable oil
6 tablespoons wine rice	2 teaspoons garlic, minced
¼ cup tomato catsup	2 teaspoons fresh ginger, minced
1 tablespoon *hoisin* sauce	½ teaspoon chili pepper flakes
2 tablespoons cornstarch	¼ cup chopped scallion, green
2 tablespoons water	part and all

PREPARATION

Shell and devein shrimp. Wash and drain. Split each shrimp in half lengthwise. Mix with 1 tablespoon of the cornstarch.

Combine the wine rice with the catsup, *hoisin* sauce, and predissolved cornstarch.

COOKING PROCEDURES

Heat 3 tablespoons of the vegetable oil in a wok or skillet and stir fry shrimp quickly for 3 to 4 minutes, or until all turn pink and opaque. Remove from the wok and set aside.

Heat the remaining vegetable oil in the same wok or frying pan and sizzle the minced garlic, ginger, chili pepper flakes, and scallions for a minute. Add the wine rice mixture, and when the mixture boils, return the reserved shrimp to the sauce and cook for another minute. Dish and serve.

Tips

The wine rice is very important to this shrimp dish. However, in areas where it is not available, the following sauce can be tried as a substitute: 4 tablespoons cooked rice soaked in 1 tablespoon sugar, 2 tablespoons wine vinegar, and 4 tablespoons sherry for 6 to 8 hours.

To make "wine rice," use the following recipe.

WINE RICE

2 cups raw glutinous rice
1 teaspoon wine yeast mixed with
  1 teaspoon all-purpose flour

Soak rice in 3 cups cold water for 4 hours. Drain. Steam rice in a steamer on a piece of paper towel 20 minutes. Rinse in warm water for 2 to 3 minutes. Drain. Before the rice is cold, sprinkle the wine yeast mixture over it. Mix well.

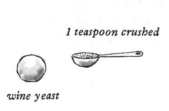

1 teaspoon crushed

wine yeast

*Place small glass
in center of casserole*

Place a small juice glass in the center of an 8-inch casserole. Pack rice all around the glass. Smooth all over with a wet hand. Remove glass, cover the casserole, and leave in a warm place for 24 to 36 hours, or until the well is filled with liquid. The wine rice can be kept in refrigerator for several weeks.

Baby Shrimp Over Sizzling Rice

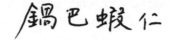

8 SERVINGS

INGREDIENTS FOR RICE PADDIES (*for sizzling rice*)

1 cup glutinous rice	2 cups vegetable oil, for deep frying

PREPARATION

Rinse glutinous rice in cold water. Place in rectangular aluminum pan, 9" x 13", and add 1¼ cups cold water. Make sure the rice is evenly distributed in the pan. Cover with foil. Bake at 375 degrees for 30 minutes. Remove foil; bake at 350 degrees for 30 to 40 minutes, till rice is dry enough to take out of pan. Break rice into squares 1½" x 1½".

COOKING PROCEDURES

Just before combining with shrimp mixture, deep-fry rice squares in 2 cups oil over medium flame until they turn slightly brown and crisp. Drain well. Place in deep bowl and keep warm.

INGREDIENTS FOR BABY SHRIMP

1 pound baby shrimps	½ cup tomato sauce
1 tablespoon salt	¼ cup diced, soaked Chinese
3 tablespoons cornstarch	mushrooms
4 tablespoons vegetable oil	½ cup diced water chestnuts
1 teaspoon sugar	½ cup cooked peas

PREPARATION

Thaw shrimps; rinse and drain. Mix with salt and cornstarch.

COOKING PROCEDURES

Stir-fry shrimps in 3 tablespoons vegetable oil for 3 minutes. Drain and dish. Thoroughly mix sugar, 2 teaspoons salt, tomato sauce, 2 tablespoons cornstarch, and 1 cup water. Heat 1 tablespoon oil in a saucepan. Add mushrooms and water chestnuts. Add the tomato sauce-cornstarch mixture and bring to boil. Add cooked peas and shrimps; mix well. Pour shrimp mixture over rice paddies at table.

Vegetables

One or two vegetables are served with every Chinese homestyle dinner. These are not the mixed meat-and-vegetable variety well known from restaurants, but vegetables only, cooked alone or combined with other vegetables. Most meals include at least one green vegetable, such as spinach, string beans, or cabbage, or one root vegetable like taro or turnips.

Chinese-style vegetables taste so good because of the method by which they are prepared. First, the vegetable is cut into bite-sized pieces. Then, it is stir fried quickly to retain both taste and nutrition. If the vegetable is leafy, such as spinach or watercress, it is cooked only until it wilts, then seasoning is added, the vegetable is tossed and served. Tubular vegetables, such as cabbage, broccoli, and string beans, are first stir fried in a little oil, then seasoned; then water or broth is added, the wok or skillet is covered, and the vegetable is cooked a few minutes longer over medium heat until just tender.

Vegetables are rarely served at banquets, because they are so strongly identified with everyday life. Sometimes, toward the end of a banquet, an unusual vegetable dish will appear, but it will always be combined with a meat or fish and served with a rich sauce to make it luxurious. Abalone with Shantung Cabbage (page 200) is this kind of dish.

Stir-Fry Red Amaranth

炒紅莧

4 SERVINGS

Amaranth is a seasonal, leafy vegetable, therefore not often served in Chinese restaurants. Red and green varieties taste the same, but the red is prettier.

INGREDIENTS

- 1 bunch amaranth
- 3 tablespoons vegetable oil
- 2 cloves garlic, crushed
- 1½ teaspoons salt
- ½ teaspoon sugar

PREPARATION

Using your hands, break the amaranth into 2-inch lengths, discarding the tough ends and roots. Wash carefully to get rid of all mud and sand.

COOKING PROCEDURES

Heat the oil in a wok or skillet and add the garlic. Cook briefly, then add the amaranth pieces and stir until all are well coated. Add salt and sugar and mix well. (If amaranth is too dry, add 2 tablespoons of cold water.)

TIPS

Amaranth is sold at Chinese grocery stores, as is chrysanthemum *choy* (page 209). Green amaranth can be used in this recipe instead of red but red is preferred for its aesthetic appeal.

Do not overcook. Like all leafy vegetables, amaranth requires only a short cooking time.

Abalone and Asparagus

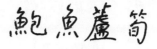

4 SERVINGS

Neither abalone nor asparagus is native to China. For years, most abalone used in China was imported from Mexico.

Asparagus is now grown in China, but it was introduced only recently and is cultivated on a limited scale. This combination is a great delicacy, served only at banquets.

INGREDIENTS

4 ounces abalone, preferably Calmex brand, liquid reserved	2 tablespoons vegetable oil
	1½ teaspoons salt
1 pound fresh asparagus	½ teaspoon sugar

PREPARATION

Slice the abalone into 1 x ½ x ⅛-inch pieces, to equal ½ cup.

Wash asparagus and break off the tough bottoms. Slant-slice asparagus into pieces ¼-inch thick.

COOKING PROCEDURES

Heat oil in skillet or wok. Add asparagus and stir fry for about 2 minutes. Add salt and sugar and mix well. Add 2 tablespoons of the reserved abalone liquid, cover, and cook for 2 minutes. Stir in the abalone slices and serve immediately.

TIPS

Abalone for this use comes only in cans, prepared. Slice the amount required for the recipe and put the leftover abalone, with its liquid, in a jar. Seal jar and keep in refrigerator. Abalone is expensive, but it has many uses, such as Abalone and Agar-Agar Salad (page 101), Abalone with Shantung Cabbage (page 200), and Abalone and Chicken Soup (*The Pleasures of Chinese Cooking*, page 158). The broth is excellent in soups and chowders.

Abalone with Shantung Cabbage

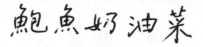

6 SERVINGS

In China, abalone is one of the few foods in the cuisine which must be imported, and milk is hard to get, as there are very few dairy cows, due to the scarcity of grazing land. Thus, when the Chinese combine both a creamed vegetable and an imported shellfish in one dish, you may be sure it is part of a highly regarded banquet.

INGREDIENTS

1 large head Shantung cabbage (2 pounds)	3 teaspoons salt
2 tablespoons cornstarch	2 tablespoons vegetable oil
½ cup milk	½ teaspoon sugar
1 can abalone, preferably Calmex brand	1 tablespoon dry sherry
	¼ cup Smithfield ham, cooked and minced

PREPARATION

Wash and drain cabbage. Quarter lengthwise.

Dissolve cornstarch in milk.

Slice the canned abalone into 1 x 1 x ¼-inch pieces. Reserve juice from can.

COOKING PROCEDURES

Pour 3 quarts water into the bottom of a large steamer and bring to a boil.

Place 4 cabbage quarters in a large bowl on a deep plate. Sprinkle with 2 teaspoons salt and place on the steamer rack, then cover and steam on high heat for 1 hour.

When ready for serving and before adding sauce, carefully drain off all liquid that has accumulated in the deep dish. Save ¼ cup of this for sauce.

To make sauce, heat oil in saucepan. Combine ½ cup of the reserved abalone juice, ¼ cup cabbage cooking juice, remaining teaspoon salt, and sugar. Stir to mix, add dry sherry and thicken immediately with the predissolved cornstarch (stirred again to make sure the milk and cornstarch are thoroughly mixed). Add abalone and mix.

Place cabbage on platter and cut into 2-inch pieces. Pour abalone sauce over cabbage. Sprinkle minced ham on top. Serve at once.

TIPS

Canned abalone is already cooked and should not be overcooked as it will get tough.

The Shantung variety of celery cabbage is becoming more readily available in American markets. For a description of this variety, see page 274.

Asparagus, Chinese Style

3 SERVINGS

At least in the Eastern United States, asparagus has a very short season. In spring it is plentiful, inexpensive, and delicious—but then it's gone, and I wish I had cooked it more often. Here is a Chinese method of preparing asparagus, which gives Americans a new way to serve the vegetable while it is on the market.

INGREDIENTS

1½ pounds fresh asparagus	2 teaspoons salt
3 tablespoons vegetable oil	½ teaspoon sugar

PREPARATION

Wash the asparagus well and break off the tough bottoms; use the tender parts only. Slant-slice each piece of asparagus tip into 1½ x ¼-inch pieces.

COOKING PROCEDURES

Stir fry asparagus in oil for about 3 minutes. Add salt and sugar. Mix well. Add 2 to 3 tablespoons cold water. Cover and cook over medium flame for 2 to 3 minutes. Mix and dish.

TIPS

To break asparagus, hold stalk lightly in one hand and strike the top sharply with the other. The stalk will break naturally at the dividing line between the tender and tough parts. Save the bottom part for soups.

When cooking a green vegetable, do not lift the cover or the color will fade.

Baby Corn and Mock Abalone

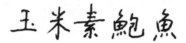

4 SERVINGS

Although this may taste like a combination of seafood and vegetables, it is entirely made of vegetables and vegetable products. Baby Corn and Mock Abalone is one of many vegetarian dishes in the Chinese repertoire. Many Chinese are vegetarians, often because they are Buddhists, sometimes for health reasons. Therefore, dishes like this one and Buddha's Delight (The Pleasures of Chinese Cooking, page 170) have been developed.

INGREDIENTS

6 medium-sized dried Chinese mushrooms
1 teaspoon dried cloud ears
1 can (about 12 ounces) mock abalone
2 ounces fresh snow peas
2 tablespoons vegetable oil
1 cup fresh lofa (loofah), in oblique pieces

½ teaspoon salt
½ teaspoon sugar
1 tablespoon light soy sauce
1 fifteen-ounce can baby corn
Few pieces red bell pepper, if available
1 tablespoon cornstarch, dissolved in 1 tablespoon water

PREPARATION

Soak mushrooms in warm water for 20 minutes, then drain and remove the stems. Cut into quarters.

Soak the cloud ears 20 minutes, in warm water. Wash thoroughly and drain. Cut larger pieces in half.

Slice mock abalone into 1 x ½-inch pieces.

Wash snow peas. Remove ends and strings. Cut into 1-inch pieces.

COOKING PROCEDURE

Heat vegetable oil in skillet or wok. Add mushrooms and stir fry for 30 seconds. Add mock abalone slices and cloud ears and stir. Add the lofa, then the salt, sugar, and soy sauce. Mix, then add baby corn and mix again. Add 2 tablespoons water and cook for 2 minutes, uncovered. Add snow peas and red pepper slices, if used. Thicken with the pre-dissolved cornstarch (stirred again to make sure the water and cornstarch are thoroughly mixed) and serve hot.

TIPS

Mock abalone, a soybean product, is sold canned in Chinese grocery stores, as is baby corn.

If lofa (loofah), a long, green vegetable with a hard, bumpy skin, is not available, substitute zucchini.

Braised Eggplant, Szechuan Style

4 TO 6 SERVINGS

This vegetable dish is prepared in the Szechuan fashion, now so popular with Americans. It is an interesting variation on the familiar, bland eggplant. However, remember that Szechuan cooking is very spicy, so be sure to serve this dish with another, milder meat or chicken dish and plenty of plain boiled rice.

INGREDIENTS

1 large eggplant
2 tablespoons bean sauce
2 tablespoons hot bean sauce with chili
1 teaspoon sugar

¼ cup vegetable oil
1 tablespoon ginger, minced
4 cloves garlic, minced
¼ pound ground fresh pork (½ cup)

PREPARATION
Peel eggplant. Cut as shown.

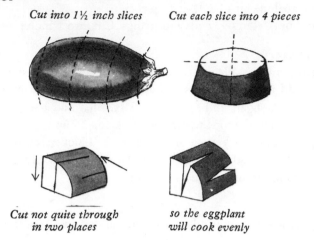

Cut into 1½ inch slices   Cut each slice into 4 pieces

Cut not quite through
in two places

so the eggplant
will cook evenly

Combine the bean sauce, hot bean sauce with chili, and sugar with ¼ cup cold water.

COOKING PROCEDURES
Heat vegetable oil in a wok or skillet, then add ginger and garlic. Mix a few times. Immediately add pork and stir fry for 2 minutes.

Add eggplant and stir fry until all eggplant is coated with oil, about 4 to 5 minutes. Add the already mixed sauce and mix well, then add 3 tablespoons water. Cover, turn the flame down to low, and cook for about 5 minutes. Serve hot.

TIPS
Prepare this dish once according to exact directions. You may wish to make it a little milder by adding less hot bean sauce when you make it a second time—or perhaps more, to make it hotter.

Braised Italian Peppers

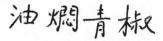

4 SERVINGS

Italian peppers are used here because they are similar to a variety of pepper which grows in China. They are long, narrow, and light green in color, but not hot in taste. Unlike green bell peppers, they taper to a point at the end. This dish is excellent either as part of a Chinese meal or accompanying an American meat course.

INGREDIENTS

3 pounds Italian peppers	1 tablespoon sugar
¼ cup vegetable oil	¼ teaspoon salt
2 tablespoons dark soy sauce	

PREPARATION

Cut each pepper in half lengthwise. Clean out seeds and membranes. Rinse and drain.

COOKING PROCEDURES

Heat vegetable oil slightly in a 3-quart saucepan. Add peppers and mix with chopsticks until oil coats all pieces, then add the salt, sugar, and soy sauce. Turn flame to medium low, cover, and let simmer for about 20 minutes. Serve warm or cold.

TIPS

This dish is best when served very cold. Prepare the day before and allow to remain in refrigerator overnight.

Broccoli Florets with Water Chestnuts

4 SERVINGS

Broccoli is classified as a tubular vegetable, so it requires a slightly longer cooking time than leafy vegetables do.

INGREDIENTS

1 large bunch broccoli	1 teaspoon sugar
¼ cup vegetable oil	½ cup canned water chestnuts, sliced
2 teaspoons salt	

PREPARATION

Cut off broccoli florets about 1½ inches long. (Save the stems for salad; see page 102.) If florets are large, subdivide them into smaller pieces, 4 cups in all.

COOKING PROCEDURES

Heat oil in a wok or frying pan. Add broccoli. Toss and turn until all florets are coated with oil. (When the vegetable is coated, it will look greener and shining.) Add salt and sugar and mix well, then add ½ cup cold water and cover, without mixing. Turn flame to medium and cook for 5 minutes, or until water is almost all absorbed. Stir in the water chestnuts and serve.

TIPS

When cooking a green vegetable, it is important not to lift the cover more than once; otherwise the vegetable will turn an unattractive yellowish green and have no eye appeal. It is just as important that food appeal to the eye as to the taste.

Brussels Sprouts with Ham Squares

炒 小 包 心 菜

6 SERVINGS

This vegetable is easy to prepare. Though Brussels sprouts are not usually thought of as Oriental, the method of cooking is typically Chinese. Ham is added both for its color and for taste appeal.

INGREDIENTS

2 boxes fresh Brussels sprouts (about 1 pound 6 ounces)
2 thin slices boiled ham, the kind used in sandwiches
3 tablespoons vegetable oil

1½ teaspoons salt
½ teaspoon sugar
½ cup chicken broth, fresh or canned

PREPARATION

Cut off the hard end of each Brussels sprout and then split in half. Rinse clean.

Cut ham into ½-inch squares.

COOKING PROCEDURES

Heat oil and stir fry the Brussels sprouts for 2 to 3 minutes, or until all sprouts are coated with oil. Add salt and sugar and mix well. Add chicken broth. Cover, turn the flame down to medium, and cook for 6 to 7 minutes.

Add ham squares. Mix thoroughly, and serve.

TIPS

If Brussels sprouts are to be served as a vegetable dish only, omit ham. Water chestnuts may be added instead, if desired. In that case, use 2 teaspoons salt instead of 1½ teaspoons.

Chinese Cabbage (Bok Choy)

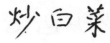

4 SERVINGS

The vegetable known as Chinese cabbage to the Chinese is also called bok choy, a Cantonese term. It can be bought only in Chinese markets in cities which have a Chinatown. Bok choy has wide green leaves and firm white stems. What Americans know as Chinese cabbage is celery cabbage, often available in supermarkets, the leaves of which are lighter green in color than bok choy.

INGREDIENTS
1½ pounds *bok choy*   2 teaspoons salt
  3 tablespoons vegetable oil ½ teaspoon sugar

PREPARATION
Wash each leaf of the *bok choy*. Cut the white part of the *bok choy* into 1-inch lengths. Split the green part lengthwise 2 or 3 times and then cut into 1-inch pieces. Keep the white and green pieces separate, in two bowls.

COOKING PROCEDURES
Heat the oil in a wok or skillet over a high flame. Add the white of the *bok choy* and mix quickly until oil coats all the pieces. After about 1 minute, add the green leaves. Mix and cook for about another 2 minutes. Add salt and sugar. Mix for another minute. Cover the wok; turn the flame to medium and cook for 5 minutes. (If the *bok choy* seems dry, add 2 tablespoons of water *before* covering and cook.)

TIPS
In cooking green vegetables, the cover should not be lifted more than once. The green will turn yellowish if uncovered and then recovered. If the top must be lifted for checking, do not cover again but cook without cover until done.

Stir-Fry *"Chrysanthemum"* Choy *(Leaves)*

炒桐蒿

8 SERVINGS

Chrysanthemum choy *is so named because its leaves resemble the leaves of the chrysanthemum flower in shape and scent. The stems of the vegetable, however, are tender, not woody like those of the flower.*

INGREDIENTS
2 bunches chrysanthemum *choy*	1 tablespoon salt
3 tablespoons vegetable oil	½ teaspoon sugar

PREPARATION
Wash chrysanthemum *choy* carefully and then break into shorter pieces with your hands to make 8 cups.

COOKING PROCEDURES
Heat the oil in a wok or skillet. Add 4 cups of the *choy* and stir until the pieces are wilted. Add the remaining 4 cups and stir again until they are wilted. Add the salt and sugar and stir-fry for 2 minutes. Dish and serve.

TIPS
Chrysanthemum *choy* is a seasonal vegetable, available in Chinese grocery stores. Like spinach and other leafy vegetables, it is very tender and does not require much cooking. Do not overcook.

Eggplant with Bean Sauce

4 SERVINGS

This is a basic home-cookery vegetable dish. I have eaten eggplant pre-pared in this manner ever since I was a child. However, because of the recent interest in spicier food, this version has been slightly modified by the addition of a little spice.

INGREDIENTS

1 to 2 eggplants (about 1½ pounds), skin left on
4 tablespoons vegetable oil
½ teaspoon salt

2 tablespoons bean sauce
1 tablespoon Koo's Hot Sauce
1 teaspoon sugar

PREPARATION

Cut eggplants into 1-inch oblique pieces, to make about 6 cups.

COOKING PROCEDURES

Add the oil to a wok or skillet. Turn on the flame and immediately add the eggplant pieces. Mix well. Sprinkle with salt. Mix. Add ¼ cup cold water and bring to a boil. Cover, turn the flame down to medium low, and cook for 10 minutes.

Dilute the bean sauce and Koo's Hot Sauce and sugar with 2 table-spoons cold water. Add to the eggplant and stir briefly. Cover again, turn the flame down to low, and cook for another 10 minutes. Serve either hot or at room temperature.

TIPS

Koo's Hot Sauce has just been put on the market. It is made, fresh, in New York City and sold in Chinese markets, mostly along the eastern seaboard. It can be used in cooking or put on the table and used, sparingly, as a condiment. If not available, substitute with same amount of hot bean sauce with chili.

Straw Mushrooms, Bamboo Shoots, and Fresh Water Chestnuts

草菇冬筍

4 SERVINGS

The elusive fresh water chestnut, while virtually unobtainable in many parts of the United States, is so much better both in flavor and in texture than the canned variety that it is worth tracking down. Most American cooks will be forced to use canned water chestnuts in this combination, looking forward to the day when fresh ones are more generally available here.

INGREDIENTS

6 fresh water chestnuts
1 cup chicken broth, fresh or canned
1½ tablespoons oyster sauce
1 tablespoon cornstarch
1 fifteen-ounce can straw mushrooms, drained

¼ cup vegetable oil
1 cup summer bamboo shoots cut in oblique pieces
2 tablespoons ½-inch squares red or green sweet pepper
1 teaspoon salt
1 teaspoon sugar

PREPARATION

Cut off both ends of each fresh water chestnut, peel off skin and slice each into 3 to 4 rounds. (If canned are used, drain, rinse, and slice.)

Mix chicken broth with oyster sauce and cornstarch. Be sure to stir well just before using.

COOKING PROCEDURES

Stir fry straw mushrooms in vegetable oil for a minute. Add bamboo shoots, water chestnuts, and pepper squares and mix well. Add salt and sugar. Mix again. Add broth mixture. Mix and cook until slightly thickened, serve hot.

TIPS

Straw mushrooms are small tan-and-brown mushrooms with caps

shaped like tall, narrow thatched roofs. They are a favorite of northern Chinese chefs and can be found, canned, in Chinese grocery stores.

The summer bamboo shoots—smaller, slimmer, and more tender than the winter variety—also come in cans. If they are not available, substitute other canned bamboo shoots.

Fresh water chestnuts are sold in Chinatown grocery stores. They are hard to get and expensive, but after peeling can be stored in the freezer for weeks.

Straw Mushrooms in Oyster Sauce

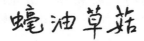

4 SERVINGS

Straw mushrooms were introduced into Chinese markets in the United States relatively recently. They have a delicate flavor and pleasing appearance, and are becoming increasingly popular with Americans. Here is a real treat, a dish in which straw mushrooms are the main feature.

INGREDIENTS

1 head lettuce
1 tablespoon cornstarch
2 tablespoons oyster sauce
¼ cup vegetable oil

1 teaspoon salt
1 fifteen-ounce can straw mushrooms, drained but liquid reserved

PREPARATION

Wash and clean lettuce and cut into 1-inch pieces.

Combine the cornstarch with the oyster sauce and ¼ cup reserved mushroom liquid, to make a paste.

COOKING PROCEDURES

Heat 2 tablespoons vegetable oil in wok or skillet. Add the lettuce and stir fry for 1 minute. Add salt. Mix and remove from pan to a serving platter. Heat the remaining 2 tablespoons oil and stir fry straw mushrooms for a minute. Add cornstarch paste and mix well. Pour mushroom mixture over lettuce and serve immediately.

TIPS
Straw mushrooms can be bought at Chinese specialty stores.

Another recipe, for Straw Mushrooms, Bamboo Shoots, and Fresh Chestnuts, is given on page 211.

The Chinese never eat raw vegetables. The lettuce in this dish is cooked just enough to wilt it, so neither it nor the already-cooked mushrooms require much last-minute cooking.

String Beans with Soy Sauce, Soochow Style

6 SERVINGS

It is unusual for the Chinese to season green vegetables with soy sauce. Usually they prefer to use salt, feeling that soy sauce destroys the green color. In Soochow, however, string beans are cooked with soy sauce instead of salt to add variety. The result is quite different and very pleasant.

INGREDIENTS
2 pounds fresh string beans
4 tablespoons vegetable oil

3 tablespoons dark soy sauce
1½ tablespoons sugar

PREPARATION
Wash string beans and break into 2-inch pieces.

COOKING PROCEDURES
Put the oil in a 3-quart saucepan. Immediately add beans and turn on heat. Mix thoroughly while beans are heating. Add soy sauce and sugar. Mix a few times with chopsticks or spoon.

Turn flame to medium low, and cover. Cook for 10 minutes. Uncover and mix a few times, then cover, turn flame to low and simmer for 20 minutes. (Do not add water.)

String beans cooked this way can be eaten either hot or at room temperature. If they were cooked a few hours early, they should be left at room temperature, not refrigerated.

String Beans, Szechuan Style

4 SERVINGS

Few Chinese vegetable dishes are prepared with meat. This dish is an exception, but the quantity of meat used is so small that it is still considered a vegetable dish. Since string beans prepared in this manner originated in Szechuan, the dish is characteristically hot in taste. In this case, chili pepper is the spice used.

INGREDIENTS

1 tablespoon Szechuan preserved kohlrabi	2 cups vegetable oil for deep frying, plus 1 tablespoon
1 clove garlic	¼ pound ground round steak (½ cup)
1 small slice fresh ginger	
1 tablespoon scallion pieces, green part and all	1 tablespoon light soy sauce
	1 teaspoon salt
1 pound fresh string beans	½ teaspoon sugar

PREPARATION

Finely mince the preserved kohlrabi, garlic, ginger, and scallion.

Break each string bean into about 2-inch lengths. Wash and drain. Heat 2 cups oil in deep-fryer or heavy pot. Deep-fry beans at 375 degrees until they start to wrinkle. Drain off oil. Save oil for future deep frying.

COOKING PROCEDURES

Stir fry garlic, ginger, and scallion in 1 tablespoon vegetable oil in a wok or skillet. Add ground beef and preserved kohlrabi. Continue stirring for another minute, or until beef appears dry. Add light soy sauce, salt, and sugar. Add string beans and mix. Add 1 tablespoon water, cover, and cook for 3 minutes or until all liquid is absorbed. Serve hot or at room temperature.

TIPS
Szechuan preserved kohlrabi is sold in cans in Chinese grocery stores. For information about storing it, see glossary.

This dish can be prepared 1 hour before serving.

Taro and Scallions

葱花芋頭

6 SERVINGS

Taro, like potato, is a root vegetable. It is found in all parts of China, and is a staple in many other areas of the world as well. Americans, who like potatoes, will find this an interesting substitute.

INGREDIENTS

1½ pounds small taro
  4 tablespoons lard or shortening
  ¼ cup scallion green, chopped

1½ teaspoons salt
  2 to 3 tablespoons broth or water

PREPARATION
Place taro in saucepan with enough water to cover. Bring to boil and boil for 30 minutes, then cool. When cool, peel and slice into ¼-inch slices.

COOKING PROCEDURES
Heat lard or shortening in a wok or skillet. Add scallion green and taro slices. Stir fry, tossing and turning until all pieces are coated with lard or shortening. Sprinkle salt over all the taro. Add 2 to 3 tablespoons broth or water and cook for 2 minutes. Dish and serve.

TIPS
Fresh taro root can be bought in Chinese supermarkets as well as in

Spanish-American markets. Canned boiled and peeled taro, sold in Oriental grocery stores, can be substituted for fresh taro in this recipe. Two 10½-ounce cans are sufficient. Since the canned taro is already prepared, the entire "preparation" section should be omitted.

If you do not use lard, substitute 4 tablespoons solid vegetable shortening, but some of the flavor will be missing.

Stir-Fry Watercress

炒西洋菜

4 SERVINGS

There are two watercress recipes in this section of the book. Although both are considered "home cooking," this is the simpler of the two. Here, the whole cress, not just the tips, is used, so the process of preparation is not time consuming. Also, when watercress is cooked in this manner, no soy sauce or sherry is added.

INGREDIENTS

2 bunches watercress
3 tablespoons vegetable oil
2 cloves garlic, peeled and
   lightly crushed

1½ teaspoons salt
½ teaspoon sugar

PREPARATION
Wash watercress and cut into 1½-inch lengths.

COOKING PROCEDURES
Heat vegetable oil, with lightly crushed garlic, in a wok or skillet. When oil is hot, add watercress pieces and stir until well coated with oil. Continue to mix until all the cress is wilted. Add salt and sugar. Mix again and dish. Discard garlic before serving.

TIPS
All the ingredients in this recipe are available in American supermarkets, and neither the preparation nor the cooking time is very long.

If this is served with another stir-fry dish, cook this dish first, as it does not need to be served piping hot but is equally tasty at room temperature.

Watercress, Shanghai Style

生煸西洋菜

4 SERVINGS

This dish is time consuming, since all the watercress leaves must be picked off by hand. However, the leaves are so tender that the resulting vegetable has a unique, delicate texture and taste, justifying the extra work.

INGREDIENTS

4 bunches watercress	1 tablespoon dry sherry
2 cloves garlic	1 teaspoon sugar
2 tablespoons vegetable oil	1½ tablespoons dark soy sauce

PREPARATION

You will use only the tips and the leaves of the watercress, so pick these off carefully; discard all the stems.

Crush the garlic with the flat side of a cleaver.

COOKING PROCEDURES

Heat vegetable oil and add the garlic. Let sizzle for a few seconds. Discard the garlic.

Add watercress, and stir fry for about 2 minutes, or until all the cress is wilted. Add the sherry, sugar, and soy sauce. Mix well with chopsticks. Cook for another minute, then serve.

Wheat Gluten and Vegetables

素什錦

6 SERVINGS

Wheat gluten is made by washing out the gluten from soaked flour. In China it is available fresh, but the dried form sold in Chinese specialty stores in the United States is a perfectly adequate substitute.

In this vegetarian dish, wheat gluten is combined with a variety of vegetables for a colorful and tasty effect.

INGREDIENTS

2 ounces dried "second layer" bean curd (*r-cho*) (¼ package)

1 eight-ounce package prepared wheat gluten

2 ounces snow peas (½ cup)

½ cup thin slices of fresh lotus root

4 tablespoons vegetable oil

1 cup *bok choy* stems in 1-inch pieces

½ cup bamboo shoot slices

1 teaspoon salt

1 teaspoon sugar

⅛ teaspoon monosodium glutamate

1 tablespoon light soy sauce

½ fifteen-ounce can baby corn (½ cup), drained

½ cup red or green bell pepper in 1-inch squares

2 tablespoons cornstarch, dissolved in 1 tablespoon cold water

PREPARATION

Soak bean curd in hot water for 15 minutes. Rinse until yellow liquid becomes clear. Cut each piece into 2 x ½-inch pieces.

Soak wheat gluten in very hot water for 3 to 4 minutes. Squeeze out water to remove grease, then drain and cut each piece in half.

String snow peas and cut into 1-inch pieces.

Scrape lotus roots. Cut into halves and then into very thin slices, to make ½ cup.

COOKING PROCEDURES

Heat the oil in a wok or skillet and add *bok choy*. Mix a few times. Add bamboo shoots, bean curd, and lotus root and mix well. Add salt, sugar, monosodium glutamate, and soy sauce and mix again. Add the snow peas, baby corn, bell pepper, and wheat gluten. Mix, then add ½ cup cold water and cook for 2 to 3 minutes. Thicken with the predissolved cornstarch (stirred again to make sure the water and cornstarch are thoroughly mixed) and serve.

TIPS

This dish can be made only in cities with a Chinese district. Try and get all the ingredients listed here at least once, so that you can taste the dish as it is made in China. If one or two vegetables are left out, it will still taste good, but it will not be authentic.

Wheat gluten, dried bean curd, and canned baby corn can be purchased at Chinese grocery stores and kept on the shelf until needed. Fresh snow peas, fresh lotus roots, and *bok choy* must be purchased just before using.

If fresh lotus roots are not available, use canned ones.

Zucchini with Water Chestnuts

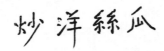

6 SERVINGS

For years, Americans have sought out Chinese restaurants to eat the crisp, tasty Chinese vegetables they believed must be entirely different from American vegetables. Actually, the difference was not in the vegetables but in the cooking method. Any common vegetable, sliced thin and stir fried, can be a "Chinese vegetable," as in this delightful zucchini dish.

INGREDIENTS

2 large zucchini	2 teaspoons salt
½ cup whole water chestnuts	½ teaspoon sugar
3 tablespoons vegetable oil	

PREPARATION

Wash zucchini but do not peel, then slice into thin rounds, to make 4 cups.

Slice water chestnuts into thin rounds.

COOKING PROCEDURES

Heat oil in wok or skillet. Add zucchini and mix until all the pieces are coated with oil. Add salt and sugar. Mix and cook for about 3 minutes. Add the water chestnut slices, and mix again. Dish and serve.

TIPS

Zucchini with water chestnuts can be eaten hot or at room temperature. Try it at least once at room temperature: you will be surprised how pleasant it tastes, and you will be spared unnecessary last-minute cooking worries.

Pickled Assorted Vegetables

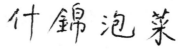

什錦泡菜

6 SERVINGS

Almost every national group has its own way of preserving in brine or "pickling" vegetables. Some people use dill and vinegar, others use oil, while still others use hot spices. Here is a typically Chinese pickled vegetable recipe, including the Szechuan peppercorns native to China. Allow at least three days for pickling.

INGREDIENTS

2 cups cauliflower florets, broken into very small pieces
½ cup string beans in 2″ lengths
½ cup carrot sticks, 2 x ¼ x ¼ inches
3 tablespoons salt

1 teaspoon Szechuan peppercorns
1 tablespoon gin
2 pickled hot cherry peppers
1 tablespoon cherry pepper juice

PREPARATION

Wash and dry all the fresh vegetables so that no water is dripping from them. Cut to sizes specified.

Dissolve salt in 2 cups warm water and add Szechuan peppercorns, gin, cherry peppers, and cherry pepper juice. Pour into a wide-mouthed quart jar and mix well with clean chopsticks. Add cauliflower, string beans, and carrots.

Leave jar at room temperature for 48 hours. Then store in refrigerator for two or three days before eating. The vegetables will keep in the refrigerator for at least a week.

TIPS

This is a very good side dish or hors d'oeuvre. It is also used as an edible garnish for a combination cold platter.

Hot cherry peppers come in glass jars and are sold in delicatessens or pickle, olive, and relish sections of grocery stores. Beware biting into one: they are very hot, and are included in this recipe for looks and for their liquid.

Desserts

The Chinese do not eat sweets at the end of a meal. Sometimes, the last dish is fresh fruit, but the last item consumed must always be tea unaccompanied by any other food. Most of the dishes listed in this book as desserts are sweet, light dishes served *between* courses of Chinese banquets.

Sweet dishes, many entirely or partially liquid and often warm, are served at intervals throughout a banquet to rest the diners and clear their palates. Since they are banquet dishes, they often contain unusual ingredients, such as wine rice (Wine Rice Mandarin Orange "Tea," page 232), or silver fungus (Silver Fungus in Syrup, page 231).

The Chinese do eat pastries, but not as part of a meal. Very few homes have a Western-style oven, so cakes are usually steamed or fried. These small cakes are eaten with tea, not as dessert after a meal. Date and Pine Nut Rolls (page 224), is one example of a fried sweet pastry, and Golden Surprise (*The Pleasures of Chinese Cooking*, page 127), is another.

Although it is not a Chinese tradition, there is no reason that these sweet dishes and pastries cannot be served at the end of the meal by those who like to eat dessert as a last course. Therefore, I have presented several dessert ideas which my students have tried and approved.

Date and Pine Nut Rolls

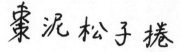

ABOUT 36 ROLLS

In China, dessert is never served at the end of the dinner. Originally, rolls like these were served between the courses of a banquet. However, these date rolls, like other Chinese sweets, can be served as a dessert by Americans, who like to finish a meal with "a sweet taste in their mouths." Prepare this dessert the day before you plan to serve it.

INGREDIENTS

- 1 pound pitted dates
- 4 tablespoons sesame seeds
- 4 tablespoons dark corn syrup
- 6 tablespoons whole pine nuts (about 2 ounces)
- 1 lemon
- ½ pound egg-roll wrappers
- 2 cups vegetable oil for deep frying, approximately
- Powdered sugar

PREPARATION

To make filling, mince dates with a cleaver or in a grinder. Combine the sesame seeds and corn syrup with the dates, then mix in the whole pine nuts. Grate the rind of the lemon into the mixture. Leave in refrigerator at least overnight.

Cut each egg-roll wrapper into 6 equal little sheets as sketched.

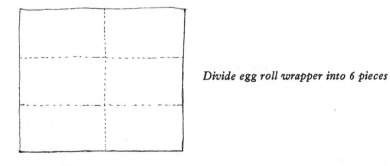

Divide egg roll wrapper into 6 pieces

224

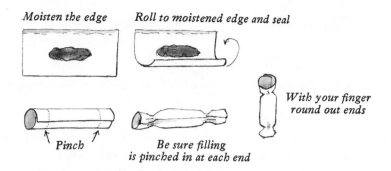

Moisten the edge   Roll to moistened edge and seal

With your finger
round out ends

Pinch

Be sure filling
is pinched in at each end

Shape 1 rounded half-teaspoon of chilled filling into an oblong roll a little over an inch in length. Repeat until all filling is used up (about 36 rolls).

Put 1 roll of filling on each piece of wrapper and roll lengthwise. Pinch at both ends about ½ inch from end and twist to seal, so that roll resembles a miniature firecracker.

Cooking Procedures

Heat oil in a deep-fryer or deep, heavy saucepan to 375 degrees. Deep fry the rolls, a few at a time, until golden brown. Cool. Sprinkle with powdered sugar.

Tips

If stored in an airtight container at room temperature, these date and pine nut rolls will keep for at least a week.

Egg-roll wrapper, which is normally found in the refrigerator cases of Chinese grocery stores, should be stored in your refrigerator, well wrapped, or in the freezer for later use. If you wish to make your own wrapper, a recipe follows:

    2 cups all-purpose flour
    ½ teaspoon salt
    ¾ cup cold water

Sift salt and flour together twice. Mix with the cold water. Knead until smooth. Sprinkle flour generously on a bread board and roll out dough paper thin. Cut into 36 rectangles, each 3 x 2 inches.

Chinese Fried Custard in Sesame Sugar

10 SERVINGS

Chinese Fried Custard in Sesame Sugar is, like most Chinese desserts, served between the courses of a banquet. Several experienced Chinese cooks usually cooperate in its preparation, as the various steps are easier to carry out that way. If you can enlist the services of a friend also skilled in Chinese cooking, this is a worthwhile dessert to try. It comes out well and is very pleasing to American tastes.

INGREDIENTS

½ cup white sesame seeds	2 tablespoons cornstarch
½ cup sugar	1 egg, lightly beaten
6 drops red food coloring	2 cups oil for deep frying, plus
1 cup sifted all-purpose flour	1 tablespoon

PREPARATION

Roast sesame seeds in an ungreased heavy skillet over a medium flame until golden brown. Crush them in a mortar and pestle. Mix with sugar, tinted with red food coloring, and set aside.

Mix sifted flour, cornstarch, and 1 cup cold water into a smooth paste. Add beaten egg and mix again.

Bring 2 cups water to a boil. Add the flour and cornstarch mixture, stirring until thickened. Pour into a 9 x 12 inch rectangular pan greased with 1 tablespoon oil and cool in the refrigerator.

When custard is cool, cut into 2 x ½ x ½-inch strips.

COOKING PROCEDURES

Heat the 2 cups oil to 350 to 375 degrees. Deep fry the custard strips, a few at a time, for about 1 minute each, then drain and roll in the sesame seed and sugar mixture.

TIPS

If necessary, the custard can be made an hour before serving and served at room temperature. However, do not make it the day before as it will taste stale.

Glazed Yucca

拔絲山葯

8 SERVINGS

Glazed yucca is the original dessert of Peking from which the glazed bananas or glazed apples so popular in Chinese restaurants in the United States have been copied. The preparation of this Peking banquet dish requires several pairs of skilled hands. Therefore, it is a real challenge, and a treat besides.

INGREDIENTS

24 pieces oblique-cut yucca, 1½-inch in size, about 2 pounds
¾ cup sifted all-purpose flour
2 cups vegetable oil for deep frying, plus 1 teaspoon

1 cup sugar
1 tablespoon sesame seeds

PREPARATION

Peel the yucca and oblique-cut into 24 small wedges, 1½ inches at the largest point. Boil in 2 cups water for 10 minutes, then cool.

Combine the flour with ½ cup cold water into a smooth paste. Dip yucca pieces into this batter.

COOKING PROCEDURES

Heat the 2 cups oil to 375 degrees in a deep-fryer or deep, heavy saucepan and fry the yucca pieces, a few at a time, until lightly brown.

Meanwhile, in another pan, heat 1 teaspoon oil. Add sugar and ¼ cup cold water and heat until the syrup reaches the "crack" stage (about 280 degrees on a candy thermometer). When all the yucca pieces have been fried and drained, place them in this syrup, sprinkle with sesame seeds, and stir until all pieces are well coated with syrup.

To serve, place on a greased plate and take hot yucca pieces to table immediately, along with a bowl of ice water with ice cubes in it. Immerse the pieces, one by one, in the water, remove immediately with tongs, and eat. The pieces should be hard on the outside, soft and fluffy on the inside.

TIPS

Yucca is a root vegetable found mostly in tropical countries. Long and somewhat like a thin horseradish root in appearance (not in taste), it can be found in Spanish-American grocery stores.

If yucca is not available, apple or banana pieces can be substituted in this recipe, but remember that yucca is the real thing. Only firm bananas should be used.

Jujube and Walnut "Drink"

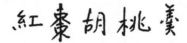

8 SERVINGS

This dessert can be served warm as a snack or in between the courses of a banquet. Many of my students have sampled it, and report that they like it. Preferably make it the day before.

INGREDIENTS

1 cup dried red jujube (Chinese red dates)
1 cup shelled walnuts

2 tablespoons long-grain rice
3 tablespoons raw sugar

PREPARATION

Soak the jujube for 6 hours or overnight in 1 cup cold water.

Soak walnuts for 1 hour with enough water to cover. Wash and drain.

Soak rice in 1 cup of water for 20 minutes.

Boil jujube in the water in which it has been soaked for about 20 minutes, then cool it until it can be handled. Remove pits. Place jujube and its water in blender and blend for 20 to 30 seconds. Pour out into a saucepan.

Into the same blender jar, put the walnuts, rice, and the water in which the rice was soaked. Blend for 20 to 30 seconds, then pour into the saucepan with the jujube. Add 1 cup of water and the raw sugar.

COOKING PROCEDURES

Bring the jujube and walnut in the saucepan to boil, watching all the time. Turn flame to medium low and cook, stirring, for 8 minutes. Serve warm. If made the day before, reheat over low flame, stirring constantly, until it is warmed through.

TIPS

Pitted jujubes (red dates without stones) are now available in Chinese grocery stores, but if neither these nor the ones with stones can be found, pitted regular dates can be substituted for them. In that case, just blend with 1 cup of water for 30 seconds without soaking. Regular white sugar can be substituted for raw if raw is not available.

If desired, this "drink" can also be served cold.

Longan and Loquat Delight

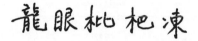

8 SERVINGS

Longan is a fruit somewhat like the lichee. It can be found fresh, in cans, or dried.

Loquats grow on trees and have an orange fuzzy skin, and pits inside. They are found fresh in California. In this dessert, however, the canned form of both fruits is used. It should be made the day before.

INGREDIENTS

1 one-pound four-ounce can *longan*

1 fifteen-ounce can loquats

¼ cup sugar

1½ packages unflavored gelatin

PREPARATION

Drain both cans of fruit and save the juice. Divide the fruits into 8 portions (if the loquats are large, cut each in half). Arrange them in 8 small custard cups. Heat the reserved juice from both cans and dissolve sugar in it. Dissolve gelatin in ½ cup cold water, add to the hot syrup, and mix well. Fill each cup with about ¼ cup of syrup and chill in refrigerator overnight, or until set.

Before serving, place each cup in a flat pan filled with 1 inch of very hot water for a few seconds. Immediately turn onto dessert plates to unmold.

TIPS

Lichees, which like loquats and *longan* are available in Chinese grocery and specialty food stores, can be used in place of *longan*. The flavor and texture of the two fruits differ, but both are tasty and fragrant.

Lotus Seeds in Syrup

4 SERVINGS

The formal Chinese banquet of many years ago consisted of thirty courses. Sweet, light dishes were served at intervals between these courses, serving as a change of taste and a rest between courses of heavier foods. This "dessert" is one of those dishes.

INGREDIENTS

2 cans prepared lotus seeds, drained	2 tablespoons sugar
	1 teaspoon almond extract

COOKING PROCEDURES

Heat the lotus seeds, ½ cup water, and sugar to the boiling point. Turn off the flame and stir in the almond extract. Serve either warm or cold.

TIPS

Every part of the lotus plant has some use in Chinese cooking. The lotus seeds in this dessert have a delicate taste. Lotus petals can be dipped in an egg-and-flour batter and deep fried. The roots can be used in salad (refer to Lotus Root Salad, page 109) or soup or dried and ground for use as a thickening agent. All products can be purchased at Chinese grocery stores or Oriental shops.

Silver Fungus in Syrup

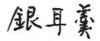

4 SERVINGS

Silver fungus, called "white tree ears" in the Szechuan district, has two uses: tonic and dessert.

In either case, the fungus is cooked slowly with rock candy. Served warm, it becomes a sweet course between the many courses of a Chinese banquet. However, some Chinese take about a quarter-cup daily in place of vitamin pills, believing it to have tonic value.

Don't tell your guests, but this is one dessert that may actually be good for them!

INGREDIENTS

2 fifteen-ounce cans silver fungus   1 teaspoon *kwei-hwa* syrup

COOKING PROCEDURES

Open both cans of prepared silver fungus, drain off 1 cup liquid, and put the fungus and remaining syrup in a saucepan. Add 2 cups cold water. Warm the liquid almost to the boiling point. Turn off the flame and stir in the *kwei-hwa* syrup. If preferred, this can be served cold.

TIPS

The canned silver fungus presently available is too sweet if all the syrup is used. If more than 2 cups of cold water are used, the flavor becomes too diluted.

Kwei-hwa in preserved form can be bought in Chinese grocery stores. A little goes a long way. It can be kept in the refrigerator for many weeks.

Wine-Rice Mandarin Orange "Tea"

酒釀橙子羹

4 SERVINGS

This is another of those so-called teas which the Chinese serve between courses of a banquet. It has to be made with wine rice, a fermented rice that is commerically produced and available in large cities that have a Chinatown.

INGREDIENTS

1 cup wine rice with juice
3 to 4 tablespoons sugar

1 eleven-ounce can mandarin
oranges, undrained

COOKING PROCEDURES

Heat the wine rice, 1 cup warm water, and sugar until the sugar dissolves.

Add the mandarin oranges, juice and all, from the can, and heat until hot but not boiling. Serve hot or chilled.

TIPS

To make wine rice, see page 195.

Eggs, Bean Curd, Noodles, Rice, and Buns: A Multipurpose Selection

The dishes included in this section have a variety of uses. They can be served as first courses or as side dishes with a dinner, or they can be served, alone or combined with each other, as a light lunch or snack.

Some of the foods in this section are regional; others are found all over China. Bean curd, for instance, is a staple, not only for the Chinese, but for most of the Orient and the South Sea Islands. Eggs, too, are popular throughout the area. Both are rich in protein and essential in supplementing the meat-poor diet.

On the other hand, buns, noodles, and dumplings come from northern China, where the climate is unsuitable for growing rice but good for the cultivation of wheat. Since the Chinese do not have ovens, wheat flour is either made into steamed buns or into noodles and dumplings, which can be steamed or boiled.

Few of these are banquet dishes. Most are served as snacks or side dishes.

Egg and Pork Roll

豬肉蛋捲

4 TO 6 SERVINGS

The truth will out: The "egg rolls" available in every Chinese-American restaurant and in the frozen food section of practically every U.S. supermarket are not egg rolls at all. They are spring rolls, traditionally eaten on New Year's Day and again in the spring.

Here is a real egg roll, more like a French-style crêpe or omelet than the crisp-skinned egg rolls so widely known throughout the Western world.

INGREDIENTS

2 ounces cellophane noodles (1 small package)	1 teaspoon cornstarch
½ pound ground fresh pork (1 cup)	4 teaspoons plus 1 tablespoon vegetable oil
1 tablespoon dry sherry	4 eggs, beaten
1 teaspoon sugar	1 tablespoon light soy sauce
1 tablespoon dark soy sauce	¼ cup chicken broth, fresh or canned, or liquid from steaming the egg rolls
1 tablespoon chopped scallion green	

PREPARATION

Soak the cellophane noodles in warm water for 20 minutes. Drain. Cut into 2-inch pieces.

Combine the pork with sherry, ½ teaspoon sugar, dark soy sauce, scallion, and cornstarch.

COOKING PROCEDURES

Heat a medium-sized skillet (about 8 to 10 inches in diameter) over a moderate flame. Add 2 teaspoons oil. After about 1 minute, pour in half the beaten eggs. Swirl the pan to let egg set before turning the pancake over. Remove from the skillet and put on a plate to cool. Repeat with 2 more teaspoons of the oil and the other half of the eggs. Spread half the pork mixture on one egg pancake and roll up. Repeat with the second pancake.

Steam egg and pork rolls in a bowl on the rack of a steamer for 15 minutes. Cool thoroughly and slant-slice into ½-inch pieces. Reserve steaming liquid.

Heat the remaining oil and add the cellophane noodles. Add the light soy sauce and remaining ½ teaspoon sugar and stir, then add ¼ cup chicken broth or ¼ cup liquid from steamed egg rolls. When mixture is boiling, carefully add the sliced egg roll and cook for 1 minute. To serve, lay the egg and pork roll with care over the cellophane noodles.

TIPS

Since the egg roll must be thoroughly cool to slice well, it should be made at least several hours in advance and can even be done the day before if more convenient. The fact that little last-minute work is necessary makes this an easy and tasty company dish. It can be served as a side dish for a main meal or as a luncheon dish, accompanied by a salad. It can even be frozen but must be thawed to room temperature before recooking.

Three-Toned Eggs

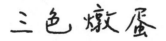

4 TO 6 SERVINGS

This is an excellent hors d'oeuvre or "light course" at a many-course dinner. Both the salted duck eggs and the thousand-year eggs are delicacies, making this a banquet dish. It is somewhat like a custard.

INGREDIENTS
4 fresh eggs

1 salted duck egg

1 thousand-year egg

½ teaspoon salt

PREPARATION
Beat the 4 fresh eggs until white and yolk are thoroughly mixed.

Shell and clean the thousand-year egg, then cut into small pieces. Mix with fresh, beaten eggs.

Break the salted egg, separating the yolk from the white. Add white to fresh egg mixture and beat a bit longer. Cut the yolk into 4 to 6 pieces and mix with the beaten eggs. Add the salt.

COOKING PROCEDURES
Place the mixture in a small, greased fireproof dish and cover with foil. Place on rack of steamer in which water has already been brought to a full boil. Wet steam in covered steamer over a high flame for 30 minutes, remove from steamer and allow to cool completely. Slice into 1 x ½ x ½-inch pieces and serve cold.

TIPS
"Thousand-year eggs" are so named because of their antique appearance, caused by preserving them in lime. Both they and the salted duck eggs can be bought in Chinese grocery stores. They keep in the refrigerator for at least a month.

Home-Style Bean Curd

4 SERVINGS

There is insufficient meat and fish in China to supply enough protein for everyone, so bean curd, made from soybeans, is used throughout the country as a primary source of protein. In fact, bean curd is inexpensive and popular throughout the Orient. Cold, it is used in salad; hot, it can be combined with fish, pork, beef, or veal. Methods of preparation vary regionally. In different areas, bean curd is served stuffed, fried, or stewed.

INGREDIENTS
4 squares fresh bean curd
½ cup vegetable oil
1 teaspoon salt

½ pound lean pork butt (1 cup, in slices 1 x 1 x ¼ inches)

1 tablespoon dry sherry
1 tablespoon dark soy sauce
1 teaspoon sugar
¼ cup dried Chinese mushrooms, soaked and cut into wedges
2 tablespoons dried cloud ears, soaked and cleaned
½ cup bamboo shoots in slices, about 1 x 1 x ¼ inches
1 clove garlic, peeled and crushed
⅛ teaspoon red chili pepper flakes
1 tablespoon *hoisin* sauce
2 scallions, cut into 2-inch lengths

PREPARATION

Cut each bean curd into 1 x 1 x ½-inch slices. Fry the slices in the oil for 3 to 4 minutes. Sprinkle with ½ teaspoon of the salt, then turn over on the other side and sprinkle with the remaining salt. When other side of bean curd is light brown, remove from the pan and set aside. Reserve the oil in the pan.

COOKING PROCEDURES

Put 2 tablespoons of the oil used to fry the bean curd in a wok or skillet. Add the pork slices and stir for about 3 minutes. (The pork must turn grayish white before anything else is added.) Add the sherry and mix. Then add the dark soy sauce and sugar. Mix a few times. Add mushrooms, cloud ears, bamboo shoots, garlic, and red pepper. Mix well. Return fried bean curd to the wok or skillet. Mix and add ½ cup cold water. Bring to a boil. Turn the flame down to medium low, cover, and cook for 2 to 3 minutes. Add *hoisin* sauce. Mix. Turn the flame to high, add scallion. Mix and dish.

TIPS

Veal or beef slices can be substituted for the pork. In that case, reduce the cooking time of meat to 2 minutes.

This dish can be reheated and served the following day.

Szechuan Spicy Bean Curd

乾 燒 荳 腐

6 SERVINGS

Szechuan cooks often, but not always, flavor dishes with chili pepper or the more subtle Szechuan peppercorn. And there are many poor people in the province of Szechuan who mash the fresh red pepper into paste and either blend it into dishes or dip food into it. However popular in this country, in Szechuan hot pepper is seldom used in rich and well-cooked dishes containing meat and seafood.

INGREDIENTS

- ¾ cup chicken broth, fresh or canned
- 1½ tablespoons dark soy sauce
- 1 teaspoon salt
- ½ teaspoon sugar
- 1½ tablespoons cornstarch
- 6 squares fresh Chinese bean curd
- 3 tablespoons vegetable oil
- 1 teaspoon minced garlic (1 or 2 cloves)
- 1 teaspoon minced ginger

- ½ cup chopped scallions, green part and all
- ½ pound ground fresh pork or veal (1 cup)
- 1 tablespoon dry sherry
- 1 tablespoon hot pepper oil
- ⅛ tablespoon crushed red pepper
- 1 tablespoon Oriental sesame seed oil
- ⅛ teaspoon five spices powder

PREPARATION

Combine broth in a bowl with ½ tablespoon of the soy sauce, the salt, sugar, and cornstarch.

Cut the bean curd into small dice, about ½ inch in size.

COOKING PROCEDURES

Heat the vegetable oil in wok or skillet for a few seconds. Then add garlic, ginger, and scallion and stir a few times. Add the ground pork and stir fry for about 2 minutes, then add the dry sherry, remaining soy sauce, hot pepper oil, and crushed red pepper. Stir, then add the bean curd and stir a few more times, gently. Add the broth mixture and bring to a boil. When it thickens, turn off the flame. Sprinkle the sesame seed oil on top, then sprinkle evenly with five spices powder. Turn into a casserole and keep warm until ready to serve.

TIPS

Five spices powder, Oriental sesame seed oil, and hot pepper oil can all be purchased in Chinese and Oriental grocery stores and sometimes in the gourmet sections of department stores. Red Devil Sauce, purchased in supermarkets, may be substituted for hot pepper oil in the same quantity.

Fresh bean curd is purchased in Chinese, Japanese, and Korean grocery stores. It may be stored for a few days in a plastic or metal container if it is submerged in cold water with a little salt sprinkled over the top. Be sure to keep it in the refrigerator.

Thinly Pressed Bean Curd Shreds with Pork Shreds

4 SERVINGS

Here is bean curd again, this time in dried form and combined with pork. This is considered a bean curd dish rather than a pork dish because the pork is not used in large quantities; it is added for flavoring.

INGREDIENTS

½ pound fresh pork
5 sheets thinly pressed bean curd (*pai-yeh*)
1 teaspoon baking soda
3 tablespoons vegetable oil
1 tablespoon dry sherry
2 tablespoons dark soy sauce
1 teaspoon salt

½ teaspoon sugar
¼ cup dried Chinese mushrooms, soaked and shredded
½ cup bamboo shoots, shredded
½ cup chicken broth, fresh or canned
1 scallion, green part and all, cut into 2-inch lengths

PREPARATION

Cut the pork, half frozen or half thawed, into matchstick-sized shreds.

Cut bean curd (*pai-yeh*) into 2 x 1¼-inch shreds, then soak in very hot water, to which the baking soda has been added, for 20 minutes. Rinse thoroughly until water is clear. Drain.

COOKING PROCEDURES

Heat the oil in a wok or skillet and add the pork. Stir fry for 3 minutes, or until all pork shreds turn grayish and no pink shows. Add the sherry, soy sauce, salt, and sugar. Mix well. Add mushrooms and bamboo shoot shreds. Mix. Add bean curd shreds and mix well with chopsticks. Add broth and bring to boil. Cover; turn flame to medium low and cook for 5 minutes. Add scallion. Mix and dish.

TIPS

Thinly pressed bean curd sheets, called *pai-yeh*, are available at Chinese specialty stores. Do not confuse them with *r-cho*, or dried "second layer" bean curd. *Pai-yeh* are prepared in oil and therefore must be soaked in baking soda and rinsed well before using.

Roast Pork Lo Mein

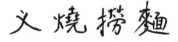

4 SERVINGS

Lo mein is a very popular noodle dish in the United States. It originated in Canton. Mein means "noodles" and lo *literally means "mixing." Less oil is needed than for the deep-fried noodles favored in other parts of China.*

INGREDIENTS

½ ten-ounce package frozen French-style string beans

¼ cup dried Chinese mushrooms

2 cups fresh bean sprouts

6 ounces Chinese roast pork (1 cup in shreds)

½ pound fresh *lo mein* noodles

5 tablespoons vegetable oil

1 teaspoon salt	1 teaspoon sugar
1½ tablespoons dark soy sauce	

PREPARATION
Thaw string beans and drain.

Soak Chinese mushrooms in ½ cup warm water for 20 minutes, drain, remove the stems and shred.

Float bean sprouts in water and skim off the green shells. Drain.

Boil 2 quarts of water in a 3-quart saucepan and add noodles. Bring to boil again and boil for 4 to 5 minutes, then rinse immediately in cold water until thoroughly chilled. Drain. Mix noodles with 1 tablespoon oil.

COOKING PROCEDURES
Heat 1 tablespoon oil and stir fry the mushroom shreds for a minute. Add the string beans and salt. Mix. Add bean sprouts and roast pork shreds. Mix again a few times, dish.

Heat the remaining oil and stir fry the noodles, breaking with spatula or spoon into 2-inch-long pieces. Add soy sauce and sugar and stir.

Return the cooked roast pork mixture and mix with the noodles for a minute. Dish into a casserole and cover. (Can be kept warm in the oven at 140 degrees for an hour.)

TIPS
Roast beef, roast lamb, or cooked chicken can also be used in this *lo mein* dish. The important part is that the meat added to the *lo mein* be precooked and cut or torn into shreds and added at the last minute.

Lo mein (noodles) may be bought fresh or dried in Oriental markets. If using dried *lo mein*, use only half the quantity required, as it will expand when cooked. The finest spaghettini can be substituted if absolutely necessary; use only half the specified quantity and follow cooking directions stipulated on box.

Roast Pork Lo Mein can be frozen. Thaw until it reaches room temperature, then preheat the oven to 250° and heat for 30 minutes.

Peking Noodles with Meat Sauce

炸 醬 麵

4 TO 6 SERVINGS

Not all Chinese live on rice.

The staple starch of northern China is wheat flour, often made into noodles. This dish, a great favorite of Americans, can only be found in restaurants specializing in the northern Chinese cuisine. Contrasting textures topped by a pleasantly spiced sauce make this an exceptionally good way to serve noodles.

INGREDIENTS

1 pound fresh *lo mein* noodles
2 tablespoons Oriental sesame seed oil
2 cucumbers
2 cups fresh bean sprouts
Sauce:
1 cup chicken broth, fresh or canned
1 teaspoon cornstarch
2 tablespoons vegetable oil

1 tablespoon minced garlic
¾ pound ground fresh pork (1½ cups)
2 tablespoons dry sherry
½ cup chopped scallion, both white and green
1 tablespoon sugar
½ cup bean sauce, canned may be used

PREPARATION

Bring 3 quarts of water to a boil in a saucepan and add the noodles. Boil for 4 minutes. Drain and mix with the sesame seed oil. Keep warm.

Peel cucumbers and cut in half lengthwise. Remove seeds. Cut into shreds, to make 2 cups.

Pour boiling water over bean sprouts. Let stand for 2 minutes. Rinse under cold water until cold, then drain.

Dissolve cornstarch in chicken broth.

To Make Sauce:

Heat the oil in a wok or frying pan and add the garlic. Mix a few times. Add pork and stir fry for about 3 minutes. Add sherry and mix.

Add scallions and mix again. Add sugar and bean sauce. Stir the chicken broth (in which cornstarch has been dissolved) and add to sauce. Bring to a boil, stirring, and when the sauce is smooth and thick, pour it into a bowl.

To serve, place noodles, cucumber shreds, bean sprouts, and sauce in separate bowls on table. Each person fills his bowl half full of noodles and adds 2 tablespoons each of cucumbers, bean sprouts, and sauce, mixing well before eating.

TIPS

This can be served for lunch, as a snack, or as part of a larger meal. If preferred, 1 teaspoon of hot bean sauce with chili may be added to noodles while mixing with sauce.

For easier handling, break noodles into 2- to 3-inch lengths before cooking.

Stir-Fry "Sha-Wo-Fun"

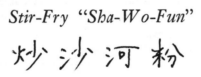

6 SERVINGS

Sha-Wo is a suburb of Canton where sha-wo-fun was originated. It is difficult to describe, besides knowing that it is made from rice flour. In taste and appearance it is similar to broad noodles.

INGREDIENTS

1 pound fresh *sha-wo-fun* (1 big round sheet)

4 to 6 fresh or canned water chestnuts

1 pound flank steak in slices 1 x ½ inches (2 cups)

1 tablespoon cornstarch

¼ cup oyster sauce

1 pound Chinese broccoli (*kai lan*)

6 tablespoons vegetable oil

½ teaspoon salt

½ teaspoon sugar

½ cup chicken broth, fresh or canned

¼ cup bamboo shoots, sliced

¼ cup Chinese roast pork slices

½ cup bean sprouts

243

PREPARATION

Cut the *sha-wo-fun* into 2 x ½-inch strips.

Cut off both ends of each fresh water chestnut, then peel and slice each into 3 to 4 pieces. (If canned are used, just drain and slice.)

Mix flank steak with the cornstarch and 3 tablespoons of the oyster sauce.

Peel the Chinese broccoli and cut into 1-inch pieces.

COOKING PROCEDURES

In a wok or skillet, heat 3 tablespoons of the oil and stir fry the Chinese broccoli. Add the salt and sugar, then ¼ cup of the chicken broth, and cook for 3 minutes. Add the water chestnuts, bamboo shoots, roast pork, and bean sprouts. Mix well; dish.

Heat the remaining 3 tablespoons of the oil and stir fry the flank steak for about 3 minutes. Return all vegetables to the wok and mix well. Spread the *sha-wo-fun* over the vegetables and steak. Mix the remaining tablespoon oyster sauce with the remaining chicken broth and sprinkle this mixture over all. Cover and cook over a low flame for about 2 minutes. Mix and dish.

TIPS

Sha-wo-fun is available only in the Chinatowns of large cities. It is typically Cantonese, made in the factories where bean curd is produced.

Fresh water chestnuts are both hard to get and expensive, but after peeling can be stored in the freezer for weeks. If unavailable, substitute canned water chestnuts.

Fresh bean sprouts, on the other hand, are not only easy to get, but can also be grown from mung beans in your kitchen. (For directions, see *The Pleasures of Chinese Cooking*, page 45.)

Bacon Fried Rice

培根 炒飯

4 SERVINGS

Fried rice, so popular with Americans, is not considered a special treat by the Chinese.

Since rice is relatively inexpensive, and too important a part of the diet to risk running short, most Chinese families cook more rice than they can consume in one meal. Fried rice, made with cold cooked rice, is an economical way of using up leftover rice and serves well for lunch and unexpected company.

INGREDIENTS

½ pound raw bacon
2 eggs
3 tablespoons vegetable oil
3 cups cold cooked rice

1½ tablespoons dark soy sauce
¼ cup scallion green, in ¼-inch pieces

PREPARATION

Cut bacon into ½-inch pieces. Fry in wok or frying pan until crisp. As bacon cooks, drain off oil. Drain bacon pieces on paper towels.

Beat eggs until yolks and whites are thoroughly mixed. Heat 1 tablespoon oil in small wok or skillet and pour in the beaten eggs. When slightly firm, remove from pan.

COOKING PROCEDURES

Heat the remaining oil in a wok or skillet. Add the 3 cups cooked rice and toss with the cooking spoon or spatula for about 2 minutes, until oil and rice are well mixed. Add the soy sauce and mix thoroughly.

Add the scallion, eggs, and bacon bits, breaking eggs up with spatula. Mix well. Dish.

TIPS

It is important that the rice be cold. It is best to cook rice the day before and leave in the refrigerator overnight.

Fried rice can be left in the oven at 140 degrees for 30 minutes. Be sure to cover the casserole. In this case use 2 tablespoons scallion while cooking and mix in another 2 tablespoons just before serving. The green of the uncooked scallion lends eye appeal to the dish.

This dish can be made in advance and frozen for several weeks. Thaw to room temperature, then warm in a 250-degree oven for 20 minutes.

Shrimp Fried Rice

蝦仁炒飯

8 SERVINGS

This delicious dish does not exactly taste like the fried rice served in the average Chinese restaurant; it is an elegant version that makes an excellent company dish.

INGREDIENTS

½ pound raw shrimp (1 cup)
5 tablespoons vegetable oil
½ teaspoon salt
3 eggs, beaten until yolk and white are mixed

6 cups cold cooked rice
3 tablespoons dark soy sauce
¼ cup chopped scallion, green part only

PREPARATION

Shell and devein the shrimp. Cut into small cubes. Stir fry in 1 tablespoon of the oil for about 2 minutes. Add the salt. Mix a few times and set aside. Heat 1 tablespoon oil in wok or skillet. Pour in eggs and cook for a minute. Dish.

COOKING PROCEDURES

Heat the remaining vegetable oil in a wok or skillet. Add rice and mix well. Add soy sauce and mix until color is even. Add shrimps, eggs, and scallion. Mix and break the eggs into smaller pieces and serve.

TIPS

This dish can be cooked just before serving, as all the preparation can be done beforehand and the last-minute cooking time is very short. Or it can be all prepared, put in a covered casserole, and kept warm in a 140-degree oven for as long as 30 minutes.

This can also be made in advance and frozen.

Chinese Pork Sausage and Mushroom Rice

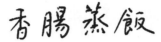

6 SERVINGS

Although plain rice is usually served with every meal in China, there are many ways rice can be dressed up for parties or simply for the sake of variety. The best pork sausages are made in Canton Province; so it is not surprising that this combination of rice with pork sausage is Cantonese.

INGREDIENTS

4 links Chinese sausage (about ⅓ pound)

4 large dried Chinese mushrooms

2 cups raw long-grain rice

¼ cup light soy sauce

½ teaspoon sugar

PREPARATION

Cut each sausage into 1-inch-long pieces.

Soak the mushrooms in hot water for 10 minutes, then drain, remove the stems, and cut each mushroom into 4 to 6 wedges.

COOKING PROCEDURES

Place the rice in a flameproof casserole and add 3¼ cups of cold water. Bring to a rolling boil on top of the range and let boil, without covering, for 3 minutes. While still boiling, add the soy sauce and sugar. Mix well. Boil another 2 to 3 minutes, place the sausage and mushrooms on top of the rice, cover, and cook over low flame for 15 minutes. Turn off flame and allow to relax for 20 minutes. Serve in casserole.

TIPS

Whenever sausage rice is served, omit plain rice. The sausages, available in Chinese grocery stores, can be kept in the refrigerator for several weeks or in the freezer for several months.

Chinese Steamed Buns

MAKES 20 BUNS

Americans, noting the absence of bread on the table at Chinese restaurants, assume that the Chinese do not eat bread at all. This is not true; one-third of the Chinese people, those who live in northern China, depend on wheat flour instead of rice for their staple food. Wheat is used to make noodles and bread, but the bread is in the form of steamed buns, as there are no ovens to bake the bread.

Chinese buns can be eaten, warm, as part of a meal, accompanying either meat or vegetable dishes. Cold buns can be sliced and toasted and eaten with either butter or jelly. In China butter is very scarce, so buns eaten for breakfast are dipped in sugar.

The following is a basic recipe for bun dough. It is quite similar to American white bread in composition. The difference comes in the manner in which it is cooked.

INGREDIENTS

2 packages active dry yeast   3 cups sifted all-purpose flour
1 tablespoon sugar

PREPARATION

Dissolve yeast and sugar in ½ cup lukewarm water in large mixing bowl. Allow the mixture to sit in a warm place for approximately 5 to 8 minutes, or until lots of bubbles have appeared in the mixture and it is of a homogenous consistency.

Add ¾ cup warm water to the mixture. Stir in the flour very gradually. Mix well. Turn onto lightly floured board and knead until smooth and elastic, about 8 to 10 minutes. Place dough in well-greased bowl, turning it over to grease the top. Cover the dough with a damp cloth and allow to rise in warm place until doubled in bulk, about 30 minutes.

When dough has doubled, punch it down with your fist and turn it onto a lightly floured board again. Knead for 5 more minutes, then place back in the greased bowl. Turn it over to grease the top, cover with a damp cloth, and allow it to rise again until doubled in bulk, about 20 minutes.

Turn half the dough onto floured board. Shape it into a long, sausagelike cylinder, about 2 feet long and 2½ inches in diameter. Cut the cylinder into 10 pieces. Cover the pieces with a damp cloth and allow to rise about 10 minutes. Repeat the procedure with remaining half of dough.

COOKING PROCEDURES
Bring water to boil in the bottom part of a large Chinese steamer, 10 to 10½ inches in diameter. Grease the floor of the top section with vegetable oil. (This section may be either metal or bamboo, but it must have holes in the bottom.) Put the pieces of dough in, ½ inch apart, with rounded part facing up and cut edges facing each other. Place the rack over rapidly boiling water, cover, and steam for 15 minutes.

Remove buns, one by one, from steamer rack while water is still boiling below, or they will fall, like a soufflé. Place them on a plate to cool. Serve at once or keep for later use.

TIPS
Steamed bread can be frozen and resteamed before using. Defrost completely at room temperature, then resteam for 5 minutes just before using.

Buns with Roast Pork Filling

MAKES 20 BUNS

Buns are made and served all over China, but each region varies its filling to suit its taste. These buns can be served as snacks, lunch, or appetizers.

INGREDIENTS

1 tablespoon vegetable oil

1 pound Chinese roast pork, cut into small dice to make 2 cups

½ teaspoon sugar

1 tablespoon *hoisin* sauce

¼ cup chopped scallion green

2 tablespoons cornstarch, dissolved in 2 tablespoons water

Basic recipe for bun dough (page 248)

PREPARATION

Heat the oil in a wok or skillet. Add the pork and stir fry over high flame for only 30 seconds (it is already cooked). Mix a few times, then add the sugar, *hoisin* sauce, and scallion. Mix again. Add the predissolved cornstarch (stirred again to make sure the water and cornstarch are completely mixed), mix thoroughly and remove from the wok. Cool to room temperature before using to fill the buns.

Use half the bun dough, previously prepared, at a time. Make a long, sausagelike roll about 1½ inches in diameter. Cut into 8 to 10 pieces. With a small rolling pin, roll each piece into a 3-inch circle about 1/6 inch thick, thinner at the edges than in the center. Put 1 tablespoon of the meat mixture into the center of the circle. Pick up the edges all around and gather them together, then twist the edges together at the top so that the filling will not escape during the steaming. Make 10 buns, then repeat with the second half of dough. Cover all the buns with a dry kitchen towel and let them stand in a warm place until they double in size, about 15 minutes.

COOKING PROCEDURES

Steam the buns according to directions given in Chinese Steamed Buns (page 248). Be sure to remove while water is still boiling.

TIPS

Do *not* try to make buns just before you need them, but make them in advance, when you have some free time, and warm them just before using.

Buns can be kept in refrigerator overnight and resteamed just before use. Or they can be frozen and thawed to room temperature and then steamed again until they are hot (5 to 10 minutes).

Chinese roast pork can be made according to the recipe given in *The Pleasures of Chinese Cooking* (page 131), or it can be bought in Chinese specialty stores. It is sometimes available frozen in American supermarkets. Do not substitute American roast pork, as the taste is altogether different.

Madame Chu's Plum Sauce (Duck Sauce)

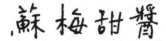

4 TWELVE-OUNCE BOTTLES

The name "duck sauce" was created in the United States, because this sauce was originally served with deep-fried pressed duck, which had no sauce of its own. Duck sauce became popular as a dip for any food, from spareribs and egg rolls to almost anything else imaginable. There are so many versions of duck sauce that it is hard to decide which kind to make. However, I have created and tested the following, which, I feel, produces the best taste.

INGREDIENTS

1 cup Chinese plum sauce
1 cup apricot preserves
1 cup peach preserves
1 cup applesauce

2 teaspoons dry mustard
½ teaspoon garlic powder
½ cup chili sauce

PREPARATION

Pick out from the canned or bottled plum sauce any solid pieces, such as ginger, pimiento, or other spices. Discard these.

Combine all the ingredients in a large mixing bowl and mix thoroughly with chopsticks or fork.

Store in jars and leave in the refrigerator. The duck sauce will keep for months.

TIPS

Chinese plum sauce can be bought in Chinese grocery stores. Some supermarkets and specialty stores also stock it.

Chinese Mustard Dip

Besides duck sauce, the other popular dip served in the Chinese restaurants is mustard sauce. Again, like duck sauce, there are ever so many versions of mustard sauce. The simplest and tastiest one is as follows:

INGREDIENTS

¼ cup dry mustard, preferably Colman's brand

3 ½ tablespoons cold water

PREPARATION

Mix the dry mustard and water into a smooth paste and let stand for 10 to 15 minutes before serving.

TIPS

Unlike duck sauce, the homemade mustard sauce does not keep. It will change color and develop a thin film on top if left overnight, even in the refrigerator. Make just enough for each use when needed.

Recipes Contributed by My Students

One of the greatest satisfactions that I get from having taught Chinese cooking for the last twenty-five years is inspiring others to teach Chinese cooking. Of course, both training and practice are necessary for a teacher to qualify. "You do not have to be Chinese" (to paraphrase a popular rye bread commercial), but to meet my standards, students must possess four qualifications:

1. They must love cooking in general.
2. They must have taken several Chinese cooking courses, with competent instructors.
3. They must be enthusiastic about spreading the gospel of Chinese food to their students.
4. They must be able teachers.

Students of mine have taught and are teaching at present in at least four states in this country. Their courses are conducted in private homes, in churches, in adult education schools, and even aboard ship. Some have even made it a career. Wherever they teach they are received enthusiastically, and their classes have continued to grow and flourish.

I have always encouraged these students to build their funds of recipes, first by studying with me and with others, and then by creating or improving recipes according to their own knowledge and taste. The following are recipes invented, adapted, or improved by my students.

Ruth Barkan's Chicken Good

INGREDIENTS

2 whole chicken breasts
1 tablespoon dry sherry
1 tablespoon dark soy sauce
1 tablespoon cornstarch
1 eight-and-one-half-ounce can water chestnuts
¼ cup vegetable oil
¾ pound celery cabbage, cut into ½-inch sections

2 tablespoons scallions cut into 1-inch pieces
2 tablespoons *hoisin* sauce
⅛ to ¼ teaspoon hot pepper flakes

PREPARATION

Skin and bone the chicken breasts. Cut into 1-inch cubes and marinate in the sherry, soy sauce, and cornstarch for 10 minutes.

Drain and slice the water chestnuts.

COOKING PROCEDURES

Heat 1 tablespoon of the oil in a wok or skillet. Stir fry the celery cabbage until just wilted, then remove from the wok to a serving platter and keep warm. Heat the remaining 3 tablespoons oil in the wok. Add chicken and stir fry until the pink color disappears, then add water chestnuts and scallions and mix well. Add the *hoisin* sauce and pepper flakes and stir fry until heated through. Put the chicken mixture on top of the celery cabbage and serve.

RUTH BARKAN teaches Chinese cooking at the Edison Adult School in Edison, New Jersey. She conducted a series of four demonstrations at the J. F. Kennedy Hospital, and also demonstrated aboard the Queen Elizabeth II *on Caribbean cruises in 1973 and 1974.*

Janet Bernstein's Shredded Chicken with Vegetables

INGREDIENTS

2 whole chicken breasts
1 egg white, unbeaten
2 teaspoons salt
¼ teaspoon monosodium glutamate
½ teaspoon sugar
2 tablespoons dry sherry

¼ cup vegetable oil
¼ cup carrots, thinly shredded
1 tablespoon ginger, thinly shredded
¼ cup green pepper slices, thinly shredded
¼ cup celery, thinly shredded

PREPARATION

Skin and bone the chicken breasts, then slice the meat, half frozen or half thawed, very thin. Cut into fine shreds, to make 2 cups. Combine chicken shreds with unbeaten egg white, salt, monosodium glutamate, sugar, and sherry.

COOKING PROCEDURES

Heat 1 tablespoon oil in skillet or wok. Add carrot, ginger, green pepper, and celery. Stir fry for 1 minute, then remove from the wok and set aside.

Heat the remaining oil in same wok. Add chicken and cook, stirring constantly, until the chicken turns white, about 2 minutes. Return the vegetables to the wok, stir well, and dish.

JANET BERNSTEIN teaches both basic and advanced classes in the Abby Gail Kirsch Gourmet Center in Chappaqua, New York.

Susan de Jong's Butterfly Shrimp with Sweet and Pungent Dip

INGREDIENTS

1 pound raw jumbo shrimp
½ cup all-purpose flour
½ cup water
½ teaspoon salt
2 teaspoons baking powder
2 tablespoons plus 2 teaspoons cornstarch
Dash of pepper
2 cups vegetable oil for deep frying
1 tablespoon soy sauce

¼ cup wine vinegar
3 tablespoons catsup
1 cup chicken broth, fresh or canned
¼ cup sugar
Lichees
Pineapple chunks
Glazed cherries
Chinese pickles
Mandarin oranges

PREPARATION

Shell shrimp except for tail section. Split down the back, three-quarters of the way through, leaving tails on. Place between pieces of waxed paper or foil and press until quite flat. Place in freezer until almost frozen.

Make a batter by combining the flour, water, salt, baking powder, the 2 teaspoons cornstarch, and a dash of pepper.

Dissolve the remaining cornstarch in 2 tablespoons cold water·

COOKING PROCEDURES

Heat the 2 cups oil to boiling (about 375 degrees). Dip each shrimp individually in batter, and then, keeping hold of it by the tail, immerse it in the deep, hot oil. When it starts to cook, let go. Fry until brown. Repeat until all shrimp are cooked, and keep warm.

Make a sauce by combining the soy sauce, vinegar, catsup, chicken broth, and sugar in a saucepan. Heat to boiling, then slowly stir in the predissolved cornstarch (stirred again to make sure the water and cornstarch are thoroughly combined). When sauce thickens, add the fruit.

Place the shrimp around the edge of large platter and heap thick sauce in the middle. Serves 3 for a whole meal, 6 or 7 as part of a dinner.

SUSAN DE JONG is a part-owner of The Gourmet Chopstick School of International Cooking. She gives Chinese and international cooking lessons there, caters, and gives demonstrations. She has taught at the Fort Lee, Northern Valley, and Riverdell adult schools in New Jersey, and gives private instruction in basic and advanced Chinese cooking in her home. In addition, she has demonstrated Chinese cooking at B. Altman's in New Jersey and aboard the Queen Elizabeth II, *and has given international cooking demonstrations in Tuxedo Park, New York.*

Grace Bloom's Jellied Steamed Fish

INGREDIENTS

1 teaspoon vegetable oil
1 pound fillets of red snapper, bass, or sole
¼ cup dry sherry
1 teaspoon salt (omit if canned broth is used)
4 water chestnuts, cut in matchstick shreds
4 snow peas, cut in similar shreds
2 medium-size dried Chinese mushrooms, soaked, drained, and cut in shreds
1 to 2 slices fresh ginger, cut in shreds

2 to 3 fresh mushrooms, cut in shreds
1 scallion, shredded lengthwise into pieces about 2 inches in length
1 envelope unflavored gelatin
¼ cup cold water
½ cup chicken broth, fresh or canned
Chinese parsley and lemon slices for garnish

PREPARATION

Spread oil evenly over the bottom and sides of heatproof dish. Place fish in container and sprinkle with the sherry, salt, water chestnuts, snow peas, Chinese mushrooms, ginger, fresh mushrooms, and scallions.

COOKING PROCEDURES

Bring water in bottom of steamer to a full boil. Place heatproof container on rack of steamer. Steam over high heat for 6 to 7 minutes, checking after 4 minutes. Cool.

257

Soften gelatin in ¼ cup cold water. Cook over low flame for 3 minutes, or until gelatin is dissolved. Combine chicken broth with gelatin mixture; add broth from fish until liquid totals 1½ cups. Simmer a few minutes. Remove from flame. Cool slightly. Add to the fish. Chill in refrigerator until jellied, 1½ to 2 hours. Decorate with Chinese parsley and lemon slices and serve.

GRACE BLOOM has taught Chinese cooking in New York City.

Eileen Marshal Fitch's Ground Beef and Walnuts

INGREDIENTS

½ pound ground steak	2 tablespoons vegetable oil
1 tablespoon dry sherry	2 ounces snow peas
1½ tablespoons dark soy sauce	½ cup bamboo shoots, shredded
2 teaspoons cornstarch	¼ cup chopped walnuts
⅓ cup chicken broth	

PREPARATION

Mix ground steak with sherry, soy sauce, and 1 teaspoon of the cornstarch.

Dissolve the remaining cornstarch in the chicken broth.

COOKING PROCEDURES

Heat 1 tablespoon oil in skillet or wok. Add snow peas, bamboo shoots, and walnuts and stir fry for 3 minutes, then remove from the wok and set aside.

Add the remaining oil to the skillet. Stir fry the steak until no red color remains, then return the vegetable mixture to the pan and mix well. Add the predissolved cornstarch (stirred again to make sure the broth and cornstarch are thoroughly mixed), and stir continuously until the mixture thickens. Serve immediately.

EILEEN MARSHAL FITCH teaches several courses in Chinese cooking in the Adult Education division at Ardsley High School in Ardsley, New York.

Bettijane Eisenpreis's Pork with Mandarin Oranges

"This dish came to be because my husband does not like canned pine-apple, an ingredient in most sweet-sour pork dishes. In searching for a substitute, I came upon mandarin oranges in my supermarket, and began experimenting with a sweet-sour pork containing them. How authentically Chinese it is I don't know, but it tastes good!"

INGREDIENTS

2 pounds lean pork, cut into
   1-inch cubes
2 cups water
1 teaspoon salt
¼ cup soy sauce
1 clove garlic

⅓ cup sugar
2 tablespoons cornstarch
¼ cup cider vinegar
1½ cups canned mandarin
   oranges, drained but juice
   reserved

COOKING PROCEDURES

Place pork, water, salt, soy sauce, and garlic in a saucepan and bring to a boil. Reduce heat and simmer 50 minutes. Discard garlic. Drain cubes, reserving broth.

In a saucepan, blend sugar, cornstarch, vinegar, and ½ cup of the reserved orange juice until smooth. Blend in the reserved meat broth and cook, stirring, until the sauce is thick, dark, and smooth. Add pork and oranges and stir again, then serve hot.

TIPS

This dish can be made the day before and reheated. It can even be frozen, thawed, and reheated in a 300-degree oven for 30 minutes. However, in both cases, do not add the oranges until immediately before serving.

Pork butt, loin, or meat from chops can be used. If you make the cubes from pork chops, reserve bones for use in meat stock for another dish.

BETTIJANE EISENPREIS teaches basic classes in Chinese cooking in New York City and was co-author with me of an article in Woman's

Day, *October 1972, entitled "Exceptionally Easy, Outstandingly Good —Chinese Party Buffets." Mrs. Eisenpreis has traveled to Pennsylvania with me to act as assistant in a series of Chinese cooking demonstrations.*

Bebe Isaacs' Banquet-Style Steak

INGREDIENTS

1 pound fillet mignon	1 fifteen-ounce can baby corn
3 tablespoons cornstarch	4 tablespoons peanut oil
2½ tablespoons soy sauce	4 slices fresh ginger
1 tablespoon dry sherry	3 tablespoons oyster sauce
½ teaspoon sugar	

PREPARATION

Cut the fillet mignon into bite-sized cubes. Combine the cubes with the cornstarch, soy sauce, sherry, and sugar and mix well.

Drain baby corn, discarding the juice. Rinse with cold water and drain.

COOKING PROCEDURES

Heat 1 tablespoon of the oil in a wok or skillet. Stir fry the corn for 1 minute, then remove from the wok and set aside.

Heat the remaining oil and add ginger. Add beef and stir fry over a high flame until meat has turned color. Return corn to pan and stir, then immediately add the oyster sauce. Mix well. Serve hot.

TIPS

Be sure not to overcook the baby corn, as it is already cooked.

BEBE ISAACS teaches Chinese Cooking in Chappaqua, New York.

Karen Lee's Beef with Black Bean Sauce, Tomatoes, and Onions

INGREDIENTS

1 pound flank or shoulder steak	2 cloves garlic
4 tablespoons dry sherry	2 slices fresh ginger
2 teaspoons light soy sauce	1 medium-sized yellow onion
1 teaspoon sugar	1 scallion
2 teaspoons cornstarch	½ pound very ripe tomatoes
½ egg white (lightly beat 1 egg white and divide in half)	(1 cup)
2 tablespoons fermented black beans	1 tablespoon dark soy sauce
	3 tablespoons vegetable oil

PREPARATION

Slice beef against the grain about ⅜-inch thick. Combine the slices with 1 tablespoon sherry, light soy sauce, sugar, 1 teaspoon cornstarch, and the egg white and refrigerate at least 30 minutes.

Mince together the black beans, garlic, and ginger.

Slice the onion, to make ¾ cup.

Shred the scallion, to make ¼ cup.

Dice the tomatoes, to make 1 cup.

Combine the dark soy sauce with the remaining sherry and cornstarch.

COOKING PROCEDURES

Place a wok or skillet over a high flame and add 2 tablespoons oil. When oil is hot, add the black beans, ginger, and garlic. Stir fry a few seconds, then add the beef mixture and stir fry over high heat until the beef has browned well, about 2 to 3 minutes. Remove from the wok and set aside.

Wash the wok out and return to high heat. Stir fry the onions and scallions in 1 tablespoon of the oil for 1 or 2 minutes. Add tomatoes and stir fry another minute.

Add the cornstarch mixture (stirred again to make sure the soy sauce, sherry, and cornstarch are thoroughly mixed) and stir fry over high heat until slightly thickened. Add beef mixture and stir to blend the flavors. Serve immediately.

KAREN LEE, who taught Chinese cuisine at St. Bartholomew's Church in New York for several years, is currently running Karen Lee's Chinese Cooking Classes in New York City. These include advanced and elementary instruction, as well as special classes in low-cholesterol Chinese cooking. She caters at private parties and conducts classes in Chinese cooking at private homes as well.

Judy Nelson's Szechuan Shrimp

INGREDIENTS

1 pound medium-sized raw shrimp
1½ tablespoons cornstarch
1 egg white, lightly beaten
¼ cup bamboo shoots, finely diced
½ cup scallions, finely sliced
1 cherry pepper, minced
1 tablespoon garlic, finely minced
1 teaspoon ginger, finely minced

½ cup chicken broth, fresh or canned
5 tablespoons catsup
½ teaspoon dark soy sauce
2 tablespoons rice wine
½ teaspoon Oriental sesame seed oil
½ cup vegetable oil
Salt to taste

PREPARATION

Shell and devein the shrimp, then rinse and dry. Combine the cornstarch and egg white, then add the shrimp. Stir to coat well and let stand.

Combine the bamboo shoots, scallions, cherry pepper, garlic, and ginger.

Combine chicken broth, catsup, soy sauce, rice wine, and sesame seed oil.

COOKING PROCEDURES

Heat the vegetable oil in a wok or skillet over a medium-high flame, not too high. Stir fry the shrimp for about 1 minute (do not wait for browning), and pour into a sieve standing in a bowl. Set the shrimp aside. Measure out 2 tablespoons of the oil in the bowl.

Wash the wok, then heat the 2 tablespoons oil. Add the shrimp, then add the bamboo shoot mixture. Cook quickly, stirring constantly. Add the catsup mixture and cook quickly until the shrimp are coated with sauce and are hot through. Taste and add salt if necessary. Serve immediately.

TIPS

Cherry peppers come in a jar and are sold in delicatessens and fine food stores. Be sure to get the hot pickled variety, not the sweet ones.

Dry sherry can be substituted for rice wine.

JUDY NELSON teaches at the East/West Cooking School, giving private lessons in basic and advanced Chinese cooking. She also instructs a basic class in Chinese cooking at the Ridgewood Adult School and at the Tenafly Adult School, both in New Jersey. She demonstrated Chinese cooking aboard the Queen Elizabeth II.

Edward Nowitzki's Steamed Crabmeat with Rice

INGREDIENTS

½ pound container frozen crabmeat	1 teaspoon salt, only if fresh broth is used
1 tablespoon dry sherry	2 cups chicken broth, fresh or canned
2 scallions, green part and all	
2 tablespoons minced Smithfield ham	8 canned straw mushrooms
	1 cup raw long-grain rice
4 eggs	1½ cups cold water

PREPARATION

Defrost crabmeat and break into small pieces. Mix with sherry.

Slice scallions into ¼-inch pieces.

Mince the ham to make 2 tablespoons.

Beat the eggs well. Add the salt (if necessary), scallions, chicken broth, crabmeat, and straw mushrooms. Mix well. Pour the mixture into a two-quart ovenproof bowl.

COOKING PROCEDURES
Bring rice to a boil in 1½ cups cold water. Lower flame, cover, and cook for 20 minutes. Remove from flame and let stand, still covered, an additional 20 minutes to rest.

Bring water in the bottom of a steamer to a full boil. Place bowl containing egg and crabmeat mixture on the steamer rack and steam over a high flame for 20 minutes.

Place cooked rice in a bowl. Place steamed crabmeat on top. Garnish with minced ham and serve.

TIPS
2 tablespoons chopped chives can be substituted for the scallions.

EDWARD NOWITZKI taught Chinese cooking courses at the River-side Church in New York City for many years, and in 1973 and 1974 he demonstrated aboard the Queen Elizabeth II *during a Caribbean cruise. Mr. Nowitzki also runs a catering service, specializing in Chinese food.*

Jerilyn M. Okin's Beef with Broccoli

INGREDIENTS

1 tablespoon fermented black beans	1 teaspoon minced garlic
1 pound flank steak	Marinade:
1 head broccoli	1 tablespoon cornstarch
3 tablespoons vegetable oil	1 tablespoon dry sherry
2 slices fresh ginger	½ teaspoon sugar
¼ teaspoon salt	4 tablespoons oyster sauce

PREPARATION
Soak black beans in hot water for 10 minutes, drain and mash.

Slice meat, half frozen or half thawed, into very thin slices, then marinate in cornstarch, sherry, sugar, and oyster sauce for at least 10 minutes.

Use both broccoli florets and stems, peeling the stems and then cutting diagonally into long, thin pieces.

COOKING PROCEDURES

Heat 1 tablespoon oil in wok or skillet and add the ginger slices. As soon as the ginger sizzles, add broccoli stems. Stir fry for a minute, then add the florets. Add salt and stir, then add 2 tablespoons water. Turn the flame down to medium, cover, and cook for 2 minutes, then set the broccoli aside in a dish and discard the ginger.

Heat the remaining oil in the wok, then add the minced garlic and black beans. Add the steak slices and stir fry for 2 to 3 minutes, or until done. Return the broccoli to wok, mix well, and serve.

JERILYN M. OKIN is co-founder of The Gourmet Chopstick School of International Cooking. There she gives lessons and demonstrations in Chinese and international cooking, and also operates a catering service. She is engaged in an ongoing series of demonstrations at Creative Cookery, an international cookware store in Fort Lee, New Jersey, and in giving private instruction in her home. In 1973 she taught Chinese cooking at Ramapo Regional High School in New Jersey. Earlier, she taught in the Fairlawn Adult Education program. She has demonstrated Chinese cooking aboard the Queen Elizabeth II *as well as at the Ringwood Library, the Skylines Lakes Woman's Club, the Pompton Lakes Woman's Club, and the River Edge ORT.*

Gloria Zimmerman's Chicken in Oyster Sauce with Three Kinds of Mushroom

INGREDIENTS

2 whole medium-sized chicken breasts
1 tablespoon dry sherry
1 tablespoon cornstarch
6 to 8 medium-sized fresh mushrooms
6 to 8 medium-sized dried Chinese mushrooms
8 to 10 dried straw mushrooms
¼ cup vegetable oil
1 teaspoon salt
1 tablespoon oyster sauce

PREPARATION

Skin and bone the chicken breasts, then cut into cubes. Combine with the sherry and cornstarch and mix well with chopsticks.

Slice the fresh mushroom stems off even with the caps and reserve stems for another use.

Soak the dried Chinese mushrooms in 1 cup warm water for 20 minutes, then drain and cut into 1-inch squares, to make ½ cup.

Soak the dried straw mushrooms in 1 cup warm water, then drain, to make ½ cup.

COOKING PROCEDURES

Heat 1 tablespoon oil in wok or skillet. Add fresh mushrooms, Chinese mushrooms, and straw mushrooms; mix. Stir fry for about 2 minutes. Remove from pan and set aside.

Heat the remaining oil. When it is very hot, add cubed chicken breast. Stir, then add the salt, and continue stirring until the chicken meat is opaque. Sprinkle oyster sauce over chicken; stir. Return all mushrooms to pan. Continue stirring until all ingredients are combined. Serve hot.

TIPS

Canned straw mushrooms may be substituted for dry ones. Drain well before using.

Remember to remove stems of Chinese mushrooms before cutting into 1-inch squares.

GLORIA ZIMMERMAN *teaches Chinese cooking in her home in Guilford, Connecticut, and at* G. Fox *in Hartford. Recently, she gave a lecture-demonstration at Bloomingdale's Stamford. She has demonstrated at many women's clubs and aboard the* Queen Elizabeth II *on several cruises. In the spring of 1973 she gave a lesson in Chinese cooking to an elementary school class as part of a course on China. She has taught at the Guilford Community Center and at Gimbel's in Bridgeport. In New Jersey, she has given instruction in Chinese cooking in the Millburn–Short Hills Adult School and the Montclair Adult School.*

Glossary of Ingredients

鮑魚

ABALONE. A mollusk found in the Pacific Ocean, especially near Mexico and Japan. Its meat is smooth-textured and pleasant-tasting. The Chinese often use it in banquet dishes, such as Abalone and Shantung Cabbage (page 200). Abalone is available fresh in California, canned or dried elsewhere. Canned abalone is precooked, so it should not be overcooked, as it will turn rubbery. The unused portion of the canned abalone can be stored, with its own juice, in a jar with a tight lid, in the refrigerator. It will keep several days.

洋菜（大菜）

AGAR-AGAR. A seaweed often found in the Pacific Ocean off Japan and in the Indian Ocean near southern India. It is processed, dried, and packaged in the form of long, translucent strips somewhat like thick cellophane noodles. Soaked in cold water, it can be used in salads, but if it is soaked in warm or hot water, it dissolves, and becomes the Chinese equivalent of gelatin. Agar-agar is sold in all Oriental specialty stores and will keep indefinitely, dried.

莧菜

AMARANTH. A seasonal Chinese vegetable, usually having fluffy, light green leaves, though there is a variety with leaves and stems tinged with red. Amaranth is sold in Chinese grocery stores in bunches somewhat like spinach. Unlike spinach, however, the stems are tough and must be removed before cooking. When red amaranth is cooked, the pot liquid will be red tinged, but red and green varieties are prepared the same way. Amaranth may be cooked as a vegetable or in combination with other vegetables or meat. Keeps 3 or 4 days in the vegetable compartment of refrigerator.

ANCIENT EGGS. *See* Thousand-year eggs.

ANGEL SHRIMP. *See* Baby shrimp.

蝦仁

BABY SHRIMP (Angel Shrimp). Tiny shrimp from South America, shelled, deveined, and frozen and sold in Chinese specialty stores and sometimes in supermarkets. These are preferred to native American shrimp for egg rolls and many stir-fried dishes. If unobtainable, use fresh shrimp or larger frozen shrimp and cut, lengthwise, into halves. Will keep for several months frozen. Once thawed, use immediately. The larger, fresh shrimp are used to make butterfly shrimp and dishes requiring the shells on.

BALSAM PEAR. *See* Bitter melon.

竹筍

BAMBOO SHOOTS. Shoots from the bamboo plant are a very common Chinese vegetable. They are sold canned, packed in water or in brine (though water is preferred), in Oriental groceries and American supermarkets. The two main kinds are winter and spring bamboo. Winter shoots are tastier, but spring bamboo is tenderer. Canned bamboo shoots can be stored, covered with water, in a jar in the refrigerator for several weeks, provided that the water is changed every few days.

珠油

BEAD MOLASSES. A thick black syrup used to color and thicken light soy sauce to make it darker. Bead molasses can be purchased in Chinese grocery stores, where it is called *soy gum*, and sometimes in Chinese food departments of supermarkets. Buy the smallest quantity possible—a little goes a a long way.

BEAN CAKE. *See* Bean Curd.

BEAN CURD (Bean Cake). Custardlike squares, manufactured from soybean milk and pressed into cakes about 3 x 3 x 1 inches. High in protein, inexpensive, and mild in taste, bean curd is a very popular food throughout the Orient. The cakes are sold fresh daily, but they can be kept refrigerated for about a week if the water is changed every two days. Bean curd is eaten cold in salads and cooked in countless meat and vegetable dishes.

Bean curd is also sold deep fried, pressed plain or seasoned with soy sauce, and in other forms, some of which are discussed later. *See also* Pressed bean curd; Fermented bean curd; Dried "second layer" bean curd; Thinly pressed bean curd.

BEAN SPROUTS, MUNG. Tiny white shoots with yellowish green hoods, used as a vegetable in salads and cooked dishes. Bean sprouts may be grown at home (see *The Pleasures of Chinese Cooking*, p. 45), purchased fresh at Chinese grocery stores, or purchased canned in supermarkets. Fresh bean sprouts are crisper than canned ones, and since they can be grown at home, fresh sprouts are preferable. They will keep 6 to 7 days in the refrigerator, if kept in an airtight container or a plastic bag with a piece of dry paper towel over them. *See also* Soybean sprouts.

BEAN THREAD. *See* Cellophane noodles.

BÊCHE DE MER. *See* Sea cucumber.

燕窩

BIRD'S NEST (Swallow's Nest). An edible gelatinous substance produced by tiny swallows or swifts that live near the South China Sea. These nests are considered a delicacy, not only because of their scarcity, but also because of the labor involved in cleaning away the down feathers and other impurities. They are light tan and somewhat resemble shredded, glazed coconut. The best-known use is in Bird's Nest Soup, which is served at many Chinese banquets. The nests, dried, are sold boxed and can be stored at room temperature.

BITTER MELON (Balsam Pear). A vegetable in the squash family which looks like a nubby cucumber. Because of its high quinine content it is bitter in taste, and fresh bitter melon must be parboiled before using. It is sold fresh in Chinese grocery stores, or canned in Oriental specialty stores. It can be used alone as a cooked vegetable or stir fried with meats. Fresh, it keeps about a week in the vegetable compartment of the refrigerator.

BOK CHOY. This is "Chinese cabbage" to the Chinese, while Americans call celery cabbage "Chinese cabbage." *Bok choy* has white stems, dark green leaves, and yellow flowers. Easily grown in many parts of the United States, it is sold mainly in Chinese grocery stores. It can be used in combinations or cooked alone as a vegetable, but it is very tender and should not be overcooked. Store in vegetable compartment of refrigerator and use soon after purchase.

油 燜 筍

BRAISED BAMBOO SHOOTS. These bamboo shoots—canned, cooked, and seasoned —can be found in Chinese grocery stores. These should not be confused with regular bamboo shoots, and should only be used for recipes that specifically call for them, such as Red-Cooked Pork Cubes with Braised Bamboo Shoots (page 138). Braised bamboo shoots are ready to eat as a side dish without heating. Just open the can and serve. Stored in a jar after opening, they can be kept in the refrigerator for several days.

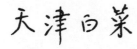

CELERY CABBAGE. Called "Chinese cabbage" by Americans, this is sold in American supermarkets and greengrocers. The most familiar variety, Tientsin cabbage, is long and light green like American celery, but has broad, flat leaves.

A short, square, white variety, now sold in Chinese groceries and a few supermarkets, is Shantung cabbage. It is more tender and tasty than Tientsin cabbage. Both types can be cooked alone or combined with meats or other vegetables.

CELLOPHANE NOODLES (Mung Bean Thread). Noodles made of mung bean flour. They are sold dried in Chinese food stores, and must be soaked before cooking. When soaked and cooked, they become transparent and take on the flavor of the other ingredients. Cellophane noodles come in packages 2 to 8 ounces in weight, are inexpensive, and keep indefinitely at room temperature. They lend texture and sheen to soups and casseroles.

CHINESE BROCCOLI (*Kai lan*). Resembles American broccoli, except that the stems are generally longer. Its flavor is also similar but somewhat more delicate. *Kai lan* can be purchased in Chinese grocery stores, usually in the summer. If not available, American broccoli can be substituted.

CHINESE CABBAGE. *See* Bok choy; Celery cabbage.

CHINESE CHIVES. Green vegetables of the onion family, similar in appearance to American chives, but much stronger in taste. Chinese chives are sold in bunches in Chinese grocery stores, especially in spring and early summer. They are minced and used to give flavor to bland dishes like scrambled eggs, bean curd, and bean sprouts.

Wash and wrap in a paper towel in a plastic bag. Will not keep for more than a week in vegetable compartment of refrigerator.

桂皮

CHINESE CINNAMON. The dried bark of the cassia tree, sold either as sticks or in ground form. This cinnamon is an important ingredient of five spices powder, used to season duck and other meat and poultry dishes. "Chinese cinnamon" is the variety of cinnamon used in the United States for American cooking, so it is easily obtainable in supermarkets and spice stores. Five spices powder is sold only in Oriental specialty stores.

蛋麵

CHINESE EGG NOODLES. Fine noodles made of egg and flour, which are the principal ingredients in *lo mein*. They are very thin, like the thinnest spaghetti, and are sold fresh as *lo mein* in Chinese food stores. Dried Chinese noodles, or thin spaghetti, may be used as a substitute, but fresh noodles do have a unique taste and should be used if possible. Will keep about a week in a plastic bag in the refrigerator, a month in the freezer. A recipe for Roast Pork Lo Mein is on page 240.

肝腸

CHINESE LIVER SAUSAGE. A sausage made from pork liver. Darker and less sweet than Chinese pork sausage, it is often cooked in combination with vegetables. See also Chinese sausage.

275

CHINESE MUSTARD GREENS. A dark-green, leafy vegetable with a slightly bitter taste, sold, both fresh and preserved in brine, in Chinese markets. A recipe for preserving mustard greens at home is given on page 119. Chinese mustard greens can be cooked fresh in dishes such as Steamed Ham with Chicken and Chinese Mustard Greens (page 153), or used in pickled form, as in Flank Steak with Preserved Mustard Greens (page 118). Both canned and fresh greens are cooked in soups.

CHINESE PARSLEY. This is not parsley at all, but fresh coriander (Italian *cilantro*). It is a green, parsley-like herb with flat, serrated leaves that can be bought in Chinese, Italian, or Spanish groceries. It is highly aromatic, used as a flavoring (see Steamed Floured Carp, page 184) and as a garnish. To store, wrap the washed Chinese parsley in a dry paper towel and store in a plastic bag in the vegetable section of the refrigerator. Keeps up to a week.

CHINESE PICKLE. *See* Tea melon.

义 烧

CHINESE ROAST PORK. Strips of pork loin, fresh ham, or other pork cut, which have been marinated in honey, soy sauce, and spices and roasted. Sold by the pound in Chinese groceries and butcher shops, and occasionally available frozen in supermarkets. Can be eaten hot or cold or added to stir-fry dishes. Do not overcook, as it is already cooked. To make roast pork at home, see *The Pleasures of Chinese Cooking,* p. 131.

CHINESE SAUSAGE. A cured, waxy, sweet pork sausage. The links are sold at Chinese food stores and butcher shops, tied in pairs. They must be cut apart and then steamed for 20 minutes before using. Chinese sausage is often used in poultry stuffings (Stuffed Boneless Duck, page 169). Wrapped in foil in a refrigerator, it keeps well. See also Chinese liver sausage.

CHINESE TURNIP. *See* Icicle radish.

杞 子

CHI-TZU. The berry of the Chinese matrimony vine, a thorny plant with dark green leaves, native to China but cultivated in the United States. The dried berries, red in color, are sold as spice in Chinese grocery stores and used in flavoring slow-cooking dishes and soups, such as Dried Lotus Root and Sparerib Soup (page 89).

桐 蒿

CHRYSANTHEMUM LEAVES (vegetable). These leaves resemble the leaves of the chrysanthemum flower, but the vegetable is not the same plant as the better-known flowering chrysanthemum. Sold in Chinese grocery stores, they give off a scent like chrysanthemums when cooked. They will keep in a plastic bag in the vegetable compartment of the refrigerator for about a week. Can be stir fried as a vegetable or in combination with meats or other vegetables.

CLOUD EARS. *See* Dried tree ears.

CRYSTALLIZED GINGER. Ginger preserved by being coated with sugar. Sold boxed in Chinese groceries and American gourmet departments. Eaten as candy or used, chopped up, in desserts.

龍眼

DRAGON'S EYE (commonly known as Longans). A cherry-sized fruit related to the lichee, but more chewy and fragrant. The flesh is pulpy and transparent; the pit, large. In the United States, longans are usually sold canned and pitted. Dried, they are used to flavor soups and desserts. Chilled, canned longans are eaten as a dessert, alone or mixed with other fruits.

冬菇

DRIED BLACK MUSHROOMS (Winter Mushrooms). Mushrooms, imported from the Orient in dried form, which must be soaked before using. Sold in Chinese or Japanese food stores. The Japanese ones are larger than the Chinese, but can be used in the same recipes. These Oriental mushrooms have a much stronger flavor than fresh American mushrooms, and can be used in many different meat and vegetable dishes. Dried, they keep indefinitely on the shelf. Do not substitute fresh mushrooms, as the taste is entirely different.

栗子乾

DRIED CHESTNUTS. Ordinary American-style chestnuts which have been peeled and dried. They must be soaked before using, but can be kept a few months in their dried state. Dried chestnuts are available in Chinese food stores and in some health food stores.

DRIED CHINESE MUSHROOMS. *See* Dried black mushrooms.

海蜇

DRIED JELLYFISH. Whole jellyfish, with tentacles removed, sold dried in Chinese grocery stores. They are yellowish brown, opaque, about 25 inches round, and must be soaked overnight, cleaned, and shredded before use. The bland flavor and crisp, crunchy texture are excellent in cold dishes. Unsoaked, jellyfish keeps indefinitely on the shelf.

蠔士

DRIED OYSTERS. A Chinese form of the shellfish, sold dried at Oriental food stores. These oysters are brown in color and have a strong, pleasing flavor. Must be soaked at least 8 hours in warm water to remove sand. Chinese oysters are cooked in soups and stews, steamed with minced pork, and stir fried.

干貝

DRIED SCALLOPS. Sea scallops, similar to those found in American waters, which have been shelled, cleaned, and dried. Amber in color, strong and "fishy" in taste, they are sold in Chinese markets. Dried scallops are used in soups and slow-cooked dishes, or to add flavor to cabbage and other vegetables. Must be soaked before using. Keep indefinitely in dried form.

二竹

DRIED "Second Layer" BEAN CURD (*R-Cho*). Long, tan, dried slices, about 2 x 4 inches in size, made by drying the residue or the second layer of creamy bean curd and sold in ½-pound packages in Chinese groceries. When soaked, the slices are bland and chewy in texture. Keeps 2 or 3 months on the shelf, before turning rancid.

蝦米

DRIED SHRIMP. Small, shelled shrimp sold dried in Oriental food shops. Used as a flavoring agent in soups and vegetable dishes and other mixed dishes. Must be soaked or steamed before using. Keep well at room temperature while dried. Do not try to substitute for fresh shrimp; they are too salty and have an entirely different use.

陳皮

DRIED TANGERINE PEEL. Tangerine peel dried by a special process until hard and tan in color. Sold in Chinese grocery stores as a spice, it keeps indefinitely and is used very sparingly, especially to flavor duck (see Orange-Spiced Duck, page 165). Also used in *congees* and soups (Dried Lotus Root and Sparerib Soup, page 89).

金針

DRIED TIGER-LILY BUDS (Golden Needles, Lily Flowers, Tiger-Lily Petals). Dried buds of the tiger-lily flower, about 3 inches long and very thin. Because of their brownish-gold color, they are often called "golden needles." Must be soaked before using in soups, vegetarian dishes, and stir-fry dishes with meat. Sold in Chinese food stores, they keep indefinitely on the shelf.

雲耳（木耳）

DRIED TREE EARS (Cloud Ears, Wood Ears). Small, dried fungus, black and irregularly shaped, sold in cellophane bags in Oriental groceries. A small bag will go a long way—they swell to four or five times their dried size after soaking. They are used in such combinations as Cassia Pork (page 126) and in spring rolls. They keep indefinitely at room temperature.

蘿蔔乾

DRIED TURNIPS. Dehydrated turnips sold in flat sheets in Chinese grocery stores. Soak before using. Used in stir-fry and slow-cooked dishes, especially in combination with pork and snow peas. Will keep many months in dried form.

DUCK SAUCE. *See* Plum sauce.

EGG-ROLL SKINS OR WRAPPERS. Thin squares of dough, about 6 inches square, sold by the pound in Chinese grocery stores. A recipe for filling them to make egg rolls is found in *The Pleasures of Chinese Cooking,* page 68. Do not confuse them with spring-roll wrappers, round pieces of flaky dough, handmade individually, each of which, when filled, makes a single spring roll. They are similar to Doilies for Cassia Pork (page 128).

To store egg-roll skins more than a few days, wrap tightly, first in foil and then in freezer paper, and freeze. To store in the refrigerator, wrap tightly in a plastic bag or plastic wrap. Do not expose the skins to the air or they will turn brittle.

FERMENTED BEAN CURD. A cheeselike form of bean curd preserved in sherry and sold in glass jars in Chinese stores. Used as a flavoring agent, especially for vegetables. Once the jar is opened it should be kept in the refrigerator. It is good for several months.

豆豉

FERMENTED BLACK BEANS. Small black beans preserved by a complicated process of fermenting, steaming, and combining with salt and spices. Often used as a spice for meats, fish, or shellfish, as in Lobster Cantonese (page 190), they should not be confused with dried black beans. Fermented black beans can be stored on a shelf in an airtight container for years.

魚肚

FISH MAW. The word "maw," like "gizzard" and "tripe," signifies the stomach, in this case belonging to some of the larger varieties of fish. The maw is removed from the freshly caught fish, cleaned thoroughly by professionals, and then dried for at least a year before it is ready for sale.

Fish maw is never the main ingredient in a Chinese dish, but is used to add flavor and make the dish more exotic. When the dried fish maw arrives at the retail grocery, the storekeeper prepares it for sale by deep frying it in oil so that it puffs up. Several recipes in this book, such as Fish Maw and Shrimp Ball Soup (page 90) contain fish maw.

It is available in 4-ounce packages and will keep for many months if frozen.

五香粉

FIVE SPICES POWDER. A light-brown, powdered combination of ground spices somewhat similar to American pumpkin-pie spices, but found only in Chinese grocery stores. The spices used are usually star anise, Szechuan peppercorn, fennel or anise seed, cloves, and Chinese cinnamon. Five spices powder is often used to season duck (Spiced Roast Duck, page 172) and fish. Keeps a long time in a glass jar on the shelf.

生薑

FRESH GINGER. Gnarled, knobby, irregularly shaped root of the ginger plant, about 3 inches in length. Once the brownish skin is scraped off with a potato peeler, the crisp, ivory-colored root has a sharp, spicy taste, much better than powdered ginger. Ginger root is used as a spice in many Oriental recipes. It can be found in Oriental, Spanish, Greek, and some American food stores. To keep fresh ginger, scrape off the skin and cover the root with sherry; keep in a covered jar under refrigeration.

FUZZY MELON. *See* Hairy melon.

GINGER. *See* Fresh ginger.

GINGKO NUT. The nut of a large, ornamental tree native to eastern China. Gingko nuts are oval, about ½ inch in diameter, with light brown shells and ivory-colored meat. They are sold in Chinese grocery stores, either already shelled and canned, or in dried form. Dried gingko nuts must be shelled and blanched before using. Widely used in vegetarian dishes and in stuffings, such as Stuffed Boneless Chicken (page 155).

GLUTINOUS RICE (Sweet Rice, Sticky Rice). A short-grained, pearly white rice that becomes very sticky when cooked. Although it is not sweet, it is used in desserts—hence the name "sweet rice"—as well as in meat balls and stuffings. Available at Chinese grocery stores, usually in 5-pound bags. A little goes a long way; so either share with another Chinese cook, or plan to store it a long time, as it keeps indefinitely in a dry place.

糯米粉

GLUTINOUS RICE FLOUR (Glutinous Rice Powder). Glutinous rice, ground to a fine powder and sold in 1-pound or 5-pound bags in Chinese grocery stores. Used for baking pastries and in steamed pork and other dishes, it keeps well on the shelf in a tightly sealed bag.

GOLDEN NEEDLES. *See* Dried tiger-lily buds.

粉皮

GREEN BEAN PASTE. A mung bean product, commercially prepared and made into transparent, round sheets, similar to dried, round spring roll wrappers. These sheets are available in Chinese food stores.

原晒豉

GROUND BROWN OR YELLOW BEAN SAUCE. A thick, pastelike sauce made from yellow soybeans, flour, and water. Sold in Chinese grocery stores in cans, either ground or containing soybean halves. Used as a seasoning in cooking meats, duck, bean curd, and bland vegetables, but never as a dip, since it is too salty. After opening can, transfer remaining sauce to a jar and store in refrigerator. Keeps several months.

髮菜

HAIRLIKE SEAWEED. Thin, black strands of seaweed dried and sold in Chinese and Japanese stores for use as a vegetable. Hairlike seaweed must be soaked and cleaned of sand before using as an ingredient in vegetarian dishes.

節瓜

HAIRY MELON (Fuzzy Melon). Cylindrical, greenish fuzz-covered vegetable of the squash family, sold in Chinese vegetable markets. Mainly available in summer, it must be peeled before using. It can be cooked in soups or used as a main ingredient in vegetable dishes. Keeps up to 2 weeks in perforated plastic bag in vegetable compartment of refrigerator.

豬肚

HOG'S MAW. This term is to pork as tripe is to beef and gizzard is to chicken. Hog's maw means the stomach of the hog. It is sold, both uncooked and precooked, in Chinese food stores.

海鮮醬

HOISIN SAUCE (Peking sauce, red seasoning sauce, red vegetable sauce, sweet vegetable paste or sauce). A thick, sweet-spicy, dark brown sauce made with soy beans, chili, garlic, and spices. Its distinctive taste adds an indescribable flavor to roast pork, roast duck, and many other cooked dishes. It is also used as a condiment for dipping and as an ingredient in cocktail dips. Sold in cans or glass jars. Once the can is opened, the contents should be transferred to glass jar and refrigerated. Keeps for many months.

辣 油

HOT PEPPER OIL. A solution of red pepper in peanut oil, used as a spice, especially in Szechuan cooking. Available at Chinese markets. A hot sauce such as Red Devil Sauce can be substituted, as it, too, is red pepper in liquid form. Use cautiously, adjusting to taste.

HUNDRED-YEAR EGGS. *See* Thousand-year eggs.

白 蘿 蔔

ICICLE RADISH (Chinese Turnip). Root vegetable sold fresh in Chinese grocery stores, resembling a giant white radish. Icicle radishes are available all year round, but are especially good in winter. Their taste is a cross between that of the American turnip and white radish. Peeled and shredded, they are used in stir-fried and braised dishes, as well as in soups (see Clam and Icicle Radish Soup, page 88) and salads (Jellyfish and Icicle Radish Salad, page 108). Will keep in vegetable compartment of refrigerator for several weeks.

紅 棗

JUJUBE (Red Dates). Small dried red fruit in the date family, native to China. Available in Chinese specialty stores and used in soups, steamed dishes, stews, and other slow-cooking dishes. They can also be soaked and served in desserts, such as Jujube and Walnut "Drink" (page 228). In dried form, will keep indefinitely at room temperature.

金 橘

KUMQUAT. Tiny, oval, orange-colored fruit of the citrus family. They grow well in the United States as well as in China. Kumquats are occasionally available fresh or dried, but can always be found in glass jars, packed in heavy syrup. Combined with loquats, lichees, mandarin oranges, etc., kumquats are served by the Chinese between courses of a banquet or as desserts. Sold in supermarkets.

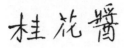

KWEI-HWA SYRUP. *Kwei-hwa* is a flower, sometimes known as "sweet olive." The petals are preserved in sugar and salt and sold as *kwei-hwa syrup* for use in dessert and cakes. The smell is similar to that of apricots. Once the can is opened, the syrup should be kept in the refrigerator in a glass jar.

LAVER (also called Purple Laver). A dark purple marine vegetable, rich in iodine, sold in dried form, in thin 7 x 8-inch sheets, in Oriental grocery stores. Laver is used in soups, such as Laver and "Egg Flower" soup (page 91). Keeps well on the shelf in dried form.

LICHEE (Litchi, Lychee). The fruit of a Chinese tree of the soapberry family, having a brittle, reddish shell, an opaque white pulp, and a single, large seed. The pulp alone is edible.

Lichees are not often available in fresh form. Canned lichees, sold in Chinese food stores, are used for dessert and in sweet and sour dishes. Dried lichees, called "lichee nuts" because of their nutlike appearance and because they are eaten like nuts, are the form in which the fruit is best known in the United States.

LILY FLOWERS. *See* Dried tiger-lily buds.

LITCHI. *See* Lichee.

LONGANS. *See* Dragon's eye.

絲瓜

LOOFAH. A long, green squash that looks somewhat like a cucumber with a rough skin and vertical ribs. Fresh loofah is found in Chinese grocery stores all year round. When the skin and ribs are removed, the meat is cut up and cooked for soup, becoming slightly sticky, like okra.

After loofahs go to seed, they are dried and sold as abrasive sponges, for stimulating the skin and for scouring.

枇杷

LOQUAT. A small, orange-colored fruit somewhat like an apricot in both color and taste. Sometimes sold fresh in California, loquats are available elsewhere in cans, packed in syrup. They are used for desserts and sometimes cooked with chicken. Sold in Chinese grocery stores.

藕

LOTUS ROOT. Root of the lotus plant, a reddish-brown-skinned, white vegetable shaped like several sweet potatoes linked together. Sold fresh, dried, or canned, available in Chinese grocery stores, the root can be peeled and stir fried as a vegetable or simmered with meats in slow-cooked dishes. Canned, water-packed lotus root is used in salads (Lotus Root Salad, page 109). The slices resemble cartwheels. Canned lotus root can be stored in a water-filled jar in the refrigerator if the water is changed every 2 or 3 days.

蓮子

LOTUS SEED. Small, oval, nutlike seeds of the lotus plant, usually sold canned or dried in Chinese food stores. Because of their delicate taste, they are used as a flavoring agent in soups or cooked with meat, such as ham. Canned, lotus seeds are ready to use; the fresh and dried forms must be blanched and skinned.

LYCHEE. *See* Lichee.

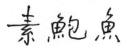

MOCK ABALONE. A soybean product, commercially manufactured. An ingredient in vegetarian dishes, it can be obtained in cans in Chinese food stores.

MONOSODIUM GLUTAMATE (MSG). A crystalline white powder, extracted from grains and vegetables. It has no flavor of its own, but when added in very small quantities, it brings out the natural flavor of foods. "Chinese restaurant syndrome," a feeling of pressure on the temples, results when persons sensitive to MSG eat foods containing large amounts of it. However, used in small quantities, it does enhance flavor. Sold in supermarkets.

MUNG BEANS. The small, smooth, brownish-green seeds sold dried in Oriental or health food stores as "mung beans" come from the pod of the mung bean plant (*Phaseolus aureus*). This member of the bean family is Oriental in origin, but is now cultivated in many parts of the world. Mung beans can be used for growing bean sprouts, and are the source of the starch used in making cellophane noodles. Dried mung beans keep 6 months in a cellophane bag or a tight jar at room temperature.

蘇 油

ORIENTAL SESAME SEED OIL. Clear, dark-brown oil distilled from toasted sesame seeds and used especially in flavoring soups and salads. Oil from untoasted seeds is clear yellow, and not to be confused with this Oriental oil. Toasted sesame seed oil is now available, not only at Chinese and Japanese, but also at health-food stores. Its taste is strong and exotic, so it should be used sparingly.

OYSTER SAUCE. A thick brown sauce made by cooking oysters in soy sauce and brine. Sold bottled in Chinese groceries, it is best known as flavoring for beef (see Flank Steak with Preserved Mustard Greens, page 118), but also used in cooking poultry and seafood and as a table condiment for cold meats and chicken. Keeps well in sealed bottles at room temperature; refrigerate for longer storage.

PAI-YEH. *See* Thinly pressed bean curd.

PEKING SAUCE. *See Hoisin* sauce.

PICKLED SCALLIONS. The white tips of green onions, preserved in vinegar, sugar, and salt and sold in glass jars in Chinese grocery stores. Used as a garnish or in sweet-sour fish dishes. Once the jar is opened, store in refrigerator.

蘇梅醬

PLUM SAUCE (Duck Sauce). A thick, preservelike sauce of plums mixed with chili and spices. Plum sauce is used in the United States as a table condiment. In China, it is used only as an ingredient in cooking. It is sold in many supermarkets, as well as in Chinese food shops. Once opened, the jar should be kept in the refrigerator.

臘鴨

PRESERVED DUCK. Precooked, pressed duck, sold immersed in peanut oil. It must be rinsed in cold water, cut into quarters, and steamed before using.

It can be served alone, chopped into bite-sized pieces, or steamed over rice, so that the rice absorbs the flavor and some of the fat. Available only at Chinese specialty stores.

PRESERVED PARSNIPS. *See* Preserved turnips.

PRESERVED RED GINGER. Gingerroot preserved in a sweet red syrup and sold in glass jars. Used to flavor fruit dishes and salads. Once opened, it will keep indefinitely in a refrigerator.

Do not confuse with the Japanese red ginger, which is covered with a thin, clear liquid and is not at all sweet.

PRESERVED SWEET MELON. *See* Tea melon.

PRESERVED TURNIPS (Preserved Parsnips). Cut-up parsnips, roots and tops, which have been steamed, salted, and dried. Three to six parsnips are packaged in one plastic bag, and are sold in Chinese grocery stores. The Cantonese use them in soup, taro cakes, *congees,* and so on, but only in very small quantities, because the taste is very strong and salty. Can be stored in a covered jar at room temperature, but must be rinsed before using to remove excess salt.

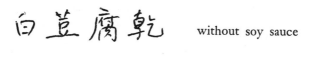 without soy sauce

PRESSED BEAN CURD (with or without soy sauce). This is a type of fresh bean curd from which moisture has been extracted by compressing. It can be found in the refrigerator case of most Chinese specialty stores, or can be made at home from fresh bean curd. A recipe for pressing fresh bean curd follows:

Wrap each piece of bean curd in cheesecloth (6 x 6 inches) and place between 2 flat boards. Put a weight, such as a large bowl of water or a heavy book, on the boards. After 10 minutes increase the weight, and after another 10 minutes increase it again. After an hour, remove the weights and unwrap the bean curd and you will have white pressed bean curd.

To make soy sauce-pressed bean curd, boil 1 tablespoon of soy sauce and ¼ cup of water in a small saucepan. Add 1 or 2 pieces pressed bean curd; bring to boil again. Turn off the flame and let the bean curd soak in the sauce for 1 hour, then drain. Can be kept in refrigerator 2 or 3 days.

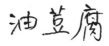

PUFFED BEAN CURD. Small pieces of bean curd, porous inside and golden brown outside. They are produced commercially by cutting pieces of bean curd into quarters and deep-frying them. Puffed bean curd is sold in packages or by the pound in Chinese food stores. To keep for several weeks, freeze in a plastic bag or container.

RED BEAN PASTE. A thick, sweetened paste made from red beans, it is sold in Chinese groceries and bakeries and used to fill pastries, especially around the New Year. Once opened, the paste should be refrigerated in a glass jar. It will keep several months.

RED DATES. *See* Jujube.

紅米

RED RICE. Long-grained rice that has been soaked in red food coloring. Used to add color to spiced duck, pork, and other dishes, it is sold by the ounce in Chinese specialty stores. While quite expensive, a little goes a long way, and it keeps a long time in a covered jar at room temperature.

RED SEASONING PASTE, RED VEGETABLE SAUCE. *See Hoisin* sauce.

米粉

RICE FLOUR. A flour ground from raw rice and sold in 1-pound packages in Oriental grocery stores. Used in sweet dishes and in the manufacture of "rice sticks" or noodles, it keeps well in an airtight bag on the shelf.

RICE NOODLES. *See* Rice sticks.

米粉乾

RICE STICKS (Rice Noodles). Fine noodles made from rice flour. They may be soaked and used in the same manner as cellophane noodles, with meat or in soup. However, their main use is deep fried as a garnish. Rice sticks are the white, stiff shreds, resembling coconut, often served as garnish in Chinese restaurants.

To deep fry rice sticks, heat vegetable oil to 375 degrees. Add rice sticks, a few at a time. Fry for literally 1 second. The sticks will puff up immediately. Remove, drain, and store in an airtight jar for future use.

米醋

RICE VINEGAR. Vinegar made from rice wine, sold in bottles in Oriental food stores. There are three varieties: white, for sweet-sour dishes, red, used as a table condiment, and black, for braised and red-cooked dishes and dipping. Keeps well on the shelf.

烤鴨

ROAST DUCK. Whole duck, marinated in spice, then roasted and sold in one piece or in pieces at Chinese grocery stores. The Chinese either serve it cold, reheat it with a sauce, or mix it with vegetables and fruits.

烤豬肉

ROAST PIG. Roasted, whole suckling pig, sold in Chinese grocery stores by the pound. Can be eaten hot or cold or steamed with sauce. A glaze is applied before roasting, making the skin very crisp, the inside well cooked and moist.

冰糖

ROCK CANDY (Rock Sugar). Crystallized sugar, either clear or amber colored, used instead of granulated sugar in chrysanthemum tea and in sauces because it gives a shiny appearance. Available in Chinese and Middle Eastern food stores, as well as many candy stores and gourmet departments. Keeps well in a covered container at room temperature.

ROCK SUGAR. *See* Rock candy.

R-CHO. *See* Dried "second layer" bean curd.

鹹蛋

SALTED, PRESERVED DUCK EGGS. Not to be confused with thousand-year eggs, these duck eggs are soaked in brine for 30 to 40 days. They are larger than chicken eggs, with a salt-and-mud mixture coated around the shell. The whites are salty; the yolks, firm. They are sold in Chinese grocery stores and must be cooked, either by boiling or by beating and using in dishes like Three-Toned Eggs (page 235). Refrigerated, they keep about 1 month.

海參

SEA CUCUMBER (Bêche-de-Mer [French: *bêche*, "spade"; *de mer* "of the sea"]). A primitive form of marine animal life that has eyes and a digestive system but no scales or fins. After the sea cucumbers are caught, they must be dried professionally before being sold. Before using, the cook must reconstitute them into a soft, workable form, a process that requires several days' cleaning and soaking. The length of time and amount of work required in preparation makes the Chinese consider sea cucumber an exotic ingredient, to be used chiefly in banquet dishes.

SESAME SEED. The dried seeds of an Asian annual herb. Unhulled, the seeds range from grayish white to black in color, but once the hull is removed, sesame seeds are flat, tiny, cream colored, and pointed on one end. The sesame plant is native to Asia but also cultivated here. Sesame seeds are valued throughout the Middle and Far East, as a flavoring agent and as a source of oil and paste. Sesame seeds can be found in spice departments of most supermarkets and in gourmet or spice stores.

SESAME SEED PASTE. A brown, thick paste resembling peanut butter in color and texture, but with a distinctive, exotic taste. Oriental sesame seed paste is made from ground, toasted sesame seeds and used in sauces and cold chicken dishes. Do not confuse it with the Middle Eastern paste, *tahini*, which is made from untoasted seeds. Store in a jar at room temperature; it will keep several months.

SHARK'S FIN. Cartilage taken from the fin of certain kinds of sharks, one of the rarest of Chinese delicacies. Originally, not only its expense but the difficulty of cleaning, removing the fishy smell, and making it edible made shark's fin a delicacy. Now the fins are available in cans, skinned and cleaned, but still costly and therefore used almost exclusively for banquets. Shark's fin is also available in dried form, but must then be soaked before using. Both varieties are sold in Chinese grocery stores.

沙 河 粉

SHA-WO-FUN. A rice-flour product, available primarily in stores that make bean curd and bean curd products. *Sha-wo-fun* is so named because it originated in the Sha-Wo district of Canton. It is sold in flat sheets, which will keep a few days in the refrigerator. Frozen, it can be kept several months.

蝦 片

SHRIMP CHIPS. Thin white or pastel-colored round slices of dough made from shrimp and flour, sold dried. When deep fried in hot oil, they puff up and look like pastel potato chips. They are used as hors d'oeuvres or snacks, and are found in Chinese food stores in some gourmet departments. Will keep dried on the shelf for 6 months or more. After frying, store left-over chips in a sealed jar or cellophane bag at room temperature. Will keep at least a week.

鹹 蝦 醬

SHRIMP SAUCE (Shrimp Paste). A thick, salty paste manufactured by pre-serving concentrated shrimps in brine. Used in small quantities as a flavor-ing similar to anchovy paste in American cooking. Sold in glass jars in Chinese groceries. Opened jar will keep in refrigerator for a long time.

SILVER EAR MUSHROOM. *See* Silver fungus.

銀 耳

SILVER FUNGUS (Silver Ear Mushroom, White Fungus, White Jelly Fungus). A dried white fungus sold in Oriental specialty stores. It is used in soups, in braised and vegetable dishes, and in desserts such as Silver Fungus in Syrup (page 231). It grows in Szechuan province and in Taiwan, and is sold in canned form as well as dried.

火腿

SMITHFIELD HAM. Smithfield ham is the American ham nearest in taste and texture to King Hwa ham, which the Chinese use for adding zest to many dishes. Smithfield ham can be bought, either cooked or uncooked, in pound pieces. Gourmet food shops may sell the cooked variety, but Chinese butcher shops usually sell it uncooked.

If the ham is bought uncooked, it must first be cleaned thoroughly to remove sand and pepper. Then soak it in cold water for 30 minutes, rinse and drain, place it in a saucepan with enough cold water to cover, bring it to a boil, and simmer it for 20 minutes. Once the ham piece is cooked, the unused portion will keep in the refrigerator for several weeks. Most recipes in this book call for only a few tablespoons of diced, shredded, or sliced Smithfield ham.

Either prosciutto or boiled ham may be substituted in recipes calling for sliced, shredded, or diced ham, if Smithfield ham is not available. Neither of these is firm enough to mince.

黄荳芽

SOYBEAN SPROUTS. Soybean sprouts are larger and coarser than mung bean sprouts and are more difficult to clean. However, they are rich in protein and have an interesting, distinctive taste. To clean, wash and pick the roots off each sprout.

Soybean sprouts are available fresh in Chinese grocery stores. They are used to make vegetarian soup stock or in mixed vegetable dishes, but never in salads like mung bean sprouts.

醬油

SOY SAUCE. A brown, salty liquid made mainly of fermented soy bean extract and salt. Soy sauce is classified as "light" or "dark," with grades in between. Actually "light" and "dark" refer more to consistency than color, and are sometimes called "light" and "heavy." The Chinese use light soy mainly as a table condiment, dark soy (to which bead molasses has been added) in cooking. Only the Cantonese cook with both varieties. Japanese soy is between light and dark. American-made soy sauce is considered inferior to the imported kind. Keeps in glass bottles at room temperature.

烏賊乾

SQUID (dried). A small, tentacled mollusk, brownish and coated with a white powder, sold dehydrated in Chinese food stores. Must be soaked before using. Used in steamed, sweet-sour, or stir-fried dishes, as well as in soup. If wrapped, will keep well on the shelf.

STICKY RICE, SWEET RICE. *See* Glutinous rice.

草菇

STRAW MUSHROOMS. Thin mushrooms with high, narrow caps, brown on top and tan on the bottom, used in meat and vegetable combinations. They are sold dried, but more frequently found canned. Transfer unused canned straw mushrooms to a glass jar, cover with water, and refrigerate. If water is changed every 2 or 3 days, they will keep about a week.

SWALLOW'S NEST. *See* Bird's nest.

SWEET TEA PICKLE. *See* Tea melon.

SWEET VEGETABLE PASTE, SWEET VEGETABLE SAUCE. *See Hoisin* sauce.

花椒

SZECHUAN PEPPERCORNS. Highly aromatic, reddish-brown peppercorns, sold whole in Chinese grocery stores. The unique taste is mildly hot, unlike common forms of pepper. It is sometimes called "anise pepper" by Americans. Used especially in cold dishes, such as Szechuan Peppercorn Chicken (page 161), and Pickled Assorted Vegetables (page 220). Keeps well in covered jars on the shelf.

SZECHUAN PRESERVED KOHLRABI (Mustard Pickle, Szechuan Preserved Vegetable). A very hot pickle made by preserving Chinese kohlrabi in Szechuan peppercorns, pepper, and brine. Available canned in Chinese grocery stores, under various titles. After opening can, store remaining kohlrabi in a glass jar in the refrigerator. Will keep for several months. Shred and use a little at a time; it adds a unique, spicy flavor to soups and stir-fry dishes (see Pork, Cellophane Noodle, and Szechuan Preserved Kohlrabi Soup, page 95, and Pork, Bamboo Shoots, and Szechuan Preserved Kohlrabi Shreds, page 134).

SZECHUAN PRESERVED VEGETABLE. *See* Szechuan preserved kohlrabi.

TARO. The root of a tropical plant, similar to a potato but larger and darker brown. Sold fresh in Chinese stores in autumn; sold canned all year round. It is steamed with duck or Chinese sausages, sliced for other uses. Fresh taro keeps in the refrigerator for about a week.

TEA MELON (Chinese Pickle, Preserved Sweet Melon, Sweet Tea Pickle). A small, brownish-colored, cucumberlike vegetable, no more than 2 inches long, sold preserved in honey and spices in Chinese specialty stores. It can be steamed with pork, beef, or fish (see Poached Fish, Canton Style, page 183) or eaten as an appetizer or snack. Once the jar is opened, keep in the refrigerator.

THINLY PRESSED BEAN CURD (*Pai-yeh*). Very thin sheets made by putting the warm "milk" skimmed off when bean curd is prepared into a special

8 x 8-inch frame, between layers of cheesecloth, and pressing these layers for 30 minutes. The sheets are then dried and refrigerated or frozen until used. They are sold in Chinese stores that specialize in bean curd products.

THOUSAND-YEAR EGGS (Hundred-Year Eggs, Ancient Eggs). These eggs are preserved in a coating of lime, salt, and ashes and cured about 100 days. The process of capillary action turns the egg white into a dark amber color and the yolks green and cheeselike. Thousand-year eggs are usually eaten alone as an hors d'oeuvre, but they may be diced and cooked in dishes like Three-Toned Eggs (page 235). They are a delicacy to Chinese and to Americans who have cultivated a taste for them. They are sold in Chinese groceries and will keep at least a month under refrigeration.

TREE EARS. *See* Dried tree ears.

VEGETABLE OIL. Unsaturated cooking oil, available at supermarkets, is recommended for Chinese cooking. In China, the most commonly used oil is made from *bok choy* seeds. Since that kind is difficult to obtain in the United States, oil made from corn, peanuts, safflower seeds, and so forth, is used instead. Oil is recommended for stir frying and deep frying. Other fats are used in small quantities for spreading and to add taste.

馬蹄粉

WATER CHESTNUT FLOUR. A fine, powdery flour made by grinding water chestnuts and then drying. Used as a thickening agent and as a coating for deep-fried foods. Formerly difficult to obtain in the United States, it is now more readily available in Oriental food stores. If unobtainable, cornstarch may be substituted. Keeps well in a tight container at room temperature.

准 山

WEI-SAN. The root of a plant that grows near the Wei River in the Honan region of China. It is sliced, dried, and sold as a spice in Chinese specialty stores. It is used in slow-cooked dishes, such as Dried Lotus Root and Sparerib Soup (page 89).

WHITE FUNGUS, WHITE JELLY FUNGUS. *See* Silver fungus.

WINE BALL, WINE CUBE. *See* Wine yeast.

酒 釀

WINE RICE. Made by combining wine yeast and glutinous rice, it can be produced at home by using the recipe given under "Shrimp in Wine Rice Sauce" (page 194) or it can be purchased in bottles in Chinese food stores. It keeps well in a glass bottle in the refrigerator. Wine rice is used in sauces and desserts.

酒 葯

WINE YEAST (Wine Ball, Wine Cube). A white ball somewhat like a camphor ball in appearance, sold in Chinese groceries, which combines with sweet rice to produce a winy-tasting rice (see Shrimp in Wine-Rice Sauce, page 194).

WINTER MELON. A very large squash, the size of a watermelon but dark green on the outside, white on the inside. Sold by the piece or the pound in Chinese grocery stores. Once cut, the whole melon must be refrigerated and used fairly quickly. Winter melon can only be eaten cooked. It is best known in the United States as the main ingredient in winter melon soup. For special occasions, the soup is cooked in the scooped-out melon itself. Winter melon is also sold candied. Fresh winter melon will keep in the refrigerator about 6 days.

WINTER MUSHROOMS. *See* Dried black mushrooms.

馄饨皮

WONTON SKINS OR WRAPPERS. Thin, square sheets of dough somewhat like egg-roll wrappers, kept refrigerated and sold in Chinese grocery stores. These contain slightly more egg than egg-roll skin to prevent the wontons from disintegrating when immersed in boiling soup. To store: Freeze, tightly wrapped, until ready to use; or keep in the refrigerator one or two days, wrapped in plastic. When exposed to air, they dry out and turn brittle.

WOOD EARS. *See* Dried tree ears.

山药

YUCCA. A root vegetable found in tropical countries. It is most commonly available in Spanish-American grocery stores. Yucca is used by the northern Chinese in desserts and as a starchy vegetable. It can be kept several weeks in the same manner as potatoes or yams.

Index